You Are Looking Live!

You Are Looking Live!
How The NFL Today *Revolutionized Sports Broadcasting*

Rich Podolsky

Foreword by Jim Nantz

LYONS
PRESS

Essex, Connecticut

An imprint of Globe Pequot, the trade division of
The Rowman & Littlefield Publishing Group, Inc.
4501 Forbes Blvd., Ste. 200
Lanham, MD 20706
www.rowman.com

Distributed by NATIONAL BOOK NETWORK

British Library Cataloguing in Publication Information available

Library of Congress Cataloging-in-Publication Data

Names: Podolsky, Rich, 1946- author. | Nantz, Jim, writer of foreword.
Title: You are looking live! : how the NFL today revolutionized sports broadcasting / Rich
    Podolsky ; foreword by Jim Nantz.
Description: Guilford, Connecticut : Lyons Press, [2021] | Includes bibliographical references and
    index.
Identifiers: LCCN 2021036030 (print) | LCCN 2021036031 (ebook) | ISBN 9781493061419
    (cloth) | ISBN 9781493063512 (epub) | ISBN 9781493073016 (paperback)
Subjects: LCSH: NFL today (Television program : 1974-) | Television broadcasting of sports—
    United States—History.
Classification: LCC GV742.3 .P63 2021 (print) | LCC GV742.3 (ebook) | DDC
    796.332/6406—dc23
LC record available at https://lccn.loc.gov/2021036030
LC ebook record available at https://lccn.loc.gov/2021036031

∞™ The paper used in this publication meets the minimum requirements of American National
Standard for Information Sciences—Permanence of Paper for Printed Library Materials, ANSI/
NISO Z39.48-1992.

For Michael Pearl, and for the hundreds of men and women who have worked on The NFL Today *and helped to make it the gold standard*

CONTENTS

FOREWORD

By Jim Nantz

WHAT IS THE AGE WHEN ONE IS MOST IMPRESSIONABLE? WHEN OUR mind is on sensory overload and our imagination can take us to wonderful and faraway places. Recently I read that the golden time for being influenced falls between ages 14 and 18. I'm not one usually given to psychobabble, but I bring this up because I've often wondered what stoked my burning desire to one day live in the world of sports storytelling.

In 1975 my family resided halfway between New York and Philadelphia in a farming community called Colts Neck, New Jersey. I was 16 years old—right in the sweet spot for impressionability—and life was good. Especially on Sunday afternoons at 12:30 when a groundbreaking studio show entered our homes. That show was *The NFL Today*.

It sounds hard to believe these days with social media and 24-hour news cycles keeping us up to date on every conceivable story—whether we want to know or not—but in 1975, information was scarce. Cable television was still a far-fetched idea, ESPN was 4 years from birth, and the Internet, or "information highway," was not even a single-lane road. If you wanted to know the latest happenings in the NFL you had few options.

You had to be enterprising. That's why I became a paperboy—delivering the *Asbury Park Press*, *Newark Star Ledger* and *Red Bank Daily Register* to just 11 homes stretched out over a 3-mile loop just to get my hands on the latest sports news. That one-hour commitment per day opened my eyes to the local papers that covered the Jets, Giants and Eagles, and they gave me enough knowledge to satiate my appetite until Sundays at 12:30 Eastern.

The NFL Today began in 1974 with Jack Whitaker as the host. Jack was an idol and would later become a beloved friend and mentor, but after one season, CBS changed the cast. What came next was the best NFL studio show of all-time with stars like Brent Musburger, Irv Cross, Phyllis George and Jimmy "The Greek" Snyder. Together, there was news, laughter and conviviality.

Brent was—and in my book remains—the greatest studio host of all time. Irv was a former star defensive back with the Eagles who brought warmth and insight to the desk. Phyllis was instantly recognized as "America's sweetheart" and would later be remembered for helping blaze a trail for women in sports television. Lastly, "The Greek" was irascible, yet lovable at times, and brought an insider look at the league that helped spark a gambler's mindset to the show. It was in short, the perfect cast with an ideal blend of information and entertainment.

There was something about their chemistry that made the viewer feel like they had a personal relationship with everyone on the show. By some stroke of good fortune, that impressionable loyal viewer from back in the '70s would later get to know everyone from that show, even becoming the host of the show 23 years later and serving in that capacity for 6 years before transitioning to the game booth. I treasure these days with Tony Romo, but there will always be a soft spot in my heart for having had the chance to sit in the chair once occupied by Brent and his remarkable running mates. Though our show never came close to reaching the popularity of the original, there remains a pride within CBS that the gigantic legacy created almost 50 years ago still lives every autumn Sunday.

Thanks to my friend Rich Podolsky for paying tribute and taking us behind the scenes. He knows as well as anyone what it was like—he was a vital part of the production team. I hope you love learning—or in some cases reliving—what it meant to be a part of *The NFL Today*. *You Are Looking Live!* will always be an important part of sports television history. I think it will leave a wonderful impression.

—Jim Nantz, September 2020

Author's Note

In 1973 I began covering the Super Bowl champion Miami Dolphins for the *Palm Beach Post*. It was a job that changed my life. During my second year there, Beano Cook became the team's public relations director, replacing Mike Rathet. Rathet had cowritten Coach Don Shula's book *The Winning Edge*, but left to become the sports editor of the *Philadelphia Daily News*. Dolphin owner Joe Robbie did not consult Shula on Rathet's replacement, which Shula was not happy about. Beano had acquired a great reputation with the press when he was at ABC Sports and the University of Pittsburgh before that, but Shula didn't care. He told Beano not to show up at any practices.

Cook still found a way to humor the press, and he became friends with many beat writers including myself. I loved hearing his stories about Roone Arledge and network sports television. On Fridays during the football season, Beano would host a lunch at the Everglades Hotel on Biscayne Boulevard in Miami, next to the Miami Dolphins headquarters. Mike Pearl and Hank Goldberg would always attend the luncheons to hear what teams Beano liked in college football that weekend. Pearl was a well-known sports producer for the CBS affiliate WTVJ in Miami, and Goldberg was the sports director at WTVJ and a radio analyst on Dolphins games. More importantly, Beano was a college football expert and they both bet on his picks.

Just before Beano would make his final pick each Friday, he would bellow out to our waiter, "EMILIO!" When Emilio arrived he would have Cook's favorite ice cream in hand. It was quite a production and we all had a great time. That was 1974.

In the spring of '75 my life changed again when I got a call informing me that my parents had been in a bad car accident. My father died a few

That's Howard Cosell right behind the author in line at the Miami Dolphins' training camp kitchen, circa 1973. (COURTESY OF THE AUTHOR)

days later from his injuries, and my mother needed six months to recover. I moved back to Philadelphia to care for her and eventually got a job for a suburban daily newspaper. Staying in touch with Beano kept me sane.

Eventually Shula forced him out of Miami and he returned to network television as the publicist for the ABC show *The Superstars*. It was a terrific show that had great athletes competing in sports that were not their specialties. The show was created by two-time Olympic skating champion Dick Button and produced by International Management Group (IMG).

Beano kept telling me that he was going to get hired at CBS Sports and when he did, somehow he'd get me an interview there. So, when former ABC Sports executive Barry Frank became the new head at CBS Sports, Beano was hired. In order to take the job he convinced Dick Button that I would be a perfect replacement to publicize *The Superstars*.

Meeting and working with Button was a thrill, and getting to work with ABC's great producer Don Ohlmeyer was incredibly enlightening. The shows were produced on the west coast of Florida from a real estate complex in Rotonda, near Sarasota. When the shows were edited back in New York, Ohlmeyer was nice enough to invite me in to watch and learn. Ohlmeyer also produced the primetime spinoff *Battle of the Network Stars*. Brilliantly he opened that show with an overhead shot of three different lines of limos converging on the game site.

In February the program's series concluded with *The Superteams*, which was taped in Honolulu. It consisted of ten members from each of the World Series and Super Bowl finalists competing against each other in sports like bike and relay races, swimming and tennis, and the obstacle course. For me, it was a dream job. I got to fly to Hawaii on a chartered jet that left from New York with Yankees like Lou Piniella, Thurman Munson, and Dock Ellis. First stop was Cincinnati, where we picked up the Reds and Johnny Bench. Next stop was Minnesota for the Vikings, and finally we stopped in Oakland to get John Madden, Kenny Stabler, and the Raiders. Madden, who suffered from claustrophobia, was still flying in February of '77.

I knew Madden from my days covering the Miami Dolphins, so we sat together in the front of the plane and swapped stories. All of the players were having a great time getting to know each other, and halfway over the Pacific Ocean, the Raiders' Ted Hendricks tapped me on the shoulder and said, "You know, Rich, there are so many famous players on this plane that if it ever went down, it would take your mother a week before she'd know you were on it." Hendricks then let out a long, loud laugh.

In Hawaii I was able to convince several of the players and their wives to be part of *The Don Ho Show* that was taped at an outdoor studio on the beach near our hotel. Ho, who was famous for recording the song "Tiny Bubbles," had a successful daytime TV variety show, and he convinced a few big linemen to put on hula skirts and makeup. Every night Madden and I met on the front porch of our hotel and talked pro football until midnight or later. It blossomed into a friendship that still exists.

When I got back to New York, Beano was true to his word. In June of 1977 I was introduced at CBS as the new writer for *The NFL Today* and *CBS Sports Spectacular*. The reason Beano had no trouble getting me in was that Mike Pearl had become the producer for *The NFL Today* in '75 and helped transform it into a groundbreaking show. Pearl remembered me and knew I could do the job.

I remained at CBS Sports for over five years, and I can safely say they were five of the happiest years of my life. Writing for *The NFL Today* was exhilarating. Meeting Brent Musburger and Irv Cross and Phyllis George and working together was a dream come true. Here I was writing for Irv Cross when sixteen years earlier, when I was fifteen in his rookie year, I was selling programs at his Eagles games just so I could get in free and sit on the top step of the 50-yard line at Franklin Field on the University of Pennsylvania campus.

Going out for drinks with *The NFL Today* production crew after the show was also a great experience. Even Phyllis came along. She may have been Miss America a few years before, but with us she was just one of the guys. A year later when Jimmy "The Greek" Snyder joined the show, he and I went to the races every Monday.

I wound up sharing an office with Beano, which soon turned into Grand Central Station. Everyone from Paul Hornung and Johnny Unitas to John Tesh and Pat O'Brien stopped by to hear Beano's stories and get his opinion. He always had a six-pack of the diet soft drink Tab under his desk along with a carton of Winstons. Everybody smoked in the '70s.

On Saturdays I would write the lead-ins and bridge material for *CBS Sports Spectacular*, which were almost all taped events. In those days the tape had a seven-second lead-in, which meant I needed to write seven seconds of material for the announcer before the tape rolled.

One Saturday, when Mike Pearl was producing, we were leading into a volleyball piece that featured an interview with Wilt Chamberlain, who was a volleyball enthusiast. The host for *Sports Spectacular* that day was an ex-NBA player in that role for the first time. For the lead-in I wrote something like ". . . and so and so had this interesting conversation with Chamberlain." Well, the poor guy just couldn't say it. Over and over we tried to tape his lead-in and he kept flubbing it. Finally Pearl said, "We're changing the lead-in to 'spoke with Wilt.'"

Most Saturdays Eddie Goren (who later became chairman of Fox Sports) was the producer, and one week we had Pete Rose as a live guest to discuss the baseball playoffs. It was October and I had obtained, with Beano's help, the phone numbers of the top college football press boxes in the country so we could get the scores faster than they came in on the Associated Press ticker. This was 1978. There was no Internet, no Sports Phone, just the wire service for results. Rose saw me calling the press boxes and walked over, pulling out his own personal pool sheet. "Could you get me the Ohio State score?" he asked. "Sure," I said, calling and saying, "This is CBS Sports—can you give us your latest score, please?" Rose asked me a few more times until we went off the air at 6:00 p.m., and as I was walking out I saw him at my desk calling Ohio State, saying, "This is CBS Sports . . ."

That same year the restaurant Runyon's, named for the famous Broadway writer Damon Runyon, opened at 305 East 50th Street in Manhattan. It became the place to be for anyone in the sports media, especially TV and newspapers. As you walked into the back room of the restaurant, there was a sign with a great quote from Runyon: "The race isn't always to the swift nor the battle to the strong, but that's the way to bet."

Joe Healey, the proprietor, treated us all like pals, and I found a clubhouse where I'd spend every weekday night for years. I recall great nights sitting with Bob Costas or John Madden or Al McGuire or Pat Summerall or Bill Brendle. Brendle was a public relations guy for CBS Sports who knew every maître d' and bartender in town. He was famous for running over on his expense account. One night as he handed his CBS-issued American Express card to a waiter, he said, "Date this for tomorrow because I used up today last night." Some say it was the story of his life.

When Bob Ryan, the Hall of Fame NBA writer for the *Boston Globe*, was in the city, he'd debate Mike Lupica of the *New York Daily*

News at the back table of Runyon's. This spurred Joe Valerio (who wrote for the *New York Post*) to later create the ESPN show *The Sports Reporters*. Runyon's was a sportswriter's dream at night, and CBS Sports was a sports fan's dream during the day. I also have fond memories of CBS because that's where I met my wife, Diana, who was on a job interview there in 1981.

In the early '80s there were rumors of cuts throughout CBS, so in 1982, when an opportunity came for me to go into management working for my former boss, Barry Frank, who was now at IMG, I took it. One thing led to another and a few years later I was in a whole new field, becoming a managing director at Bear Stearns on Wall Street.

I remained on Wall Street for sixteen years but kept my hand in sports, writing a column that ran for two decades at *College and Pro Football Newsweekly*. In the early 2000s I began researching a book on rock 'n' roll icon Don Kirshner, and all the great songwriters he discovered, including Bobby Darin, Neil Sedaka, and Carole King. In 2011 *Don Kirshner: The Man with the Golden Ear* became a reality, and my second book followed that on Neil Sedaka's great comeback. I was fortunate to get Elton John to write the foreword for that one.

My CBS years were great years, and recently when we found out that Phyllis George had passed away, we were all so saddened. Like so many others, I wished that I had kept in better touch with her. I had seen her a few years earlier at Saratoga, and she invited me to sit in her clubhouse box. It was as if no time had ever passed. She was the same wonderful person. She was always one of the great people to work with. Sweet and always kind. She died of a rare blood disease that she kept secret for most of the thirty-five years she had it. Her passing and the recent induction of both Mike Pearl and Bob Fishman into the Sports Broadcasting Hall of Fame spurred me to write about the tremendous impact *The NFL Today* had, not only on me, but also probably on anyone who has loved pro football. It was a show that changed pro football, and it certainly changed my life.

—Rich Podolsky, August 2021

CHAPTER ONE

CBS Sports: And That's the Way It Was

WHEN BILL FITTS GRADUATED FROM SWARTHMORE IN 1953 AND GOT a job at WCAU-TV in Philadelphia, he had no idea that many years later he would be instrumental in both the growth of the National Football League on CBS and the rise of ESPN.

WCAU would soon become one of five stations in the country that were owned and operated by the CBS Television Network, which was still run by its founder, William Paley. If you worked at WCAU and if you were good at your job, sooner or later you'd wind up working in New York for the network. This was the case for announcer Jack Whitaker, programmer Jack Dolph, directors Frank Chirkinian and Tony Verna, and later Tom Brookshier. They all wound up working for CBS Sports.

"Jack Dolph was the program director at WCAU," said Fitts when contacted for this book. "I basically became his operations manager, and he brought me with him when he came to New York to work for the network Sports division in 1962."[1]

One of Fitts's first jobs in New York was to set up CBS's NFL regional network. CBS had strong, established teams in most of the country's largest markets. Among them were the New York Giants, the Philadelphia Eagles, the Washington Redskins, the Chicago Bears, the Detroit Lions, the San Francisco 49ers, and the Los Angeles Rams.

At the time there were no satellites, so Fitts had to develop a solid relationship with the phone company, which made carriage of the games possible. "The phone company was extremely important," he said. "They helped out and understood what was going on. It became pretty complicated, especially during the times we had two different announce booths going on."

Talk about being complicated! Yes, if you can believe it, in the early '60s CBS had two different sets of announcers calling the games—one pair whose call would go to the home city, and the other call would go to the visitors.

"In fact, we did closed-circuit rehearsals on Saturdays just so everyone could understand what would happen on Sundays," Fitts said. "All that helped out later [when he produced *The NFL Today*], getting signals to the locations for the 'whip-around,' and then back to the [production] truck."

NBC, realizing what it was missing by not having part of the NFL package, began telecasting games from the new American Football League (AFL) in 1965. Although the markets weren't nearly as strong, they could see the potential.

A bidding war for players emerged, and after six years the two leagues worked out a compromise and merged, with the champions of each league playing each other for the first time on January 15, 1967, in a game promoted as Super Bowl I.

NFL commissioner Pete Rozelle decided to allow both CBS and NBC to broadcast Super Bowl I. The game, played at the Los Angeles Coliseum, wasn't a sellout. That was partly due to the high-ticket price at the time of $12. CBS would do the main camera work and share the feed with NBC, while NBC would have their own cameras for sideline reports. CBS felt they had two great play-by-play announcers in Ray Scott and Jack Whitaker, so they had Scott take the first half and Whitaker the second. Frank Gifford did the color commentary during the game for CBS. Pat Summerall was their sideline reporter.

Over at NBC, Curt Gowdy, on play-by-play, and Paul Christman, doing color, did the entire game, with Charlie Jones reporting from the sidelines. Apparently, tensions grew high between the two networks during the week before the game, and a fence was constructed separating each network's production trucks and personnel.

Bill Creasy was assigned as the producer for CBS, but according to many, Creasy did not get to the truck until halftime. It didn't matter.

Executive producer Bill Fitts was there for CBS, and he was in charge when a few unusual things happened at halftime.

"[NBC analyst] Paul Christman came down at halftime and shouted at me, 'Way too many replays. Way too many,'" recalled Fitts. "I said, 'Paul, those aren't my replays, those are your network's replays.' They had their own tape truck. I said, 'It's your guys who are running those [replays] in, not me.'" Christman turned sheepishly and returned to his booth.

Then something very unusual happened at the start of the second half. Right after the halftime entertainment of trumpeter Al Hirt, marching bands, and high school drill teams, NBC missed the second-half kickoff because they were still airing an interview with Bob Hope.

"Mark Duncan, the head of officials, was a hard-nosed guy," said Fitts. "He came over to me and said, 'Bill, I'm allowing you twenty minutes for this halftime, and I'm warning you that after twenty minutes I'm kicking off, so you better be ready.'"

Fitts took him seriously and assumed he said the same thing to the guys at NBC. He got all of his commercials in with five minutes to spare and was ready in plenty of time for the kickoff. "So I called the NBC producer Lou Kusserow and said, 'You better go to commercial cause they're gonna kick off.' Well, sure enough he didn't and they got caught.'"

Perplexed, the NFL decided to re-kick so NBC wouldn't have egg on their face. "The league said that there was no signal for the kickoff and that's why they re-kicked it," Fitts explained. "But they did signal. We had a camera on the shag man [the official who signals ready for kickoff] down in the end zone and he did signal. There was no question about it."

After the death of Bert Bell, who had been the NFL commissioner from 1946 through October of 1959, the twelve NFL owners argued for a week over who would succeed him. On the twenty-third ballot in January of 1960, they selected Pete Rozelle, the former general manager of the Los Angeles Rams. It was probably the best decision they ever made.

Rozelle, an incredibly smart businessman, saw the popularity of professional football growing and he wanted it on all three networks. So in 1969 he carved out a package of games to be broadcast on Monday nights and offered the package not just to ABC, but to CBS and NBC too.

"CBS and NBC turned it down immediately," said Fitts, "because they had great prime-time programming. ABC was also inclined to turn it down. That's when Rozelle started thinking out of the box.

"He and Bill MacPhail [the head of the CBS Sports division] were great friends. He went to MacPhail and asked him if he could talk to me about setting up his own network, because he was worried that ABC wasn't going to do it. He initiated a couple of conversations with me about it, and I didn't think it would be a huge problem to do. Then ABC got wind of it and realized that if he did his own syndicated network, that most of the stations that joined it would be ABC affiliates. So ABC went ahead and did it, and took all the credit for *Monday Night Football*, when actually it was something they were forced into."

After the AFL won Super Bowl III, Joe Namath and the New York Jets became enormously popular. In a sense, they were America's team. Regardless, CBS was still killing NBC in ratings, mainly because they had the top five markets in the country. In an attempt to level the playing field, Rozelle came up with the brilliant idea of having a double-header game. It would be a chance for NBC to get an exclusive game window without competition from CBS. He wanted NBC's ratings to go up enough that they wouldn't be discouraged enough to drop the package.

"I told the CBS brass, 'Don't okay that,'" said Fitts, "but they did. Now that Rozelle had the NFL on as many different networks as possible, he correctly wanted them all to succeed."

In 1956 CBS hired thirty-six-year-old Bill MacPhail to run its Sports division. At the time, it seemed like his only qualification was that his father, Lee MacPhail, was a tough-minded, well-respected baseball executive. Before arriving at CBS, Bill MacPhail had been the traveling secretary for the Yankees and was the director of publicity for the Kansas City A's.

Living in his father's shadow wasn't easy for Bill, and getting the CBS job proved to be the perfect solution. It also didn't take him long to figure out what the job was. By the early '60s he had hired an all-star list of broadcasters including Jack Whitaker, Jim McKay, Chris Schenkel, Pat Summerall, and Frank Gifford.

MacPhail was exactly where he wanted to be and stayed at CBS Sports for seventeen years before he quietly retired in 1973. During that time he may have been the most-liked executive in sports television. He acquired the rights to the NFL, the NBA, the Triple Crown of horse racing, and the Masters. CBS was loaded with great events.

Of all of MacPhail's great hires, Whitaker may have been the most interesting. Jack had begun his college education at St. Joseph's College in Philadelphia in 1942 when he heard from Uncle Sam. Before he knew it, his dreams of working in radio were on the back burner. With his army platoon, Whitaker landed on the beaches of Normandy June 8, 1944, on the third day of the invasion, and survived being wounded twice.

Once he was honorably discharged, he finished college and got a job at a 1,000-watt station in Allentown, Pennsylvania, where he read the news and interviewed the mayor and pastor on a regular basis. One day in June of 1950 he heard coverage of Ben Hogan's U.S. Open at Merion coming from the newsroom. Only it wasn't on radio but on the new medium of television. His immediate thought was, "That's what I should be doing." The next day he quit his job and returned to Philly, looking for a job in TV.

He interviewed at WCAU-TV, where they asked him if he knew anything about sports because their sportscaster had just given his notice. "I said yes," Whitaker replied. "That's when I realized I didn't."[2]

Nine months earlier Ed McMahon joined the station, and the two became good friends. Whitaker and McMahon were featured nightly on the 11:00 p.m. newscast, led by John Facenda, the future voice of NFL Films. Whitaker did the sports and McMahon did a commentary each night at the end of the broadcast. With their newscast No. 1 in the ratings book, things seemed to be going great, until the CBS Network bought the station in 1957.

The network executives had other ideas. They cut the newscast back to fifteen minutes and got rid of sports and the commentaries altogether. They made Whitaker the weatherman. Can you believe it? Thinking their careers at 'CAU were just about over, McMahon and Whitaker began taking the train every weekday morning to New York, looking for work at the ad agencies that controlled network television. They'd make their rounds then take the train back to Philly in time for the 11 o'clock news.

Whitaker landed work with the CBS Network doing color on weekend NFL games, and McMahon landed a job as the announcer for a new game show called *Who Do You Trust?* The host of that show was a comedian from the Midwest—someone named Johnny Carson—and when NBC hired Carson for *The Tonight Show*, he took McMahon with him.

Whitaker excelled doing color and later play-by-play, and by 1960 the network had hired him to do golf and horse racing too. Soon he was hosting *CBS Sports Spectacular* and *The NFL Today*. Along with Walter Cronkite, he was becoming the face of the network.

To work at CBS Sports in those days was a dream for many. With a staff of just twenty-five, everyone knew everyone else and they didn't need much of an excuse to party. Ellen Beckwith was one of them.

She came to CBS Sports in December of 1966, just a few weeks before the first Super Bowl. She was twenty-one, fresh from a year working as an assistant at WNEW radio for former New York Giants receiver Kyle Rote and also for disc jockey William B. Williams, famous for his program, *Make Believe Ballroom.*

"I came the day of their Christmas party," Beckwith said. "I worked for producers and directors. After a while I moved to the front [of the office] to work for Bill Fitts. Under MacPhail, CBS was a blast and everybody drank. We never knew how the shows would get on the air. On Thursdays we had cocktail hour [after work] and Pat Summerall, or one of the guys, would usually come by and pick up the tab."[3]

She also worked for Jack Dolph, a brilliant programmer who would later become the commissioner of the American Basketball Association (ABA). Dolph had a strange sense of humor. Whenever someone would question his instructions, he'd bellow out, "WHICH WORD DIDN'T YOU UNDERSTAND?" Dolph also liked to wager on many of the events CBS broadcast. He did not do well betting, however. Part of Ellen Beckwith's job was to keep the bookies away.

"He had a great personality and everybody loved him, except the bookies," she said. "The bookies started coming up to CBS [to collect]. At that time, Yvonne Connors was working for him and she would have to fend off the bookies. They would come up to the office and sit there waiting for their money."

After his stint as commissioner of the ABA, Jack opened his own production company, and Beckwith went to work for him there. The bookies, however, kept coming for Dolph. "One Sunday night," said Beckwith, "I was in Runyon's and I remember calling my mother crying. She said, 'What's the matter?' I said, 'Jack can't pay me anymore and I don't know what to do.'" Eventually she went to work for Bill Fitts at ESPN.

"Jack Dolph was one of the smartest programming guys in the business," said Fitts. "His reactions were always right. I loved working for him because he'd trust me to do what I had to do. I just loved the guy. Unfortunately, he did have a few personal habits that weren't so great [betting, drinking]."

Yvonne Connors came to work at CBS in the late '60s as a producer on the Foreign desk. She soon switched over to Sports, where the camaraderie was much better. One of the places the ladies would go after work was Toots Shor's, which was at the corner of 52nd and Sixth Avenue, directly across from CBS. Jackie Gleason was a regular there.

"At Toots Shor's a woman couldn't sit at the bar unescorted," Connors recalled. "Sam Klein was the maître d' and he knew and liked all of the ladies from CBS Sports. When we came in, he was like our father. We'd sit at a table and no man could come over and try to buy us a drink or talk to us. He'd be right there saying, 'Excuse me. You don't talk to these women.'"[4]

The ladies rarely paid for their drinks, though, because Summerall or Bill MacPhail or Bill Creasy would come by and do so. "When I went to work for Jack Dolph, my interview went like this," Connors recalled:

Dolph: "Do you smoke Marlboros?"
Connors: "Yes, I do."
Dolph: "Okay, you're hired."

"Jack was an Army intelligence officer in the Second World War," Connors said. "He was smart but he had that one problem—he loved to gamble. I remember we were dealing with the Bank of New York downstairs [on the ground floor of CBS Black Rock] and there was a man there named Paul Perillo. He'd call me and say, 'I can't keep covering for Jack. The checking account is bouncing.' So I went up to Jack, as mad as I've ever been, and I said, 'We were just kicked out of the Bank of New York. If you keep this up, we'll be dealing with Shanghai National next.'"

Most of the watering holes the CBS gang stopped at were within a block or two of the office. They included Rose's, Kee Wah Yen, Mike Manuche's, and P.J. Clarke's. "We all used to go to Mike Manuche's on Fridays," Yvonne said, "and one Friday Pete Rozelle was there. When we asked for the bill they said that the commissioner had picked it up."

Robin Beck was just nineteen when she moved into the Barbizon Hotel for Women in Manhattan to take daily classes at the Katharine Gibbs Secretarial School. At the Barbizon no man was allowed beyond the first floor. It was where actresses Lauren Bacall and Grace Kelly stayed early in their careers. After nearly a year, Robin graduated and got a job at CBS Sports in 1972. Two years later she was promoted to production assistant, and loved the camaraderie the department had.

"I thought it might be fun one day to bring in a batch of chocolate brownies laced with pot," Beck said when contacted for this book. During a break, several friends went into an empty office and started snacking. Then producer Charles (Chuck) Milton III walked in. "Oh brownies," he said, grabbing one, not knowing their contents.

"He quickly downed one and walked out with another. Nobody said a word," Beck continued. "An hour later they called an ambulance to rush him to the hospital. He thought he was having a heart attack. Turned out he was okay."

Several years later when Robin got married and was leaving the job, everyone signed a big card for her. When she got to Chuck Milton's signature, he added, "P.S. Loved the brownies."[5]

Bill Creasy came from a wealthy family and joined CBS Sports in 1962. Tall and suave, with an all-year tan, Creasy reminded many of the actor George Hamilton. He had a way with the ladies too, and once took actress Sue Lyon in a limo to a Willie Nelson concert. He usually produced games in San Francisco. On the TWA flights he was known as "Mr. Charm." The flight attendants would call him at the office, and he'd tell Yvonne which ones he'd talk to and which ones he wouldn't.

When Creasy was sober he was a charming, clever gentleman and a fantastic producer. In fact, he was assigned to produce some of CBS Sports' top events, including Super Bowls I and II and six Triple Crowns. However, once he started drinking his personality often changed.

"He was a nasty drunk," recalled Connors. "He was awful, AWFUL! I remember Jack Whitaker calling me from downstairs once. Creasy was yelling and screaming. 'Yvonne, get down here,' Whitaker yelled. 'He'll listen to you.'

"At Toots Shor's once Creasy slugged somebody at the bar. I saw this man go crashing over the bar stool onto the floor after Creasy hit him. I think Toots banned him after that. They had to escort him out."

"It was a time," said Yvonne Connors, "to never be seen again."

On September 17, 1961, CBS broadcast its first-ever NFL pregame show. Just fifteen minutes in length, it was hosted by former Notre Dame quarterback Johnny Lujack. The show was called *Pro Football Kickoff*.

In 1962 and '63 Kyle Rote hosted it. The show was still fifteen minutes long but was now called *NFL Kickoff*. In '64 Frank Gifford, the former star New York Giants running back and wide receiver, took over the hosting duties. The only other change was the program's name. It began the season known as *NFL Report*, and halfway through the name was changed to *The NFL Today*.

Gifford remained the host through the 1970 season, with little change in format until it was stretched to a half hour beginning in 1967. In 1968 *The NFL Today* was produced on Thursday nights, with features taped and sent to the different remotes. The sports columnist Dave Anderson of the *New York Times* came in Thursday nights to write some copy. He later won a Pulitzer Prize at the *Times*.

In 1970 a young woman named Marjorie Margolies came up from WCAU to help write segments for the show. A University of Pennsylvania graduate, she impressed enough people at the Philadelphia station that they allowed her to represent WCAU at the 1968 Mexico City Olympics. There, with a cameraman at her disposal, she wrote and appeared on camera doing several human interest pieces that were a big success back at that station.

"I went by myself," Margolies said when contacted by the author. "I told my bosses at 'CAU that I spoke Spanish and could send back stories. I did features on [John] Carlos and [Tommie] Smith, Tommy Waddell and Bill Toomey. Tommy Waddell was a doctor taking a break from his residency. He came in sixth in the decathlon. They were offbeat, human interest stories. The bosses at 'CAU liked them."[6]

"I was friendly with the sports guys at 'CAU," she said, "like [former Eagles defensive back] Tom Brookshier and [former Eagles tight end] Pete Retzlaff, who became my best friend."

In '70 they sent her to New York to write and produce features for *The NFL Today*. The first few weeks of the season she was also the on-air talent presenting the features, which, according to Bill Fitts, were good. "She was a terrific writer and a good [on-air] talent," said Fitts.

"After the second week MacPhail called me in," recalled Fitts, "and said, 'You've got to replace her on the air. We want to use the Winston cigarette girl.'"

The Winston cigarette girl was a very sexy brunette named Carole Howey. She was featured in a thirty-second song-and-dance number called "Me and My Winstons." But on April 1, 1970, she was out of a job when President Nixon signed the Public Health Cigarette Smoking Act, banning cigarette advertising on television. So she and her husband (who happened to be a CBS executive) asked their good friend Frank Gifford, the host, if there was anything he could do. The next thing you know, she was on the show. "I produced Carole's features," said Margolies. "She was lovely, but she was a work in progress."

It was enough of an angle, though, that both *TV Guide* and the *New York Times* wrote feature stories about the two women working together on a football show. "We were trying to appeal to women," Margolies told *TV Guide*'s Elinor Kaine for the December 5, 1970 issue. "We didn't want the women just sitting there knitting or opening beers [for their husband]."

Among the items Howey offered to *TV Guide* were that she thought Rams quarterback Roman Gabriel was "kind of cute," and that Gifford had introduced her to her husband.

ZEROING IN
ON A BROAD AUDIENCE

CBS sends out a couple of girls—
to scout for female football fans

By Elinor Kaine

This year, for the first time, *The NFL Today*, a 30-minute program preceding Sunday pro football games on CBS, includes a weekly segment written, produced and reported by a two-girl production team. These features take direct aim at a female audience.

"We hired Marjorie Margolies as the writer-producer, and an actress, Carole Howey, as reporter," said Bill Fitts, who has been producing NFL football on CBS since 1962. "No one is interfering with what the girls have in mind. We want it to →

Football for females: Marjorie Margolies (top) and Carole Howey are trying to make women into professional football fans.

That's Marjorie Margolies (top) in this 1970 *TV Guide* feature on women in football. Below is Carole Howey, the former "Winston Cigarette Girl" who replaced Margolies on *The NFL Today* because she was a friend of host Frank Gifford. (COURTESY MARJORIE MARGOLIES)

"I stayed for the rest of the season," Margolies continued. "She [Howey] was just okay. She didn't come up to Phyllis George's ankles [in talent], but no one did. And I was much more of a news person."

Margolies left CBS after that year and went to work for NBC and *The Today Show*, writing and producing her own pieces out of WRC-TV in Washington, D.C. She won five Emmy Awards along the way and in 1992 ran for Congress from Pennsylvania and won.

Margolies usually got emotionally connected to the people she did stories on. When she did a piece on a Korean orphanage, she later wound up adopting one Korean child and another from Vietnam.

"One of the stories I did for *The Today Show*," she said, "was about a heart surgeon who I wound up trying to fix up with Katie Couric. He did a transplant for a NBC sports cameraman who got the heart of a twenty-two-year-old Korean kid. Turns out the kid's parents owned a deli across from the Redskins training center. Every day that cameraman had walked into his parents' deli."

After interviewing congressman Edward Mezvinsky, Marjorie Margolies married him, and in 2010 their son Marc Mezvinsky married Chelsea Clinton. For the last twenty years Margolies has taught Political Science at Penn. As far as working for Bill Fitts on *The NFL Today* went, Margolies said, "I just loved working for him. He was such a decent guy."

Future Hall of Fame director Bob Fishman also worked at WCAU in Philly in the summer of 1969, just after graduating from Boston University. "Here's the craziest thing," Fishman said. "I was running Tele-PrompTer for [Tom] Brookshier, [sports director] Andy Musser, and [newscaster] John Facenda [who was the voice of NFL Films]. And I went on shoots as a production assistant for Marjorie Margolies."[7]

In the early '70s he worked weekends for Bill Fitts helping with film transfers from NFL Films, and he also worked as a production assistant on horse racing with Bill Creasy. "Before [Bob] Wussler [became the head of CBS Sports], I wanted to work full time," Fishman said, "but it seemed to me that the sports department was a closed Irish drinking fraternity."

In 1971 Frank Gifford left to become the play-by-play announcer on *Monday Night Football* and work with Don Meredith and Howard

Cosell. Cosell did voice-over highlights of Sunday's games during *Monday Night's* halftime, and his presentation was well received by viewers.

To replace Gifford, CBS brought Summerall and Whitaker in from the field to cohost in the studio. As before, everything was taped on Thursday nights, but that all changed in 1974. That year, as a response to ABC's *Monday Night* halftime highlights, executive producer Fitts decided to go live with *The NFL Today* for the first time. Whitaker was now cohosting with Lee Leonard from two separate studios. It was an experiment that didn't go well due to timing and coordination issues.

But Fitts did break ground in several ways. Besides going live, he was able to show what the game sites looked like with the "whip-around," which was at the start of the show. "In terms of the whip-around," said Fitts, "it was a way to quickly establish the scope of the show. Since special effects were lacking, there was a problem with the quad split [showing four different game sites at the same time]. We had to stack four monitors and shoot them with a camera. There had to be careful technical control or the pictures would roll." But it did work.

His entire intention with going live was to show halftime audiences across the country same-day highlights of other games for the very first time. To some extent it worked, but it wasn't organized well enough to be an easy voice-over for Whitaker when the highlights popped up. As Fitts said, "The pace was just too fast for him, and I didn't adapt fast enough to help him."

Although MacPhail had been at CBS seventeen years, he was still only fifty-three years old when he was forced into retirement in 1973. According to executive Kevin O'Malley, here's what happened:

"I had written a column for a Boston College alumni newspaper," O'Malley recalled, "saying, 'If you like college football on television, you probably can't stand watching Chris Schenkel and Bud Wilkinson [on ABC], especially if you've heard Lindsey Nelson.'"[8]

An executive at CBS News read it and sent it to MacPhail, who arranged a meeting with O'Malley and eventually hired him, creating the position of Director of Program Development at CBS Sports.

"You have to remember," said O'Malley, "that CBS Sports started out as kind of a poor relative in the whole spectrum of CBS. They were No. 1 in prime time, they were No. 1 in News, they were No. 1 in children's programming. They were No. 1 in everything. In Sports they had the NFL, the Masters, but only four other tournaments, none of which were any good. They had the U.S. Open Tennis championships, but tennis was hardly a big winner in the late '60s. But Bill MacPhail was the sweetest man you'd ever meet in the business, and he had a whole cadre of friends in the business that loved him personally. One of his closest friends was Pete Rozelle."

CBS was perfectly happy with MacPhail because they didn't prioritize Sports. Everything else made so much money. They weren't known as "The Tiffany Network" for nothing. It was because they made so much *more* money than the other networks. Their stars included Mary Tyler Moore, Lucille Ball, and Walter Cronkite.

"He was a very lovable figure," O'Malley said of MacPhail. "But Bill had an alcohol problem, which is why he left. Larry MacPhail was his father and a tyrant. He made the lives of his sons miserable. Bill was cowed and beaten down by his father. When he would invite Bill to meet him for lunch at the [stodgy] Metropolitan Club [on Fifth Avenue], Bill literally couldn't sleep the night before. He'd be in the office shaking with the door closed in fear of having lunch with his father. People with that kind of family experience are rarely as accomplished as Bill. He had a marvelous ability to get along with everybody. They respected him and liked him.

"I came [to CBS Sports] in June of '73 and Bill was gone by the end of the year. The alcohol thing got out of hand to the point that Pat Summerall and Bob Wood [who was the president of the CBS Television Network] did an intervention and brought him to a place in Westchester to kind of dry out. The company eased the way for him to resign, and nobody ever wrote a thing about it in the newspapers."

MacPhail recovered well enough to go to work for Ted Turner at CNN and help start a sports department for the new cable channel. After seventeen years the easy-going beloved leader in the CBS Sports division was gone. In a sense, the party was over.

In mid-1974 visionary CBS executive Bob Wussler arrived, replacing MacPhail, and nothing would be quite the same again—especially *The NFL Today*.

Before Wussler arrived at CBS Sports, wrote former *New York Times* sports editor Neil Amdur in a December 7, 1982, article, "*The NFL Today* was limited technically and artistically. The first person who understood the importance of combining the technical capabilities of sports broadcasting with live editorial responsibilities was Bob Wussler."

His first move was to make Brent Musburger a star.

CHAPTER TWO

Brent Musburger: The Natural

THINGS TOOK A DRAMATIC TURN FOR BRENT MUSBURGER BEGINNING the autumn of '68. While employed as a sports columnist for the *Chicago American* newspaper, he had been doing some part-time work for WBBM Radio when the station decided they wanted a man at the Mexico City Olympics.

It was too late to request a credential, so, according to *Sports Illustrated*: "Musburger passed himself off as Al Silverman, then the editor of *Sport Magazine*, who hadn't gone to the Games. Gliding around with his tape recorder, Musburger cornered John Carlos and Tommie Smith in an area off-limits to the press, minutes after their famous black-power salute. The 12-minute tape made airwaves across the country, and WBBM wanted to hire him full-time the minute he got home."[1]

Part of the allure was that Brent had written a column ripping Carlos and Smith's actions, calling them "black-skinned [Nazi] storm troopers." John Carlos, to this day, is still waiting for an apology, but at the time the black power salute on the Olympic medal stand was not favorably received in the United States.[2]

Brent loved his job at the *Chicago American*. By then he had moved all the way up to full-time columnist and was making $13,500 a year (equivalent to $117,000 today), when WBBM offered to double his salary. He went to his editor at the newspaper hoping he'd offer a nice raise so he could stay. Instead he got a lecture.

"Oh, you're crazy," his sports editor yelled at Musburger, who at that moment felt much smaller than his six-foot-two-inch frame. "Nobody gives away a newspaper column." Brent knew he'd never make that kind of money working in the newspaper business. He was married to Arlene, and they had plans for starting a family. "Had they offered me $10,000 a year more I would have stayed," he said.[3]

"I wanted to take the chance," Musburger told VSiN (Vegas Stats and Information Network) in 2017. "I figured I could always come back [to writing]. I had always felt the biggest weakness in radio was the absence of good reporting."

In retrospect, it was an easy decision. And maybe the most important one he made his entire career. He excelled at WBBM Radio and soon he was on WBBM-TV, doing sports news and highlights with ease and flair. Meanwhile, just five years later, in September of 1974, the *Chicago American* printed its final edition and went quietly into the night.

Before long Musburger was doing four radio shows and three commentaries a day.

"I would be surprised if we only paid him double his newspaper salary," said Van Gordon Sauter, who was the news director at WBBM Radio at that time. "But he came full time and was a tremendous asset to the station."[4]

"He was a wonderful hire," Sauter continued. "He had great energy. He was very sophisticated about his audience, and he was incredibly effective. He was a natural from the moment he started radio [in 1968]. I met him and liked him. He was ambitious, as he has always been, and I don't say that as a criticism. He wanted to do things."

Soon thereafter Sauter became news director at WBBM-TV and also hired Brent there. Later, he left to become the general manager of the CBS-owned-and-operated KNXT-TV in Los Angeles, and in 1980 became president of CBS Sports for two years.

He did recall one unusual thing about Musburger. "While most people in the news business drove around in a four-year-old Chevy," Sauter said, releasing a small chuckle, "Brent drove a butterscotch-colored Porsche."

That drive and that energy of Musburger's that Sauter spoke of goes all the way back to his father, Cec Musburger, and Brent's days growing up in Billings, Montana.

When Brent was in first grade, his father Cecil, or "Cec" as he liked to be called, took him to Chicago to see the Harlem Globetrotters play. Cec pulled some strings and got seats right down near the floor. It turned out that the kid wound up sitting next to one of the most famous sportswriters in the country, Arch Ward, the sports editor of the *Chicago Tribune*. Ward was the man credited for creating the baseball All-Star Game, back in 1933. Sitting next to and chatting with Ward during the game must've made some impression on Brent.

"From that point on, my life's ambition was to be a newspaperman," Musburger told former *Tribune* columnist Ed Sherman.[5]

Cecil C. Musburger was born in North Dakota in 1912, the son of Milo and Anna Musburger. His mother died when he was just a year old, and by 1930 his father had moved Cec, his brother Leo, and his stepmother to Lockwood, Montana, a suburb of Billings, where they rented a farm.

Several years later Cec married Beryl Ruth Woody, and in 1939 Brent was born in Portland, Oregon. The family moved back to Billings when Brent was a toddler, and in 1944 Todd was born, five years Brent's junior.

To understand Brent Musburger you have to know who Cec Musburger was. Cec was a man who liked to get things done. He was a striver. He owned and operated his own appliance business in Billings, and when his son wanted to play Little League baseball, Cec organized the first Little League teams in Billings.

"My father was born in Bismarck (N.D.), but moved at a very young age to Ashland," Musburger told the *Great Falls Tribune* in 2010. "He lived all over the state of Montana and his father drove stagecoaches into Yellowstone from Gardiner. . . . My mother grew up outside of Jackson [Wyoming] on a ranch."[6]

In a January 16, 1984, profile, *Sports Illustrated* described Brent's parents as "two rugged individualists who would have fit well in a Zane Grey novel."

"My dad (Cecil) owned an appliance store in Billings and briefly had one in Great Falls, on Central Avenue," Musburger said in the *Great Falls Tribune* article. "I was working for my dad and whatever appliances they'd need to get from Billings to Great Falls, I'd truck 'em up. I made that [three-and-a-half-hour] drive way too often."

When Brent was eight, in 1947, he was already a huge baseball fan. "I grew up reading the *Billings Gazette* every day," Brent said in an August 12, 2011, article in that newspaper, "trying to outrace my father to the sports page so that I could study those box scores. And I guess, that's when I decided I wanted to become a sportswriter."

That summer Cec took him back to Chicago, to Wrigley Field, to see Jackie Robinson and the Brooklyn Dodgers play the Cubs. "My father took a 16-millimeter picture of Jackie, who came over and posed," Musburger recalled.[7] It was a moment a boy would never forget.

Around the time Brent was twelve, he was a bit mischievous and convinced his brother Todd to accompany him as he "borrowed" the car of the family's cleaning lady for a half-hour drive. Another time, Brent's dog Flicka was impounded for not wearing the proper tag. One night soon after, Brent and his pals broke into the pound and not only set Flicka free, but also thirty-five other dogs. He figured it would be a lot more difficult to blame him if all the dogs were gone.[8]

To teach him better behavior, Cec and Beryl decided to send Brent away to the Shattuck Military Academy in Faribault, Minnesota, where he would learn some discipline and spend his high school years.

But before sending him away, Cec wanted to give him the feel of playing for a Little League team. The only trouble was that Billings didn't have one. So after reading an article in the *Saturday Evening Post*, Cec wrote to Little League founder Carl Stotz. Stotz responded with some encouraging words and also sent him a price list for everything he'd need to establish a four-team league, including uniforms at $6 each, caps for 75 cents each, $8 catcher's mitts, and baseballs, which were then $18 per dozen.

Sixty-four years later, in 2016, the Billings Chamber of Commerce renamed their Little League field in Cec Musburger's honor. At the ceremony Brent waved that original price list and said, "My, how times have changed!" Cec Musburger not only started the league in Billings, he also gave the kids proper instruction and taught them baseball fundamentals. Dick Cox, who was one of the boys who played alongside Brent that summer, was at the ceremony and talked about the time Cec drove the team two hours to Miles City to play against a team of reform school kids.

"I asked one kid what he was in for," Cox told the *Billings Gazette*. "He said, 'Reading comic books in church.'"

Cec also taught the Boy Scouts how to raise money. "He taught us how to sell candy," said one former Scout. "Ask them to buy three," Cec suggested. "We sold a lot of candy that year."

Dave McNally, who was two years younger than Brent, used to tag along that summer. McNally, who wound up being a star pitcher for the Baltimore Orioles and a World Series winner, would show up at the field with his black Labrador and take over the field maintenance duties that Brent didn't particularly care for. "I was allergic to manual labor, and I am to this day," Brent Musburger told the crowd during the sixty-minute ceremony. "Dave became one of Cec's favorites. He was a hardworking kid."

Musburger loved growing up in Billings, a town where you didn't have to lock your car or your front door. "It was an unbelievable place to grow up," Brent said. "We didn't have a TV, so we used our imaginations. We made stuff up."[9]

Taking a cue from Cec, Brent also sold programs and popcorn at the Billings Mustangs games. The Mustangs were the Pioneer League Rookie affiliate for the Cincinnati Reds and the closest thing to big-time baseball they had in Billings.

"Growing up I just wanted to play baseball," Brent said, looking back. "I wasn't that good, but I sure did like playing. I would have preferred to be a player, to be right alongside Dave McNally, but I think I knew at an early age that wasn't going to happen. I doubt that I'd have this kind of life of leisure if I'd grown up somewhere else."[10]

After graduating high school, he was accepted into Northwestern, where he ran into a bit of trouble again. He was suspended after his freshman year for having a car on campus that wasn't properly licensed.

Dejected, Brent was set to go back to Billings, when his dad suggested he try the Al Somers School for Umpires in Daytona Beach. Cec had umpired Little League and he knew Brent wasn't going to be a star athlete, yet he loved baseball. While in Daytona, Brent supported himself by selling tickets to the Daytona 500 and also working at Cleveland Indians exhibition games in Florida. After graduating umpire school, he spent that next summer umpiring in the Class D Midwest League. He ejected a lot of players that summer, but one incident convinced him to quit.

"It was 1958, in Michigan City, Ind.," Musburger explained to the Montana Hall of Fame folks. "Juan Marichal, a super prospect in the San Francisco Giants farm system, was pitching and the game was tied at 1–1 in the eighth inning.

"A batter hit a ball that bounced over the fence, but I lost it in the lights and called it a home run. I ended up kicking three guys out of the game. I led the league in ejections that year with 15. I needed a police escort to get off the field. It was at that point in my young life that I decided to go into sports writing because I could use an eraser when I made a mistake."[11]

Musburger eventually returned to Northwestern for two more years. He then became a sports editor in DeKalb, Illinois. "I had promised [my parents] that I would come back and finish school," he said, "but I never made it."[12]

In 1962, Musburger landed a job with the *Chicago American* newspaper as a sports reporter. Just twenty-two, he showed an ability to write sports immediately. He quickly got promoted and was assigned the Chicago White Sox beat, which was a job anyone on the paper would have loved. The White Sox were good in those days and battled the Yankees for the pennant, year in and year out.

It was his first time covering big-time professional teams, which he found far different from interviewing high school or college athletes.

Dave DeBusschere, a pitcher for the White Sox, was one of the young athletes Musburger got to know. DeBusschere also played for the Detroit Pistons in the NBA and more famously helped the New York Knicks win NBA championships in 1970 and 1973.

"We had some late nights," Brent recalled. "You learned about the pressures and insecurities of being an athlete, and what their families go through. I thought I knew it, but I didn't. I don't think those relationships happen today."[13]

In 1963 he'd also be covering the Chicago Bears. It was a good year to be covering them because the Bears only lost one game all season behind No. 89 Mike Ditka. They went on to beat the New York Giants in the championship game, 14–10.

"I didn't tell anyone, but I had seen only one pro (football) game in my life," he said. "I was lucky, though. The Bears won the championship that year and I became a good reporter."[14]

That year the NFL decided to play their games the Sunday after President John F. Kennedy was shot. While the entire country was mourning, the NFL played, but the TV networks did not cover the games. Musburger, however, was told to be at Forbes Field in Pittsburgh, where the Bears were playing the Steelers.

"I was really, really going off," Brent said. "'Who in the world would think of playing football today?' [he said, half out loud where others in the press box could hear him]. An older man in a topcoat heard me and reached for a bottle of Jack Daniels. He said, 'Young man, maybe this will make you feel better.' . . . Later, I asked someone, 'Who was that old guy?' He said, 'Brent, that's Art Rooney [owner of the Steelers].'"[15]

Covering the Bears certainly laid the groundwork for Brent to feel totally comfortable when *The NFL Today* opportunity happened. He had spent time not just with the players, but also with coaches like George Allen (then the defensive coordinator in Chicago).

In 1969 it didn't take Brent long to become the WBBM-TV sports anchor in Chicago as well. "I would say that my being a TV sportscaster is more luck," he told sixteen-year-old high school interviewer Todd Salen in 1972. "I didn't study broadcasting at Northwestern and I don't consider myself a professional broadcaster at all."[16]

It might have been luck and just might have been, as Sauter pointed out, that Brent was a natural talent. By 1973 he was a rising star with the CBS Television Network. He proved his versatility by doing play-by-play on a full slate of NFL games that season. In four short years at WBBM he was now getting network assignments. His on-air partners that year were ex-Minnesota running back Tommy Mason, former Detroit Lions linebacker Wayne Walker, and Green Bay Packers legend Bart Starr. Although Musburger did not get the most attractive games, his work was still first-rate and impressed some of the producers at CBS Sports. He was on the verge of breaking through.

In 1974 CBS Sports executive producer Bill Fitts tried taking the network's pregame show live for the first time. Hosting the show that year was Jack Whitaker. While Whitaker was a splendid sportscaster, he wasn't suited for the quick pace of the live show with highlights being thrown at him from every angle at halftime.

One weekend, however, Whitaker was scheduled to be in Ireland covering the Irish Derby for the network's anthology show, *CBS Sports Spectacular*. Fitts decided to bring Mr. Musburger in from Chicago to try his hand at doing the pregame show live.

"Whitaker struggled so much it's a miracle he didn't have a nervous breakdown," said Tommy O'Neill, one of the producers that year for the pregame show. "Jack was doing something that no one had ever tried before, including no one on the production end of it.

"When Brent came in that week he thought he was in heaven. He was phenomenal. He caught on so quickly and adjusted to all the different problems. He had such enthusiasm. He was like a kid in a candy store. When they'd be setting up for the next segment, he'd be laughing and he'd say, 'Look at all that I have here. I've got this, I've got that,' and he just ate it up."[17]

Ed Goren, who was the associate producer of the show, agreed. "He just sold it," Goren said. "He then showed that he didn't need a Tele-PrompTer and had a clock in his head to say the right thing in the proper time frame."[18]

Bill Fitts, though, deserves a lot of credit for implementing the live format in '74. Through trial and error he put together little pieces of the show that worked and eliminated those that didn't.

"By going live," Fitts said, "the show got a lot more complicated, particularly at halftime, with remotes coming in at different times. The No. 1 problem was that I didn't have Brent. I had Jack, and the show was just too fast for him. Jack was a great guy and a great writer, but this show was just not designed for him."[19]

But Fitts wasn't about to embarrass Whitaker by replacing him for the second half of the season. By 1974 Jack Whitaker was already an icon at CBS. He was so well thought of that he shared play-by-play duties with Ray Scott on Super Bowl I. Before that he had done everything imaginable at WCAU, the CBS owned-and-operated station in Philadelphia, including the local sports, the weather, and appearing in the late-afternoon soap opera *Action in the Afternoon*, before the network brought him to New York. At times in the '60s he was the face of CBS Sports, especially hosting the annual Masters golf tournament, a prized possession for the network.

While Whitaker was covering the Monday playoff round of the 1966 Masters, Jack Nicklaus was closing in on his third green jacket. After Nicklaus hit his shot to the green on the 18th hole and started walking toward it, the throngs on either side of the fairway ropes broke through and rushed into the fairway to get position for the final shots. The broadcast was already running late, and Whitaker was feeling pressure from the Walter Cronkite news group to throw it to them ASAP. In his haste, Jack described the throngs of spectators rushing into the fairway behind Nicklaus as a "mob," and then after Nicklaus putted out, he immediately sent the audience to Cronkite in New York.

Clifford Roberts, who ran the Masters, was infuriated by the "mob" comment and also that CBS didn't show the green jacket ceremony. He told CBS that if they wanted to keep the event, they could no longer have Jack Whitaker on the broadcast. CBS might have loved Whitaker, but they couldn't afford to lose the Masters. Whitaker spent the next four years watching the event from home before Roberts allowed him to rejoin the broadcast team. That was 1971 when he returned. The sting was still fresh in everyone's memory.

The brass at CBS knew Whitaker was not at fault, yet they allowed him to take the heat after he had given them so many years of great calls and masterful essays. Bill Fitts had this in mind when he brought Jack Whitaker back to finish the 1974 season, although he now knew it would be a better show with Brent.

Musburger's boss at WBBM in Chicago was a young executive named Robert (Bob) Wussler. In 1972 Wussler was promoted to general manager of the CBS-owned-and-operated station. He watched Musburger progress right under his nose and knew what a great talent he was. Then in 1974 the network asked Wussler to move to New York and become the new head of CBS Sports. It was a dream job for Wussler, who was a big sports fan, and for Musburger, it was his passport to celebrity.

Chapter Three

Phyllis George: More Than a Pretty Face

THE YEAR BEFORE PHYLLIS GEORGE WON MISS AMERICA, SHE THOUGHT she was a lock to go to Atlantic City as Miss Texas, but she lost.

"I came in second to a drummer from Longview," Phyllis told *Texas Monthly*. "The local papers had to retrieve their original headline of 'Miss Denton Becomes Miss Texas.'" The experience soured her on the thought of trying again in 1970. "It hurt my pride and I said I don't want to do this again."[1]

She had grown up in Denton, a small town just forty-two miles north of Dallas. Her parents were hard-working Methodist people. As a young girl every year she watched the Miss America pageant with her mom.

"Back in the day, it was the biggest thing on television," she told the University of Texas in 2018. "And I would walk around with books on my head, so I'd have that perfect posture. My dad always said, 'Eat your carrots, Phyl. Your eyes will sparkle.' I hated carrots, but I ate them."[2]

She started taking piano lessons when she was seven, and she could throw a ball farther than most of the guys. She was one of those high school kids everybody liked. She was Miss Denton High School, president of the junior class, and in all of the plays. "My mother used to say, 'Phyllis, settle down and smell the roses.'"[3] So it was no surprise when the Denton Chamber of Commerce asked her to enter the Miss Texas pageant.

The following year, 1970, the Miss Dallas contingent kept asking her to run for their title. She kept saying no. Late one Friday night she stopped by her Zeta Tau Alpha sorority house, where her sorority sisters

Teenage Phyllis George poses with her mom, Diantha Cogdell George. The two always watched the Miss America Pageant together every year. (COURTESY OF PAMELA BROWN)

tried to talk her into running without success. She grabbed her dirty laundry and headed home. Shortly after arriving, the phone rang.

"I ran over and answered it, and I was like, 'Hello?' I thought, 'Who's calling at midnight?' Sure enough, it was an official from the Miss Dallas pageant, who said, 'I'm just going to give you this one last chance, Phyllis. You were so close last year that we really think you could win this year.' And I said, 'Are you kidding me?' The preliminaries were the next morning! But the scholarship money was important enough to me, that he flat talked me into it."

Somehow she got her gown and shoes and swimsuit together in time to arrive in Dallas the next day. Her mother didn't quite understand what was happening. "But I did it, and I won Miss Dallas."[4]

She did it by switching her talent and playing an arrangement of swing tunes on the same flute she'd had since fifth grade. "After I won, the stories all referred to me as a flautist," she says. "I wasn't a flautist—I was a Texas flute tooter!"[5]

"And you know what? Had I won the year before, I wouldn't have won Miss America. I just wasn't ready. I needed the loss. I needed to lose to win. I came back and went on to be the fiftieth Miss America—the first one with a gold crown."[6]

That night, as a sign of the times, a group of feminists were protesting outside the Boardwalk Hall in Atlantic City, where the pageant was held. This was something Phyllis would have to get used to almost everywhere she stopped on her Miss America travels.

Although she had a beautiful singing voice, and played the flute successfully to win Miss Texas, in the Miss America pageant she decided to use her experience of fourteen years taking piano. She played the popular Burt Bacharach tune "Raindrops Keep Fallin' on My Head" while smiling the entire time and swaying back and forth as if she was having a grand old time. Eighty million viewers had tuned in.

When Bert Parks announced that she had won, the dimpled five-foot-eight-inch beauty was handed flowers, a robe, and the Miss America scepter, and the gold crown was loosely placed on her head. It was a real balancing act in a very emotional moment. As she started to walk the runway in her long gown—even before Parks could get the first words of the song out—her gold crown fell. Luckily it was by her side. The stones went everywhere and the audience gasped.

"All I could think was, 'This is your moment, Phyllis—all your friends and family are watching—and look what you did!' But even then I could laugh about it."[7]

Without a sign of panic, she calmly picked the crown up and smartly decided to hold on to it rather than try to replace it on her head. As she walked, Parks sang the famous song written by Bernie Wayne sixteen years earlier. (Wayne, by the way, also wrote the classic Bobby Vinton

Phyllis George, with her trademark smile and dimples, after accepting the 1971 Miss America crown and scepter. (COURTESY PAMELA BROWN)

tune "Blue Velvet.") Along the runway she stopped and smiled for long periods for the cameras and managed to return to the stage in one piece, just as Parks was completing the song's final lines:

There she is,
Walking on air she is,
Fairest of the fair she is,
Miss A-mer-i-ca.

Three nights later she told Johnny Carson, "You'll remember me. I'm the klutzy Miss America," which only made the viewers and the press love her even more.

The victory meant she would lead six other state winners on a twenty-two-day USO tour of Vietnam. It sounded more like a life sentence than a reward. Although she won in September of 1970, the title was for the year 1971, which was right in the heart of America's controversial participation in the Vietnam War. At each stop they made, the girls would put on a show, singing and dancing in little white outfits—short skirts and go-go boots—for two and a half hours before a mob of soldiers, starving for something from home.

One army clerk, Neil Dobos, in An Khê, Vietnam, was lucky enough to be chosen to escort Miss America 200 yards from the airstrip to the stage. "I could not believe that I was the one picked for such an honor and privilege," Dobos said in a YouTube post. "So I asked the lieutenant why the commanding officer chose me. He said, 'You just got to Vietnam, right? That makes you the least horny.'"

He then saluted the major who brought Phyllis over to him. "I came to attention and held my salute for him, but I looked right at Phyllis and she was looking at me. I noticed her head was up, chin pulled in and a little tiny wrinkle on her brow. God, I thought, my appearance was so impressive that it registered on her face. She didn't realize it, but I knew that that is what I looked like to her. I wanted to run down the steps and tell her, 'No, no. I'm not really the soldier you think I am. I was drafted.'

"At the moment the major returned my salute she angled off the path from him, and with a big, bright smile on her face she climbed up the steps, held out her hand to me, and in a sweet Southern accent said, 'Hi, I'm Phyllis George from Texas.' I grabbed her hand and said, 'Hi, I'm Neil from the western part of Connecticut.' And then as if we were going out for ice cream, she grabbed my arm and asked if we were ready to go.

"There I was walking the runway with Miss America. If anything happened to her then, the entire country would want to know, who let it happen. With Miss America walking at my side, I felt like John Wayne. If we were going to be attacked, I thought, let it be now. Walking beside Phyllis makes you feel like you can defeat the entire North Vietnamese army."

He escorted her to the stage and waited by the side door until the show was over to escort her back. "When she met me," he said, "she said something that endeared her to me forever. She said, 'Did you enjoy the show, Neil?' She remembered my name. I walked her back up the runway, stopping for pictures and autographs along the way, and before she went back inside she signed my flyer and we said good-bye. I was too shy to hug her, but when I got back home I married my own 'Miss America.'"[8]

One month into the rugged schedule, Phyllis called home and whined, "Oh, Mother, I'm tired of having to be pretty." Her mother reminded her how resilient she could be, and she toughened up when the press started getting tough. At press conferences back in the States, questions about how she felt about Vietnam and other social issues of the time came up on a regular basis.

"Everyone expects me to be a universal authority," she told *Family Weekly*, "not only on teen problems and fashions but also on world affairs. As a student at North Texas State University I discussed contemporary issues in class and among friends, but nothing I ever said was astounding enough to be printed."[9]

Back in 1971, the feminist groups would picket anywhere Miss America went. Phyllis quickly learned how to deal with it in a very peaceful way.

"The 'women's libbers'—we didn't call them 'feminists'—would follow me around," she said. "I was in DeKalb, Illinois, I kept saying, 'They're not picketing me, they're picketing what they think this program stands for.' So I went outside and said, 'It's really cold out here. Why don't you guys come in and let's have some coffee and talk about this?'

"So they all came in. And I said, 'Look, I don't feel like I'm exploited. I'm from a small town in Texas. This is great for me. I won scholarship money. I've done something with my life, and I can show my talent. I want to be in broadcasting. This is going to help me, so I want you to look at it that way.' Did I like being in a swimsuit? Absolutely not. I hated it. And now they wear these little Band-Aids!"[10]

During that year on the road she appeared on *The Tonight Show Starring Johnny Carson* several times, and along the way she got to meet some famous people, including President Lyndon Johnson and his wife Lady Bird. She also got to meet John Wayne. "He heard that I did a great John Wayne imitation and he dared me to do it, and I did," she said laughing.[11]

When the year was up, she crowned the 51st Miss America and then returned to college, thanks to her $10,000 scholarship, this time at Texas Christian University in Fort Worth. She didn't finish the year, however, and instead packed up and headed to New York, where a new world of opportunities awaited her. Soon she'd be starring in a thirty-second cotton commercial modeling a cotton towel, a cotton T-shirt, and that million-dollar smile.

In 1972, when Phyllis George arrived in New York after her year as Miss America, she was hoping to land a job in broadcasting. She began by doing some modeling. "I always thought I was the cute one. You've got these gorgeous, thin, tall models who walk in and I'd go, 'Whoa, what am I doing here?'"[12]

Making the rounds, she ran into two young, handsome producers from CBS Sports, Tommy O'Neill and Bob Stenner.

"She was trying to get some commercial work and kind of struggling a little," said O'Neill. "We all became friends, and while she was hanging out with us, she was just one of the guys. Like Monday nights when we'd go to Il Vagabondo and some of the neighborhood places like Mr. Laffs."[13]

Il Vagabondo was an old-world red-sauce Italian restaurant on East 61st Street in Manhattan. It launched as an Italian social club with an in-house bocce court in 1910, and then slowly became a restaurant in the

1960s. By the early 1970s, the place was so popular that it expanded to the townhouse next door. The three or four or five of them would have a standing date there every Monday night.

Mr. Laffs was a popular saloon on First Avenue in Manhattan, owned by former Yankee star Phil Linz. Sports stars, models, and television people flocked there and were always greeted warmly by bartender Joe Healy.

O'Neill and Stenner introduced Phyllis to some of their pals, who included New York Rangers star Rod Gilbert and former New York Giants running back Tucker Frederickson, whom she dated for a while. Those two could have been two of the most eligible bachelors in New York at the time. Gilbert was always a fun-loving guy, and even caught the attention of Andy Warhol, who painted his portrait. And Frederickson, with his blond hair and southern drawl, was the basis for the Billy Clyde Puckett character in Dan Jenkins's bestseller *Semi-Tough*. Burt Reynolds played the character based on Tucker in the film version.

After Phyllis and Tucker stopped dating, they all settled into a comfortable friendship. "She was just delightful and fun," said O'Neill. Bob Stenner added, "She was not only beautiful but she was also a great friend."[14]

When the Miss America pageant invited her back to cohost with Bert Parks, it gave her a chance to be seen on TV, and in '74 Allen Funt hired her as a cohost for his *Candid Camera* show in New York. But working as the second banana to Funt wasn't exactly what Phyllis had in mind when she sought out a job in broadcasting.

Near the end of that year, CBS decided to make a change at the top of CBS Sports. Longtime president Bill MacPhail was quietly retired and Bob Wussler, just thirty-eight years old, was brought in. Wussler had been the head of the Special Events unit at CBS News, in charge of such things as space shots, moon landings, elections, and political conventions. He was known as a man who knew talent and who people liked working for.

"Casually Bob Stenner and I went to Wussler," O'Neill said, "and we told him about Phyllis. Wussler liked her right away."

Officially, her agent arranged a meeting over drinks. Phyllis was even more vivacious in person than she was on camera: great smile, flashing her dimples, and a warm, outgoing personality. You could hardly see a speck of makeup. And while she still had that Miss America glamour, she was totally approachable. Almost immediately Wussler realized that audiences could identify with her.

After some small talk, Wussler asked her, "What do you know about sports?" It was a loaded question. Phyllis thought for a moment.

"Well," she said with a smile, "I've dated some athletes, and coming from Texas, of course I love the Dallas Cowboys."[15]

Bingo! Wussler, who was normally cool and reserved, was taken by her charm. A thirteen-week contract was drawn up with the promise that if things worked out, it would become permanent.

When Bob Wussler was running the Special Events unit for CBS News, one of the events they covered every year was the Miss America Pageant. "My dad loved Miss Americas," said Rosemary Wussler Boorman when contacted for this book. "And one of the reasons he thought Phyllis could be successful was because that year she had been touring as Miss America prepared her for the press. She was used to having questions fired at her."[16]

"I accepted Bob Wussler's offer," Phyllis said, "partly because I needed a job—always a good incentive—and partly because something inside told me I could do it."[17]

One of the first people to work with her from CBS was producer Neil Amdur, who later became sports editor of the *New York Times*. "I think she had a bit of culture shock when she first came to New York," Amdur said. "She was this pure Denton, Texas girl thrust into a totally different society, so she had to adapt and quickly. That included forming impressions, standing up for herself, to dating Jewish guys she didn't know existed as a naïve beauty queen from the Lone Star state."[18]

One of her first assignments was the Fiesta Bowl in Arizona. At the game CBS dressed her in a Western outfit but didn't give her much to do. Irked, she returned to New York, asking CBS to clarify her role. Soon it became clear that her role would be to interview star athletes.

For her next assignment she was sent to Boston to interview Celtics star Dave Cowens, who was never known for being glib. Cowens, who cherished his privacy and disliked interviews, had reluctantly agreed to the CBS request because the team management insisted it was good public relations. He also had no idea they were sending a woman. He took one look at her when she and her camera crew arrived at practice, according to Phyllis, and rolled his eyes.

"Hey Dave, how are you?" she called out to him, but he didn't respond. She tried again, and again he ignored her.

"As soon as practice was over, Cowens made a beeline for his Jeep," Phyllis wrote in her memoir, *Never Say Never*. "I followed, and my producer urged me to hop in. I did.

"My career was on the line, and I had no intention of going back to New York without talking with him. I'm not going away, I thought to myself. I am getting this interview! So off we went to his log cabin on the outskirts of Boston."

She kept peppering him on the forty-five-minute drive to his cabin, firing questions at him and getting very few answers. When they got there, he took a beer out of the fridge, offered her one, which she declined, and they settled into a couple of rocking chairs on the porch. By the time the CBS crew arrived, she had slowly started to draw him out and the interview turned into more of a conversation.

"He rocked back and forth in his old chair," she wrote. "And he talked and talked. As the camera rolled, I instinctively tossed aside my formal questions and talked to him like a regular human being, not like a superstar. Mostly I asked him what I was interested to know as a curious fan, questions like: What would you do if it were all over tomorrow? Are there some days you just don't want to suit up? What if you had an injury? Where would you go, what would you do? Do you ever want to settle down and get married?"

These weren't typical questions guys like Cowens were accustomed to hearing. Asking a player about his feelings was almost unheard of. When the piece got edited, it was obvious that Phyllis had captured a side of Dave Cowens that few people had ever seen. As she introduced the interview on the air, she said that Cowens had "a little bit of Huck Finn lingering inside him."

"I was astounded by the overwhelmingly positive response," Phyllis said of the interview.[19]

Sports Illustrated's Melissa Ludtke called it "probably the best national television piece ever done on him." Ludtke should know. She was one of the very first women permitted to report from a pro locker room.[20]

So why did Cowens open up to her? What changed his mind? When reached by email, he had this to say: "As a bachelor in 1975, I certainly would not pass up an opportunity to talk to Miss America. We had a good time and the entire session was professionally conducted." And then he added, "Phyllis was way out of my league, if you catch my drift."[21]

Cowens can't really take all the credit for that success, because she was a tough, determined young lady. Her year as Miss America, dealing with camp after camp of screaming soldiers in Vietnam, taught her patience. And back in the States she learned how to deal with the press, answering questions about the war and the drug culture. By the time she got to Cowens, she was a veteran at age twenty-five, ready to take on any battle.

"The only thing I can take credit for," Cowens wrote, "is that I told her she had a piece of food in her teeth after lunch. I'm just pleased to know that she did a good job and got rewarded for it."

After the Cowens interview she had similar positive experiences interviewing hard-nosed Jimmy Connors and NBA star Elvin Hayes. Her interviewing style was working. "The producers realized something new and distinctive was happening," she said. "I had gotten a sports star to remove his armor. I went for the heart and the athletes gave heart back."[22]

Wussler later told *USA Today* that he knew she'd be great all along. "In my gut, I thought Phyllis was pretty special," he said. "I thought there was a role for her, as somebody who could talk to guys who knew something about sports."[23]

In August of '75, Ludtke of *Sports Illustrated* pronounced her ready for prime time. "George is still no sports expert," she wrote, "nor does she pretend to be. But she is rapidly becoming more than just another pretty face."[24]

Her thirteen-week tryout quickly turned into a three-year deal, and Phyllis Ann George was on her way. Little did she know that only one month later she'd be starring on the hottest sports show on TV and within a year be adorning the cover of *People* magazine.

CHAPTER FOUR

Bob Wussler: The Visionary

IN OCTOBER OF 1972, FRESH OFF OF HIS SUCCESS MANAGING THE broadcasts of the Democratic and Republican conventions—both in Miami Beach—thirty-six-year-old Bob Wussler was looking for a new challenge. He got it when the network asked him to become manager of the CBS-owned-and-operated television station in Chicago, WBBM.

It was a station whose newscast had become the laughing stock of the city. Think of Howard Beale at UBS in the movie *Network*, and you'll have the general idea of where WBBM stood in public opinion. When Wussler took over, he brought Van Gordon Sauter along with him from WBBM Radio to be his news director.

"In July of 1972, three months before I arrived," Wussler later told the *Chicago Sun-Times'* Robert Feder, "WBBM was in *fourth* place, behind even WGN and Cubs baseball. There were people at CBS who were ready to swap the station altogether for one in Houston or Phoenix. So risk-taking [for me] was a little easier to do."[1]

The risk he took was teaming silky smooth CBS News correspondent Bill Kurtis with Walter Jacobson, a tough-as-nails reporter known for his blistering commentaries. Then they moved the newscast out of the studio and into the newsroom, a completely new concept at that time. When the two debuted on the 10:00 p.m. newscast in March of '73, the station's slogan was "It's Not Pretty, But It's Real." Further promotional ads said, "In Chicago, if it's news, Kurtis and Jacobson are there, because they're newsmen not announcers."

"Bob was superb at live television," said Sauter. "He was incredibly effective at mixing a pool—putting together unique people who could find a relationship between themselves—a relationship that was definitive that the audience could view. You were looking at real people, not dummies."[2]

The strategy worked. It certainly didn't hurt that Kurtis and Jacobson were very appealing. "Their success would set a new standard for the industry, making journalistic icons out of Bill & Walter, and helping advance Wussler's career," wrote Feder in the *Sun-Times*. But that newscast success didn't sit well at first with some of the CBS brass.

CBS did not appreciate it, at first. Both William Paley, who owned the CBS Network, and his No. 2 Frank Stanton firmly believed that news people should not being doing editorials or commentary of any kind.

"They wanted a complete separation of church and state," said Wussler. "However, I was in the fortunate position of having taken over a television station that had fallen on very difficult times. Quite frankly, I slipped it by them. I just told them I wanted to hire this guy who'd worked at WBBM previously [Kurtis] and who I felt was one of the few personalities then in Chicago who lit up the screen whenever he came on. I sold them on Jacobson as Mr. Rough-and-Tumble and Kurtis as a gentleman."

"After four or five weeks on the air," Wussler continued, "somebody [from CBS] in New York called and asked, 'Is Jacobson doing commentary?' I said yes. They said, 'By whose authority? That really flies against company policy.' I told them, 'By mine.'

"My argument was that Chicago is the kind of town where news, viewpoint, commentary and editorializing are very important. More important than, say, in New York or Los Angeles, where people perhaps are not as passionate about local politics and local issues. Chicago takes itself, quite properly, very seriously."[3]

Of course, when the results yielded higher ratings and more advertising dollars, the New York brass made an exception, and Wussler crept higher on the company ladder. The path to the top went through the Stations division. You had to run one of the owned-and-operated stations, particularly in New York, Chicago, or Los Angeles, to make your bones as a businessman and get the approval of those who ran sales and programming. Now that he had done that successfully, he was ready for the next step.

Bob Wussler grew up in the Vailsburg section of Newark, New Jersey. It was a tough neighborhood, to say the least. According to CBS broadcaster Bill Raftery, by growing up in Vailsburg, Wussler became aware of things like segregation, gambling, and the Mob-run rackets.

"I'm sure that played into his open-mindedness," said Raftery, "and for his wanting to have the first woman and the first Black [on a live football program]."[4]

When Wussler attended Seton Hall University in the early '50s, the Pirates were a national basketball power. The team went 25–3 in 1951–52 and 31–2 in 1952–53 and won the National Invitation Tournament (NIT), which was college basketball's most prestigious postseason event in those years.

"I believe that Bobby called some of the games for [campus radio station] WSOU," said Raftery, "and when I coached there [1970–81] he'd come with a friend and we'd have give-and-take before and after the games."

While at Seton Hall, Bob became the sports editor of the *Pirate* newspaper and moved up to run WSOU before he left. "After graduation he briefly worked at a Black radio station in Harlem," said the Reverend Mike Russo, who was hired as an intern for Wussler at CBS, thanks to a friendship of both men's parents.[5] Russo went on to become Walter Cronkite's desk assistant before leaving for the priesthood. Today he is a retired professor of Communication Studies at Saint Mary's College of California and the past chairman of the school's Communication Department.

Bob Wussler first joined CBS at its New York headquarters in 1957. He started in the mailroom and quickly worked his way up at CBS News. By the early '60s he was producing and was instrumental in the broadcast of John F. Kennedy's funeral. By the mid-'60s he had become the head of the new Special Events unit at CBS News, in charge of broadcasting space shots, moon landings, funerals, elections, and political conventions.

"He was still in his twenties when he became an executive producer," said the former CBS writer Gary Paul Gates. "Everybody who was at CBS and NBC in the late '50s and early '60s had meteoric rises because that's when television exploded. He caught a wave of that, and the brass loved working for him."[6]

At that time he was still known as "Bobby" Wussler, but his youth didn't lose him any respect. Everyone in the Special Events unit loved working for him. He had a big corner office that later became the office from where Andy Rooney did his commentaries. When he was producing an event, there was no doubt that he was in charge. He also had two very important mentors: producer Don Hewitt, who created the CBS news magazine show *60 Minutes*, and Bill Leonard, who later became the head of the CBS News division.

Gates wrote glowingly about Wussler in his book, *Air Time: The Inside Story of CBS News*, published in 1978. "But all hands agreed," Gates wrote, "that given the combination of qualities that Wussler had going for him—youth, talent, resourcefulness, and charm—that Wussler's career had not yet come close to reaching its peak."[7]

While working at CBS, Russo was taken with the complete confidence Wussler had in just about everything he did. "When he was in a control room he was basically directing the program," said Father Russo. "Wussler was the intermediary between Cronkite and the directors and news people. He'd tell them exactly what to do. He'd call every shot. He maintained remarkable poise and an aura of great certainty, as he gave directions to his crew with the precision of a quarterback."

"Years later," Russo continued, "when I watched episodes of *Mad Men*, and I saw Jon Hamm play [the program's great visionary] Don Draper, I said to myself, 'That's Bob Wussler.'"

When contacted for this book, Bob Wussler's son Rob offered this: "Those who knew him best, said he had three distinct qualities: (1) he always looked forward and was courageous, (2) he embraced technology, and (3) he had a great eye for talent."[8]

Wussler's curiosity and innovation intrigued all those in his sphere. He clearly had a vision for what television should be. He wanted that Special Events unit to be the biggest and the best. "So it had the biggest control rooms and everything was carpeted," said a former CBS News executive who wished to remain anonymous, "and after every event there was a fabulous party, and all of that was at his instigation because he wanted everybody who was there to be involved."[9]

Occasionally those parties were held at Wussler's luxury townhouse on Central Park South. It was next door to the art deco building where Candice Bergen lived. You'd get off the elevator and you'd be in his apartment.

It was during the 1969 moon landing by Neil Armstrong that Wussler's work became well known. Twenty-five years later, he penned an essay for the June 27, 1994, edition of *Broadcasting & Cable Magazine*. It began:

> *July 16, 1969, the launch date of Apollo 11, and July 20, the day Neil Armstrong and Buzz Aldrin landed on the moon and stepped onto its surface, are events etched into the memories of the world's population. Most adults can tell you where they were and what they were doing when John F. Kennedy was assassinated and when the first lunar landing and moonwalk took place. For television the world over, it was a high point: re-establishing for broadcasters everywhere their ability to bring human drama into the home.*

When Apollo 11 launched there was no cable industry to speak of, no VCRs, and only a few channels to select from. The three networks spent millions on their coverage. One of the biggest problems for Wussler was what CBS would show once the rocket was out of sight. Director Joel Banow, who had stagecraft experience, wanted to build costly simulations.

"No matter what I asked for," said Banow, "Bobby said yes."[10] Banow had miniature lunar and command modules of Apollo 11 built that were filmed in front of a green screen. For the simulation of the rocket engines and the burning and sparking of the spacecraft's heat shield when it reentered the atmosphere, a Bunsen burner was used. Banow then hired a former Disney animator to depict the Apollo 11 spacecraft orbiting the moon. While CBS waited for the first sighting of Neil Armstrong walking on the lunar surface, a NASA technician in a hangar in Long Island City, New York, dressed in a spacesuit, simulated Armstrong's descent from the lunar lander. It was breathtaking television.

"We knew that NBC would cover the hardware, the rocket, the astronauts from top to bottom," Wussler wrote in *Broadcasting & Cable*. "We decided to provide a different angle. We wanted to take advantage of Walter Cronkite's ease in doing homey events. Like a fine wine, the longer we went, the better Walter got. Money was no problem. The networks were doing exceptionally well, and extra dollars went into News. At CBS, we spent over $3 million on Apollo 11—a very healthy sum for 1969, and at least $1 million over budget. [In 2020 that sum would be $21 million in the CPI Index.] Following glowing reviews of Walter Cronkite and the CBS News coverage, no one ever mentioned the cost to me again."

Both Wussler and Cronkite won Emmys for their work, and Wussler's ultimate reward came in 1974 when he was asked to take over the CBS Sports division of the network, a division that according to Van Sauter, "had been run like a country club for years."

Bob Wussler walking the beach with JFK during Wussler's days as head of the CBS News Special Events unit. (COURTESY ROB WUSSLER)

Bob Wussler married Grace Charlotte Harlow on April 24, 1960, and they had six children, including two sets of twins. In the late '60s, when he had achieved success as executive producer of CBS's Special Events unit, he bought a small beach house in Avalon, New Jersey, for $37,000. His son Rob recalls what it was like.

"I hardly got to know my dad until I got out of college because he was always traveling," said Rob Wussler, "but when we would go to the beach, there were six of us. Somebody would have the umbrella, somebody would have the beach bag, and somebody would have the shortwave radio because he was always listening to the international news. And if you weren't fast enough to grab one of those things, you had to take Dad's briefcase, which contained a phone that weighed about twenty pounds. This was the late '60s and nobody had a portable phone, except my dad."

If you asked Bob Wussler what job he wanted next at CBS, he certainly would have put running the CBS Sports division at the top of the list.

"My father was a news man but he was a sports fan," said Rob Wussler. "At his heart he was a sports fanatic, and that's putting it mildly. He was thrilled to get that job."

When Wussler first arrived at CBS Sports, midyear in 1974, he interviewed all the top producers and executives. One was Kevin O'Malley, a recent Boston College graduate whom Bill MacPhail had hired a year earlier as Director of Program Development. MacPhail had run CBS Sports since 1956, and many of the producers had become a little too comfortable in their jobs. One was Bill Creasy, a senior producer who had been CBS's producer for the joint coverage of Super Bowl I with NBC. But Creasy failed to make it to the production truck until halftime. Rumors were that he overdid it the night before. "No comment," said executive producer Bill Fitts, while recalling the incident fifty-one years later.[11]

"I first met Bob Wussler at Super Bowl VIII in Houston," said O'Malley. "He came up to me and said, 'You're the guy who bought the Irish Sweepstakes for Sports Spectacular.' So when he came in as head of Sports, there were a few people who had it in for me. One of them being Bill Creasy. Creasy told him he had to get rid of me."

"Why would he say that?" Wussler asked O'Malley.

"I don't want to tell any tales out of school," O'Malley said.

"School's open," Wussler responded with a smile. "I'm your boss."

O'Malley continued: "Soon after arriving, Wussler observed Creasy in the control room one Sunday afternoon during a rehearsal for CBS Sports' *Sports Illustrated* show. Bill was completely hung over and pitched a fit, not realizing that it was a rehearsal. He had to leave the control room sheepishly sick. He was a bad drinker. Not long after that he tried to go after Wussler with a beer bottle at P.J. Clarke's."[12]

Another time Creasy lost his temper in the control room and took it out on twenty-one-year-old production assistant Janet "Muffy" Renz. For no apparent reason he grabbed Renz by the throat and slammed her against the control room wall. "He was crazy," she said when contacted by this author. "He did stuff like that all the time."[13]

Bill Fitts had been the executive producer for CBS Sports for several years and did a remarkable job, especially figuring out on NFL Sundays what programming was going to which markets. In '74 he tried going live for the first time with *The NFL Today* with little success.

Fitts was a pioneer. He did the tough, dirty work getting live NFL games on the air back in the '60s before the advent of satellites. He saw the future and understood the importance of going live with the pregame show; he just couldn't execute it with Whitaker at the helm.

Musburger, on the other hand, was a completely different type of anchor. He could visualize and compute eight different things happening at the same time and tell an audience of millions which of those were most important and in what order. He probably would have also made a great air-traffic controller.

When any general manager is hired to run a professional team, he always wants to hire his own guy as manager or coach. That might have been the case with Wussler bringing Michael Pearl in from WTVJ in Miami to produce *The NFL Today* in 1975.

Regardless, Fitts was out.

"Wussler came in and he immediately wanted to get rid of me," Fitts continued. "He wanted his own people. I don't have any hard feelings about that except he could have been a little more receptive to what I was doing.

[After he hired Phyllis] he brought her into my office and said, 'Make her a star.' So I took her to Puerto Rico where we were taping a tennis show, and when I got back my office was moved to way down the hall. The handwriting was on the wall. He basically gave me nothing to do."

Mike Pearl became Wussler's most trusted producer. He learned the job from the bottom up. A communications student at the University of Miami, he began interning there for station manager Bernie Rosen at WTVJ-TV, a CBS affiliate.

"I started out getting coffee. Then I moved up to be a cameraman," Pearl said. "If you shot a story you brought the film back and took it next door where they developed the film. You wrote the story and then you got the film, you spliced it and edited it, and then you gave it to Bernie [Rosen] to look at. From that I went on to doing weekends, and I got the job as the weekend producer. There you'd do everything yourself, including what I just said, covering all the stories, writing all the shows—the early show and the late show—and producing them also. Bernie's goal was to beat the *Miami News* and the *Miami Herald* on stories."[14]

When Pearl finally got to sit down with Wussler for an interview in the summer of '75, and he told him everything he did to produce all those live shows in Miami, Wussler hired him on the spot. "I was excited," said Pearl, "because I was aware of all the things he did at CBS News with the space program, and I had a feeling that he'd take that ingenuity to Sports."

It turned out that Wussler was just as excited about bringing Pearl to New York. At Super Bowl X in Miami after the 1975 football season, Wussler said this about Pearl to media archivist Tom Weinberg: "When I came into the Sports division, what I lacked was a very knowledgeable journalistic guy [producer]. I went out and I found Mike Pearl. When I hired him I never thought he was going to be as good as he is. The guy is terrific. He's a very knowledgeable unassuming guy. You look at him and you wonder, 'Who is this guy?' He happens to be terrific."[15]

Smart women did not intimidate Bob Wussler. In fact, he was a promoter of women in the business. Joan Richman, the person who was his No. 2 at CBS News, was a very strong, tough woman who ultimately went on to become an executive vice president at CBS News.

So one of the first things he did when arriving in New York was send Jane Chastain, a sports reporter from WTVJ-TV in Miami, to Denver to be the third in the booth with Don Criqui and Irv Cross. Although Chastain was a proven football reporter, it did not go over well with sexist viewers. "Get That Broad Out of the Booth" was the title of a *TV Guide* piece that followed.[16] The title was reflective of the mail that CBS received, which was heavily against her presence.

"The problem was that she was the first," said Wussler, not willing to accept the verdict. So the next thing he did was to hire Phyllis George. He felt strongly that there was a place for a woman in sports, even if no one had yet tried it.

"I wanted to get more women into sports," Wussler told interviewers at Super Bowl X in Miami, "because I thought sports on television was starting to become a male ghetto. I wanted to get some life into it. It's not necessarily true that women will watch women, but it's getting better chemistry, and better chemistry will attract more people—and that's what that Musburger, Phyllis George, Irv Cross thing is about."[17]

Phyllis George was the recipient of a lot of publicity in the beginning, when it seemed more like on-the-job-training for her. As the season wore on, she became more and more confident of what she was doing and CBS became more and more confident in her.

"She got all that publicity because she was the first woman who really made it in sports," said Wussler, "and people didn't hate her, and people liked her. And while all that was going on she had the ability to become a better broadcaster. She's got commitment now. She saw it as an opportunity.

"Her future? She'll continue to remain within the framework. She'll remain in the fringe, if you will—pregames and halftimes and postgames. It's something she's very comfortable with and it's something that she likes. How long we continue to go with that, I don't know. She has a good future as a broadcaster, though. That's the more important thing."[18]

In the summer of '75 Pearl found out he was going to produce *The NFL Today*. Wussler told him of his plans to have three cohosts, with Musburger, Irv Cross, and Phyllis, and he also wanted to make a place for Jack Whitaker to do his essays. Wussler wasn't concerned that Cross

Brent Musburger and Phyllis George share smiles and football for debut of *The NFL Today* in 1975. Brent's wardrobe improved considerably by 1980. (COURTESY CBS SPORTS)

would be the first Black cohost of a live sports studio show. Cross had already been doing NFL games for the network as an analyst, and his easy style seemed a perfect blend. For Pearl, working with a woman in sports was nothing new. He had worked with Jane Chastain in Miami.

"To me, I didn't think it was that big a deal [adding Phyllis] because I had worked with Jane [Chastain] before," said Pearl. "As long as we found a role for her and not have her just sit there on the set, we'd be fine. When CBS signed its deal with the NFL, they agreed to spend X amount of dollars with NFL Films. So we had her do features with them and she got to excel at it. Also we had Irv do a feature each week using them, and Phyllis would often do a music piece."

Another thing Wussler encouraged was the use of music pieces in the show. NFL Films would string together highlights of a player or a particular theme to match a popular song of the day. Phyllis usually introduced these features. A perfect example was "Nobody Does It Better," written by Marvin Hamlisch and Carole Bayer Sager and produced by Richard Perry for the James Bond film *The Spy Who Loved Me*. NFL Films adapted the song to highlights of the Chicago Bears' star running back Walter Payton gallivanting over and through the opposition. In 1977 *The NFL Today* wore out that song.

Phyllis was unsure of how she would fit in, sitting between Irv and Brent. Brent was a hundred-mile-an-hour guy, and Irv just sat back and leaned on his knowledge of the game. So everybody had their role, and the feature (piece) was a good way of giving her something to do.

"I felt the most important goal in creating a chemistry," Pearl continued, "was *not* to put Phyllis in a role where she would embarrass herself or insult the hard-core viewer. Director Bob Fishman helped by shooting the set so that the viewer wouldn't see Phyllis sitting there doing nothing. After a few weeks she realized she didn't have to pretend to know the Xs and Os to be successful. She even found that occasionally she could partake in studio jabber."

Musburger looked back on that first year together on the NFL Network's *Rich Eisen Show*, on March 1, 2021. "I was a total unknown," he said. "It was a time of great excitement for me. The big difference was that we were live. When Phyllis George was added to me and Irv, we rehearsed and it was like we were friends for a long, long time. As I look back I was blessed with Irv, Phyllis, and even The Greek. Bob Wussler made great hiring decisions."

Pearl's partner Fishman said he owes his career to Wussler.

"He was a very approachable guy," said Fishman. "He was a thinker, so you always wouldn't get your answer right away, but he'd obviously think about it. I had this wonderful relationship with him based on my time as a young commercial coordinator working the moon shots. We met and talked about how much he loved the [San Francisco] Giants and I loved the [Los Angeles] Dodgers. We had a great relationship. And then he hired me to be his production assistant in the Special Events unit, and I wasn't even in News at the time."[19]

"He wanted to do a show that embraced a leader in Brent," Fishman continued. "He saw to it that a former pro [Irv] was part of it. He saw the entertainment value in bringing Phyllis to the set. He kept Jack Whitaker on the show as an essayist, which he was brilliant at."

Keeping Whitaker involved was important because he had previously been the face of CBS Sports and had a tough time managing the host role in the new live version of *The NFL Today* the year before. Musburger, however, made it look easy. Bob Costas saw it clearly when contacted for this book.

"Here's the thing," Costas said. "Brent Musburger could never do what Jack did so brilliantly, but Jack could never do what Brent did. It's all horses for courses."[20]

"It was a brilliant cast when you go back and think about it," Fishman said. "He just had a knack for that kind of stuff. He knew he was taking a chance, but that was part of his brilliance. I remember how he would manipulate a show in News. He would go from point A to point B to point C and do it all so effortlessly. Which is why his greatest strength, besides being in the studio, was reacting on the fly. In a very calm but firm way, he'd let us know where we were going and for how long. He'd say, 'One minute to this remote, then to that remote, then to that interview,' etc., etc. Pearl learned that from him.

"He had an uncanny ability of putting the right people in the right places and letting you do your job without any interference. And he had an eye for talent and understanding that a pregame show needed to be more than just scores and highlights. Hiring Phyllis was an example. Hiring Jimmy [The Greek] and letting him do his picks pissed off the league, because they didn't want any mention of point spreads. Instead he'd say, 'They'd win by a field goal.' Wussler knew the public would take to him. He was a great leader."

NFL commissioner Pete Rozelle knew that gambling was helping the league's ratings, but publicly disdained it. He testified before Congress that he thought only 2 percent of viewers bet on the games. In response, CBS publicist Beano Cook, who was known for his humor, said, "If that's true, then they all live on my block."

The show was an enormous success. That first year, 1975, it won an astounding thirteen Emmy Awards. Wussler could afford to take risks and to follow his gut, because he had the equity built up from his success at WBBM in Chicago and before that running the Special Events unit at CBS News. He also wasn't afraid to hire new faces. One of them was *New York Times* sportswriter Neil Amdur, who later, for fifteen years was its sports editor.

"He was aggressive," said Amdur. "He knew what he wanted and had the license and authority to hire and set policy. He was willing to follow through on ideas, like Jimmy The Greek and Phyllis, as unconventional as they were. Even when he took some heat for it, he knew he had struck a chord. People were talking about the show."[21]

They were more than talking about it. They were watching it, and it would go on to be the highest rated NFL pregame show for the next eighteen years.

Former *Washington Post* columnist Tony Kornheiser, who is now a star on ESPN, was also paying attention at that time. "In 1975 CBS put together the greatest pregame show in American history," he said. "Each member of that cast was the perfect choice. On Sundays tens of millions tuned in to see and hear what they had to say. It was simply great, and for the last forty years everybody has tried to copy it."[22]

Chapter Five

Pearl and Fishman: They Made the Magic

On his way to becoming one of the most successful producers in the history of Sports television, Michael Pearl learned how to do it the hard way at WTVJ-TV in Miami. This is what was involved when he would meet a fighter at the 5th Street Gym in Miami Beach for an interview: "I'll always remember," said Pearl, "that there were about twenty steps [at the 5th Street Gym] that you had to walk up and *schlep* the camera and the lights and do it by yourself. Often I was alone and had to do the interview.

"I'd put the person on a chair. Once it was [Muhammad] Ali. He was [Cassius] Clay then. I'd put him in the chair, frame him up, start the camera, then run around, ask him a couple questions, then stop, run back around, take a different angle [with the camera], loosen the shot or tighten the shot, run back around, and ask a couple more questions. You'd wind up setting up the lights, doing the interview, setting up the camera, then go back and do all the rest."[1]

Then he'd have to pack up all the equipment and *schlep* it back down the twenty steps and back to the station, where, of course, he would cut, edit, splice, and fully produce the piece for the 6 o'clock news.

"I decided," said Pearl, "that after working at TVJ as an intern after my sophomore year, that I could get more out of working when offered a full-time job than going back to school. I figured I could always go back and take courses. When I got the job at CBS, those thoughts went out the door." (The University of Miami made him an honorary alumnus in 1990.)

In 1965 while working in the Sports department at WTVJ, Pearl was perplexed as to why the station's News department wasn't covering the Beatles' arrival in Nassau, just a short flight away. The Beatles were there to make their second film, *Help*, and Pearl thought it was something any newsworthy News department would undertake. He decided to take things into his own hands. Here's how he explained what happened next, to the Sports Broadcasting Hall of Fame audience during his 2015 induction:

"My roommate's father owned an airplane and both he and I had a pilot's license, and on a whim I asked a friend of mine to get a camera crew together, and we would fly over to Nassau, cold, hoping to get some shots of the Beatles on the set. When we got to their hotel—I don't remember why I did this—but when we got there, I went directly to the house phone and asked for [the Beatles'] manager Brian Epstein's room, expecting no answer. But to my surprise and my shock, he did answer. I told him I was from a local station and asked if there was an opportunity for us to get some shots of some of the guys around the hotel. His answer was, 'Would you like to interview them?'"

"Well, after I was looking for somewhere to get rid of my wet underwear," Pearl said while the audience laughed. "I told him I'd call him once we found a room to set up. They arrived and they gave us as much time as we wanted. We shot the interview [with Pearl on camera doing the interviewing] and it was on the air that night. Let's see you try and do something like that today."[2]

In addition to his other assignments, in 1973 Pearl also produced Jimmy The Greek's radio spots. By then he and The Greek had become friends, and Pearl understood the magnetism and respect the bettors had for Jimmy. But getting to CBS Sports in New York was Pearl's main goal, and he saw the appointment of Bob Wussler as the new head of the Sports division as his way in.

"I first met Bob Wussler when he came to Miami for a golf tournament at Doral," Pearl recalled. "I asked him if we could sit down and talk about me becoming a producer in New York. He said, 'Well, I just started, let me get situated then give me a call.' I waited a month or so and then I must've made twenty calls before I got an appointment to see him in February of 1975."

At five feet three inches, twenty-four-year-old Janis Delson may have been little, but she was mighty. The green-eyed brunette joined the department in 1972 and quickly rose to become director of operations for *The NFL Today*. During the week she shared an office at CBS's Black Rock location on the 26th floor at 52nd Street and Sixth Avenue with a young guy from Miami named David Berman.

"Pearl had been calling trying to get a meeting with Wussler," Delson said in her distinct New York accent. "He was dying to come to work for us. Dave Berman was at CBS, and Pearl knew him from Miami at TVJ. Pearl would always call Dave trying to find out when it would be a good time to call Bob Wussler."[3]

Since Delson and Berman shared an office, he would answer her phone when she wasn't around, and she would answer his. So it didn't take long until she started talking to this guy named Mike Pearl.

"From the seat that I had I could see directly into Wussler's office," Delson continued. "We chatted a few times that I picked up Dave's line and we got friendly over the phone. Once he realized I had the best view of Wussler's office, Pearl started calling me instead of Berman.

"He'd call me and he'd say, 'Is Wussler in his office? Can I call him now?' This went on for a while and I'd say, 'Yes he's in there,' or 'The door is closed,' and so on."

Eventually Pearl got through to Wussler and he came up for an interview. He flew to New York and stayed nearby at the Hilton Hotel at 54th and Sixth Avenue. "I walked across the street," said Pearl, "for my appointment with him in the morning, and when I walked back across to the hotel, I had a job at CBS. He hired me on the spot. I started almost immediately after that meeting.

"I think he had heard about me from Bernie [Rosen] and he came from News. In the meeting I described the work I did at TVJ as far as covering stories, and what covering the story meant. In my meeting I went into quite a bit of detail. We talked for quite a while."

While Pearl was thrilled to have finally landed his dream job, Janis Delson was a little disappointed, at first, after seeing him.

"Here's how you can get misconceived perceptions from a phone conversation," she said with a laugh. "He presented himself over the phone as a globetrotter, which he was, and a guy coming from Miami driving fancy cars. So I thought he was going to be this fancy hunk. And then he comes in to the office and I see him walking into Wussler's office with this sloppy-looking sports coat on and pants that were too long and didn't fit, and dragging some duffle bag. I couldn't believe it. I remember turning to Berman, and saying to him, 'THAT'S MIKE PEARL? That wasn't what I expected at all.'"

When Pearl moved to New York he shared a three-bedroom apartment on the East Side at 56th Street and First Avenue with CBS Sports executive Kevin O'Malley and O'Malley's Boston College buddy Mike Lupica, a columnist for the *New York Daily News*. It was an easy walk to work. Shortly after that, when Phyllis George was hired she decided to take an apartment a few floors above Pearl's.

Pearl never concerned himself with being a fashion plate. His close friend Hank Goldberg, who was the sports director at WTVJ-TV, related this story: "Phyllis called me one time and said, 'I know you're close to Michael. Can you get his pants size for me? I can't stand to look at those pants he wears anymore.' I told Bob Fishman that story. Fishman laughed and said, 'He's still wearing those pants.'"[4]

Janis Delson got over her first impression of Mike Pearl and they soon became friends. "My impression of him at the time," she said, "was that he was very smart, a little bit low-key, which I didn't expect, unlike Wussler, who was forceful. He was laid back, very quiet, very bright, and he wanted to socialize with all of us too. So he fit right in with that pack of wolves. He was also very generous—always picking up checks. And he never had a cross word to say to anyone."

Working with Pearl as the director of *The NFL Today* after that first year was Bob Fishman. They formed a very tight, cohesive duo, and each had love and respect for the other.

"He was a great partner," Fishman related of Pearl. "We did so much more than just a pregame show. Sometimes you always didn't know what Mike was thinking. I'd say, 'Mike, you're too quiet.' Or I'd say, 'Where are we going? What are you doing?' And then he'd figure it out and tell you."[5]

"We were as close as any producer-director team could be," Fishman continued. "Sometimes it could be frustrating because I wanted

In 1975 low-key Michael Pearl became the producer of *The NFL Today.* (COURTESY CBS SPORTS)

information, now, now, now, now, now, and he may have been still thinking about it or reworking the format. But he had an ability to fly by the seat of his pants. He was just an incredible partner."

On September 21, 1970, ABC launched *Monday Night Football*, with Howard Cosell as a surprise analyst. The games were an instant hit. Then at halftime Cosell did something that had never been seen before—highlights of the previous day's games, as edited by NFL Films.

With Cosell overdoing the calls with dramatic flair—saying things like "Right there!" or "He [pause] could [pause] go [pause] all [pause] the way!"—these highlights became so popular and Cosell's calls became so imitated that more than a decade later Chris Berman used them on ESPN, crediting Cosell.

At sports bars like Runyon's in New York, which were packed for the Monday night games, customers were ordered to shush so everyone could hear Cosell at halftime. It even got to the point that fans in some cities felt slighted when their team's highlights weren't chosen.

This phenomenon continued for years. One reason was that it was nearly impossible for CBS and NBC to get highlights to their fans of other Sunday games at halftime. On Sundays at 1 o'clock Eastern time there were as many as eight games rolling on tape machines at the same time. There just wasn't enough time to take in the highlights—a few specific plays to show—then edit them, then write down for the announcer who was identified on each play, then send them up to the control room, separate them from the other seven games, get them in an order, cue the announcer, and roll the tape.

Until 1974 every remote at every game would simply do their own game's highlights at halftime for their viewers. Other than that, all they could provide were the scores of other games, sometimes not on a very timely basis. In 1974 executive producer Bill Fitts tried to go live with *The NFL Today* in hopes of bringing halftime highlights of other games to the entire country for the very first time. With Jack Whitaker hosting, Fitts just couldn't pull it off. At first he tried going live using two different studios, with Lee Leonard hosting from the other. It didn't work. "Using two different studios was one of the stupider things I tried," said Fitts.[6]

But at least he tried. Some of the things that he tried did work, like opening the show with the "whip-around" showing live the weather at each game site. In '75 Bob Wussler's team perfected it, and Musburger patented it by saying "YOU ARE LOOKING LIVE," but it was Fitts who figured out how to do it.

A year later, Bob Wussler knew exactly how to make the halftime highlights work. With Mike Pearl producing and Joel Banow, coming over with Wussler from News, directing that first year, it might not have been easy, but it was organized nearly to the second. According to Mike Pearl, this is how they did it.

All the tape machines were in the basement of the CBS Broadcast Center, and CBS Sports used every available tape machine except those being used by News. These machines were huge and they were open, with one bleeding sound into the one right next it, which made it difficult for the person taking in the highlights to hear what was going on. They were also clumsy to use.

Director Bob Fishman explained: "If you wanted to go back and add a certain play [for the highlights], you couldn't see what you were rewinding. You had to go back ten seconds and estimate where the play was that you wanted, relying on a time code or the game clock. If you wanted to edit from one play to another, both your edit machine and your playback machine had to go back ten seconds."

Pearl added: "Each game was assigned to a machine. And as each game's highlight package was finished, associate directors Joan Vitrano and Colleen Kolibas would gather the highlights and take them over to one of two designated machines [which always were machines 74 and 75].

"Joan and Colleen would write up the highlights for each game on a piece of paper that was sent up to Brent so he knew what was coming."

If they were doing highlights of six other games at halftime, Pearl would shout out the order in the control room. He'd yell something like, "All right, we're coming up to halftime and this will be seen in Atlanta, Kansas City, and Chicago" (because those games' halftimes all ended close to each other, and could be synched up). Then he'd dictate the order of the six games' highlights.

After that director Fishman would roll the tape that was sent up from machines 74 and 75. The associate director, Peter Bleckner, would count Fishman down (out loud) how much time remained in each highlight package.

Just to make things even more difficult, once the technician pushed the button to roll the tape, the machines needed seven seconds before the tape actually appeared on the home screen, so Brent would have to vamp until it did. "From there they were rolled to air," Pearl said. "Brent saw them at the same time Fish rolled them."

Then we saw them at home. Nothing to it, right? And this happened several times for the 1 o'clock games then for the 2 o'clock games and for the 4 o'clock games. When the games were over, final highlight packages were redone as games were completed.

It might not have been easy, but it was exactly what the public had been wishing for. And for the very first time in 1975, *The NFL Today* gave them same-day highlights.

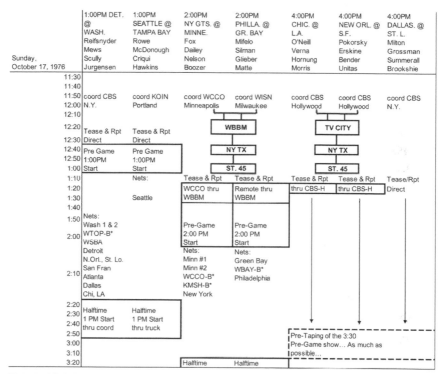

This is CBS Sports' partial NFL production schedule for Sunday, October 17, 1976. It gives you an idea of just how complex it was for *The NFL Today* to coordinate eight games starting at the same time, along with halftimes and postgame shows.

In 1959, when Bob Fishman was ten years old living in the Virgin Islands, it wasn't easy being a Dodgers fan. The move by the Dodgers from Brooklyn to Southern California left Fishman scrambling to find a station via Armed Forces Radio, which carried the Dodgers.

Sometimes he could get the Dodgers via the NBC Game of the Week in Puerto Rico, dubbed in Spanish. "But for me," Fishman said, "it was radio, and the man who made it all come to life, Vin Scully."

It was a dream come true twenty years later when, for two seasons, Bob Fishman directed Vin Scully's NFL games on CBS. After one Sunday game in 1981, Scully asked Fishman if he wouldn't mind doing him a favor. He asked Fishman to take his big blue Dodgers suitcase home with him to New York, while Vin flew to do a Dodgers-Expos playoff game the next day. If the Dodgers won, Bob could drop it at the Dodgers hotel in New York since they'd be playing the Yankees next. If they lost, he could have CBS send the suitcase back to L.A. for him.

Fishman was telling this story at the Sports Broadcasting Hall of Fame ceremonies in early 2020, at the Hilton Hotel in Manhattan, where he was being inducted.

"That's when my loving wife Margaret suggested—jokingly I think—that this was my chance to open his suitcase and sleep in Vin Scully's pajamas." The audience roared with laughter. "For the record," Fishman said with a grin, "I didn't."

Bob Fishman grew up wanting to be a play-by-play announcer, à la Vin Scully, but when he got to Boston University, it became clear to him that he "was never going to be good enough behind the microphone."

Instead, his interests turned toward directing. His first job was in 1970 as a stage manager at the CBS-owned-and-operated station in Philadelphia, WCAU. There, on Saturday mornings, one of Bob's tasks was to drop confetti on the head of children's show host Gene London.

Three months later a job opened in New York as a commercial coordinator. Fishman jumped at it. "It was the only opening they had," he said. As fate would have it, he was assigned to coordinate the commercials during space shots. Bob Wussler, who later became president of the network at age forty, ran the Special Events unit then at CBS News. It was Fishman's job to notify Wussler when they had to insert a commercial.

"I'd follow him [Wussler] around the studio," Fishman said, "and I kept reminding him that we were three Tang commercials behind schedule. He'd say something to me like, 'Can't you see they're walking on the moon?'" Fortunately there was enough downtime for Wussler to get to know Fishman.

In 1972 Wussler chose Fishman as his production assistant, and Bob had a ringside seat for CBS's coverage of space shots, political campaigns, and election nights. When his directing mentor, Joel Banow, took ill the night before the launch of Apollo 17, Fishman was thrust into the director's chair for the first time at the tender age of twenty-four, directing segments for *The CBS Morning News*.

"I overcame my panic," Fishman said, "the first time I cued Walter Cronkite and realized, 'Hey, I can do this!'"[7]

When Wussler became president of CBS Sports in 1974, he took young Mr. Fishman with him. After a year he paired Fishman with Pearl. In 1975 Fishman was the videotape associate director.

"Wussler was so in control and so calm about everything," Fishman said. "I never saw him get angry except one time when he got angry at Joel Banow and me. We were arguing loudly about something stupid. He grabbed us both by the necks and said, 'If I ever see you two ever act like this again in a control room, you won't be working for me very long.' And that told me right then and there that he's in control, he knows what he wants. He never allows his people to act in any way that is detrimental to putting the best product on the air."

In '76 Wussler made Fishman the director, but he still didn't have a director's title or pay rank. Then Wussler left to become president of the network, and Barry Frank was in charge. So right before the '77 season was about to start, Bob went into Frank's office and asked him if he'd promote him to director. Frank was shocked he had never gotten the promotion and said to Bob, "Go down the hall [to Business Affairs] and make a deal."

Fishman was more than just interested in the director's shot—he was also very interested in content.

"He cared about the content of the show," Pearl said. "He had ideas, sometimes, that we would put in on the fly. We'd throw them in and they would work. The first year I produced the show, I had to sit on the set and Wussler was in the control room, which was too small for both us."

To get to Studio 43 where *The NFL Today* was broadcast from, you walked up to the second floor after entering the CBS Broadcast Center, and then walked down a long hallway to the end. Along the way you'd pass several rooms, including one labeled "2E6." This room had a big bank of monitors that pulled in all the games simultaneously. With no other way to see a game outside of your home market, 2E6 became very popular with friends of the network. Sandwiches and drinks would be provided.

One of these guests was *Newsweek* writer Pete Axthelm, who later would appear on NBC's competing pregame show. "Axe" loved to bet on every game and was grateful CBS allowed him to watch. When the first set of pregame shows were over, Jimmy The Greek would join Axthelm. Sometimes you could hear them cheering or moaning. "Oh, I just got screwed by three zebras at the same time," Axthelm once cried out.

"The way we communicated [in the tight control room]," said Pearl, "was by shouting to each other. There were four people on our right and four on our left, all talking to the various remotes. I had a music stand next to me that I had my show script on, and I had a baton. When I wanted to tell him [Fishman] something, I'd hit him on the elbow to communicate. Next to me I had what we called a Wussler box. It was

That's a young and handsome director Bob Fishman (open shirt on the right) next to associate director Peter Bleckner. Due to lack of space in the control room, producer Mike Pearl sat behind Fishman. (COURTESY CBS SPORTS)

something he brought over from doing the conventions. I could talk or listen to every talent [announcer] and producer or director in the field. We used that to synch up halftimes and the 3:15 to 4 o'clock end of games. I could talk to anyone I wanted to in the field no problem, but to talk to Fishman, who was the director, I had to hit him on the shoulder with a stick."

Somehow it all worked. Wussler had not only put together the perfect cast of characters to broadcast the show, he also had a roomful of production people who were inspired by him. Pearl knew he was producing the perfect combination of talent.

"I have always believed," said Pearl, "that, with the right mix of [on-air] talent, anything is possible. When you find personalities that have great chemistry and complement each other, the rest is a walk in the park. That was truly the case with *The NFL Today*. With personalities like that, you couldn't lose."

CHAPTER SIX

Jimmy The Greek: His Life and Times

DEMETRIOS SYNODINOS WAS BORN SEPTEMBER 9, 1918, IN STEUBEN-ville, Ohio. At the age of nine, while he was playing outside, his mother and his aunt were shot to death. The shooter was his aunt's deranged husband. The young boy, whom friends started calling Jimmy, learned to grow up fast.

When he was twelve, the Eastman Kodak Company, in a promotion, gave a Kodak box camera to every seventh grader in Steubenville and offered a $25 prize for whoever took the best photo. Determined to win, Jimmy stopped at Dan Miller's camera store and asked for advice. Miller was glad to give it and even showed the young Greek boy how to develop his pictures in Miller's dark room.

Jimmy would stop at Miller's on the way home for lunch or the way back to school. One day Miller asked the kid if he wouldn't mind picking up the *Racing Form* for him on the way home, and also dropping off a few bets for him at Money O'Brien's Academy Poolroom on the way back. Jimmy obliged, sneaking in O'Brien's back door because his uncle had a barber chair in the front of the poolroom.

Steubenville was a wide-open steelworkers' town of about 40,000. It had eleven different bookmaking establishments. Recounting his youth many years later, Jimmy would say, "I was twenty-five before I found out that gambling was illegal."

Jimmy soon realized that Dan Miller lost nearly all his bets by trying to parlay long shots. It didn't take the kid long before he started booking some of Miller's bets himself, without letting Miller know.

Besides his bookmaking operation, O'Brien had a craps table, a Big Six wheel, and a few poker tables. Jimmy, who was an arithmetic whiz, not only taught himself how to handicap the *Racing Form*, but also spotted a flaw in the way the dealer ran O'Brien's Big Six wheel. By the time he was fourteen, O'Brien had put Jimmy in charge of the wheel at night, and gave him the parking concession at a nightclub he owned. Before long Jimmy was bringing home more money every week than his father, who owned a small grocery store.

When Jimmy was sixteen, he looked twenty-one, tall and handsome with that smile and that great cleft in his chin. He also started spending money on clothes to look more sophisticated. He wore $70 suits from Denmark and $30 Bostonian shoes. Across town, a kid he knew named Dino Crocetti was the Romero (blackjack) dealer at the Rex, an Italian casino. A few years later, as a singer, that kid changed his name to Dean Martin.

It may have been the Depression, but it wasn't one for Jimmy Synodinos. He was already respected for the numbers he made on football and baseball. It didn't take him long to figure out that no matter how good he was at picking horses or winning football teams, he wouldn't be successful unless he concentrated on one thing. To do that he knew he needed an edge, and in handicapping college football games he found one.

In the 1930s, besides what was written in local newspapers or occasionally mentioned on the radio, there was no way of knowing how good teams were in other parts of the country. Research was the answer to The Greek's quest to be the best college football handicapper in the country. He had already started making his own odds on the games, which turned out to be better than those made by the bookmakers.

So he began spending time at the train station in Steubenville, where trains would arrive from different parts of the country. He paid railroad porters 50 cents each for all the newspaper sports sections they could gather that customers left behind. Soon Jimmy knew what Grantland Rice was writing in Nashville about Vanderbilt and the Southern Conference, and what Blackie Sherrod was writing about Texas and the teams in the Southwest. He now had his edge and began building a bankroll.

One of his biggest scores occurred Thanksgiving weekend, 1943. He had just turned twenty-five. This was when an undefeated (9–0) Notre

Dame team lost to Great Lakes Naval Training Station, 19–14. Notre Dame had a great team that year, led by All-American Johnny Lujack, but most people didn't realize that Great Lakes had some superior, older players. Nobody really knew much about them.

Betting on the game opened with the Irish listed as a 17-point favorite. The Greek bet $12,000 altogether on Great Lakes—but most of it taking 13–1 odds that Great Lakes would win the game outright. Great Lakes pulled it off on a last-second 46-yard pass and Jimmy cleared over $100,000 in profit (CPI value of $1,491,161).

Jimmy Snyder first came to the attention of the country in 1948 after Harry Truman pulled off an amazing upset to defeat New York governor Thomas Dewey for the presidency.

The next morning, November 3, 1948, the headline of the *Chicago Daily Tribune* blared out, "DEWEY DEFEATS TRUMAN." Truman, who looked like the little man on top of the wedding cake, held the headline high, because, of course, it was wrong. Truman, who was a 20–1 underdog only days before the election, somehow won.

Even more elated was twenty-nine-year-old Jimmy Snyder, who won the biggest bet ever recorded until then on the upset. Two nights before the election, Snyder traveled to New York and met a friend, Miami gambler Harold Salvey. "We met at Lindy's—you know the cheesecake place—on Broadway," Snyder said.[1] Lindy's was the favorite hangout of both Damon Runyon and every major bookie on Broadway.

With Salvey's help The Greek bet $50,000 at odds ranging from 17–1 to 22–1 on Truman to win the election. "I took the 17–1 bet because he advised me that the guy will definitely pay off," he said. It turned out they all paid off, and a few nights later Jimmy's secret was not a secret anymore.

The next night syndicated columnist Walter Winchell made Snyder a legend. Tapping on a telegraph key, Winchell began his radio broadcast: *"Good evening Mr. and Mrs. North and South America, and all the ships at sea. Let's go to press.* Harry Truman won the election but the biggest winner may have been Jimmy The Greek Snyder, a young gambler from Steubenville, Ohio, who won over one million dollars taking the underdog."

This was the first introduction of Jimmy The Greek to the nation. What Winchell didn't know was that The Greek won the bet because his sister Mary told him not to grow a mustache. "Women don't like men with a mustache," she told him. "It reminds them of Hitler." A minute later Jimmy noticed that the front page of the *Chicago Tribune* had a picture of presidential frontrunner Thomas Dewey. "Dewey was smiling but all I saw was Dewey's mustache," Jimmy said. "Then it hit me that Dewey could lose."

He first hired three ladies for $15 apiece to stand in front of the local A&P in Steubenville and canvass a total of 500 women. The Greek was amazed at the results: 122 liked mustaches, 347 did not, and 31 didn't care one way or the other.

The wheels started turning. Jimmy had been betting politics in Ohio since he was twenty and won nearly $250,000 on FDR's 1940 election win. He knew that women comprised 52 percent of all voters and that women also influenced their husbands. If these results were right, he had a hell of a live underdog in Truman. They were and he did.

A decade later The Greek had landed in Las Vegas running one of the most successful sports books in the city, the Hollywood Sports Service, handling close to $2 million a week. His reputation was such that *Sports Illustrated*'s Gilbert Rogin interviewed The Greek for a 1961 feature story, "The Greek Who Makes the Odds."

"I'm not a crook. I'm not a thief. I'm a gambler—and a damn good one," Jimmy told Rogin. "The oddsmaker is the most vulnerable guy in the world. He sits there like a pigeon. If the bettor thinks he's got you beat, he shoots [bets against] you. If he doesn't, he doesn't shoot. Is there anything more hazardous?"

After his big score betting on the 1948 election, Snyder took a good chunk of his money and invested it in oil. He drilled twenty-two straight dry holes. "I matched my wits with Mother Earth," he said, "and she got the decision. My handicapping wasn't too good." That's when he moved to Las Vegas to concentrate on football.

"If you follow the coach's opinion," he said, "he'll break you. He's too close to it. The coach is only good in August, when he looks at his schedule realistically. After that the outside has much more information than the inside."[2]

At that time Bobby Kennedy was making a name for himself as Attorney General, going after underworld characters and labor leader Jimmy Hoffa. Unable to pin something on Hoffa, he went after the gamblers in Las Vegas. Snyder was furious.

"They lost in Laos, they lost in Cuba, they lost in East Berlin," Jimmy said to anyone who was listening, "but they sure are giving the gamblers a beating."

Kennedy then slapped Snyder down for "interstate transmission of gambling information for purposes of betting." Jimmy's sin was simply taking a call from a friend in Salt Lake City who asked him what Utah should be favored by in a college football game against Utah State. After pleading *nolo contendere*, The Greek paid a fine and had to give up his gambling license. Eleven years later, on December 19, 1974, Gerald Ford issued Snyder a presidential pardon.

Reinventing himself, Jimmy walked into the *Las Vegas Sun* and convinced publisher Hank Greenspun to give him a column where he would publish the baseball and football numbers that he computed. The Greek's odds became a weekly staple and soon became syndicated in over 300 newspapers.

Unable to work in a gambling establishment, he got the idea to open a public relations business in Las Vegas, and soon he had Caesars Palace as a client. It didn't take long before Howard Hughes became Jimmy's biggest client. Hughes owned the Desert Inn, the Sands, and the Landmark hotels, among others in the city. The Greek was contacted through ex-FBI man Bob Maheu, who was in charge of Howard Hughes's Nevada holdings. No one actually saw Hughes in those days, including The Greek and Maheu, but many thought he occupied the entire top floor of the Desert Inn.

It turned out that Hughes and Maheu needed Jimmy to successfully lobby against underground atomic testing in Nevada. The Greek's PR machine flooded news outlets with stories of the consequences of radiation as a result of similar tests. Within six months the Atomic Energy Commission announced that it was halting all such tests in Nevada.

Jimmy thought he had a job for life, but in 1970, after four years in Las Vegas and spending approximately a half-billion dollars on Nevada real estate, Hughes abruptly left the state. Once more The Greek needed to find a way to support his family.

In 1968, he gave a summary of his analytical techniques in football. The gamblers and sports books took notice. "Overall team speed is the biggest factor," he said matter-of-factly. "Then comes the front four on defense, then the back defense, especially the cornerbacks. Then the quarterbacks, and then I have to consider the intangibles."[3]

He wasn't just guessing, he was assigning points for each area. The gamblers liked it, and the public loved it. His column became more popular than ever.

By the early '70s his syndicated odds column ran three times a week and The Greek was as famous as he'd ever been. In 1969 he got more publicity for being wrong for making the Baltimore Colts a 17-point favorite in Super Bowl III over Joe Namath and the New York Jets than if he had been exactly right.

On Thanksgiving Day 1973, the Super Bowl champion Miami Dolphins were playing a late-afternoon game in Dallas. The Dolphins, who went undefeated in '72, had now won 26 of their last 27 games, with their lone loss coming at Oakland early in the season, 12–7. Five days earlier they had traveled to Buffalo and slammed the door shut on O. J. Simpson and the Bills in a crushing 17–0 defeat. Despite Miami's incredible record, the Las Vegas oddsmakers made the Cowboys a 2-point favorite, but it was Jimmy The Greek who spread it across 300 newspapers.

In the game, which the Dolphins dominated with their running game, Miami took an early 14–0 lead. Roger Staubach's Cowboys couldn't penetrate the great Dolphin defense until they finally scored in the fourth quarter, tightening the game to 14–7. But with 9:45 remaining, Dallas never saw the ball again. Miami took the kickoff and slowly marched down the field getting first down after first down by handing the ball off to Larry Csonka and Mercury Morris. When the final seconds ticked off, Miami was at the Dallas 1-yard line.

That they were underdogs didn't sit well with the Dolphins, who played like they had something to prove. I was one of the reporters waiting for them as they entered the locker room, but it was not the Cowboys whom the Dolphins wanted to talk about. "Fuck Jimmy The Greek!" shouted one prominent Dolphin. "How in the fucking world could they have made us underdogs?"

That's how big The Greek's recognition factor had become.

Living part-time in Miami, Jimmy met Mike Pearl and they became friends. Pearl then began producing The Greek's weekly radio shows.

"I wrote his daily show for Mutual Radio and produced it," recalled Pearl. "Half the time he'd rip it up and say, 'I don't like it.' I didn't bring him to CBS. This is how it happened:

El Producto Cigars was a PR client of his firm. He thought they could become a sponsor on *The NFL Today*, and that with me being there [in 1975] I could help put it together [produce it]. They met with the CBS sales people and it happened. We took that board with him that he used to end each newspaper column with, that board that had the eighteen strengths and weaknesses of each team in matchups."[4]

When Pearl took over as the producer on *The NFL Today*, he recommended his pal Hank Goldberg to take over writing and producing Jimmy's radio show. "At first we did it from Miami," Goldberg said. "When he moved to New York we had dinner every Friday night at Dewey Wong's restaurant with Walt Michaels of the [New York] Jets."[5]

With Pearl hired as *The NFL Today* producer, it made it easier for Jimmy to be part of the show. Bob Wussler agreed and approved it. The Greek would bring in a whole new audience. In his segment he'd talk about the information that his sources were giving him. In 1976 Jimmy "The Greek" Snyder became the fourth member of the cast, and the show's popularity shot up to another level.

But Jimmy was an enigma. Sometimes he could be fun and engaging, and other times he could be an outright scoundrel and tactless. One of the first assignments he had for CBS was venturing an opinion on the Belmont Stakes. Phyllis George was also assigned to the show, and together the two of them walked the backstretch at Belmont Park along with producer Chuck Milton.

The Greek must have been in a bad mood that day, because he began letting out f-bombs as they walked. "Please," said Phyllis to producer Milton, "ask Jimmy to stop saying 'fuck' in front of me."[6]

Reined in, The Greek got off to a good start on *The NFL Today* until the time he made Phyllis cry by calling her husband, John Y. Brown, "a son of a bitch" on the air.

"This probably happened her third year [1977]," said Mike Pearl. "He did it on purpose because he knew it would upset her." The Greek had insisted that John Y. owed his public relations company $100,000 for past work on the Kentucky Fried Chicken account. Brown, who owned KFC, disagreed and refused to pay. Phyllis, stuck in the middle, took the brunt of it.

Foreshadowing what was ahead for The Greek, Pearl said, "I knew the time would eventually come when he would burn himself."

"There were two Jimmys," said Bob Fishman. "There was the gruff, obnoxious guy who had no television talent whatsoever, and there was the guy who had a way of getting his opinions across to the gambling world, who wanted to hear what he had to say. He had his faults, like always trying to air rumors that Al Davis [owner of the Oakland Raiders] fed him, and we got sick and tired of him picking the Raiders every weekend."[7]

"I'd see him at Saratoga," continued Fishman, "and he could be as obnoxious as a person could be. 'Hey you,' he'd say, 'give me a cigarette.' And then he'd turn around and tip the guy a hundred dollars. He was also extremely generous. But in the end he added so much to the show because nobody else was really doing that kind of thing. I think the visual of his board [with eighteen categories] and his checkmarks was really, really fun. He couldn't mention point spreads, but The Greek had a way to get them across. 'I like the Cowboys by, oh, what does a golfer say when he's hitting a ball out of bounds—oh, fore!' And that would be a signal to his people to lay the four. He had a great sense of humor when it came to that stuff."

At Saratoga he'd do his own unique research while others were still sound asleep. He'd wake up at 5:00 a.m. every day and walk the backstretch, talking to trainers, jockeys, and clockers. In the afternoon he'd have one of the few tables high up in the clubhouse, where he'd buy lunch for anyone who would walk up and down the staircase to the betting windows for him. When he lost he'd tell that person, "You're bad luck to a huntin' dog." When he won, he'd be overjoyed, and as his horse crossed the finish line, he'd smack his hand down on the table and bellow out, "That's me!"[8]

And fans asking him for his autograph were surprised to see that this big, gruff teddy bear of a character not only had silky-smooth manicured hands, but was writing his autograph as perfectly as a professional calligrapher.

With Jimmy The Greek you got the good with the bad. The good included his astounding prediction that quarterback Jim Plunkett, who was injured and completely out of football for over a year, would not only return, but lead the Oakland Raiders to a Super Bowl, which he wound up doing in 1980.

Jimmy also had his own pain in life. In 1952 he married the lovely and personable Joan Specht. It was his second and last marriage. They had five children, but tragically three of them died from cystic fibrosis. Florence died after thirty days, Tina at age two and a half. The last was his son Jamie.

"First off," said Jimmy, "who knew what CF was? I came from people born and raised in Greece, and I can't remember anybody ever being sick in our family. My great-grandmother was 116 when she died, and my grandfather was 98."[9]

Approximately one out of every four children born to Caucasian parents who both carry the CF gene have serious digestive and respiratory problems. There is no test to determine CF-carrying parents, and, according to experts, the disease remains costly to treat and ultimately incurable.

"I had a son. I lost him," he told Peter Richmond of *The National Sports Daily* in 1990. "So brilliant, he was a mathematical marvel. He was something. Tried so hard to live. He was 26. He was supposed to be dead at 2."[10]

The late *Sports Illustrated* writer Frank Deford, who also had a child who suffered from CF, wrote a long piece about Jimmy's life and tribulations.[11] The Greek's family secret was a secret no more, and everyone at

The 1980 *NFL Today* cast photo after Phyllis George returned to the show. From left, Brent Musburger, Phyllis, Jimmy The Greek, and Irv Cross. (COURTESY CBS SPORTS)

CBS felt terrible for him. But somehow he got past it and could put it aside and have joy in his work on the show, especially the times he was right.

Along the way his handicapping of the political world continued to be something people were interested in. After betting on Truman, his reputation stayed with him. In 1972 Jim Berry featured The Greek in his syndicated editorial cartoon. It showed President Richard Nixon saying to his Attorney General, John Mitchell, "Frankly John, I don't care about the Gallup Poll or the Harris Poll—What does Jimmy The Greek say?"

Occasionally Jimmy would talk about political odds on *The NFL Today*, and politicians sought him for advice. In 1985, two years before she won her first congressional seat, Nancy Pelosi was interested in becoming the head of the Democratic Party. In doing so, she sought out a breakfast meeting with Snyder. They met at the Park Lane Hotel on Central Park South in Manhattan. She wanted his knowledge on the Democratic powers in the South.

Good or bad, naughty or not, The Greek was a hit, and nobody else had anyone like him. The gamblers loved him. Jimmy had a mystique and the public was fascinated with him. In the meantime, *The NFL Today* kept cashing in.

CHAPTER SEVEN

Irv Cross: Mr. Reliable

IN 1949, WHEN IRV CROSS WAS IN FIFTH GRADE, HIS TEACHER, RUTH Ewing, told him, "You're the kind of young man who can go to college." Her words came at a comforting time for the ten-year-old. His mother had just died during childbirth, leaving Irv and his fourteen brothers and sisters to practically raise themselves.

Ruth Ewing might have been aware of his mother's passing when she whispered those words to the young boy. She continued to give him special attention, when she made him the editor of the class's practice radio station, with the call letters WGCR, which stood for Good Citizen Room.

These inspiring words from a white teacher in her forties to a ten-year-old Black child were a turning point in Irv's life. "I knew if I could get to college, it would open doors for me that reached far beyond Hammond, Indiana," Cross wrote (along with Clifton Brown) in his 2017 autobiography *Bearing the Cross*—a book that he dedicated to Ruth Ewing.

His father was a steelworker. He would wake up every morning at 5:30 and walk to work. Irv had to get up even earlier. "My chore was to take care of the coal stove. We had coal delivered and they'd leave it on the sidewalk. I'd bring it to the basement. I'd get up at 5 a.m., start the fire, and get the house warm by the time everyone woke up."[1]

When contacted for this book, Irv added, "We were raised to take care of each other. We all had chores and duties around the house. The older kids took care of the younger kids, and we sort of grew up attached

73

to one another. You always had big brothers around to help you through it. It was a big plus."[2]

One of his first jobs was stacking pins at a bowling alley. He made $5.75 for the day and would spend 75 cents of it at the White Castle hamburger stand, next to the bowling alley. White Castle is famous for its sliders, and for 75 cents you'd get a dozen of those burgers. When he'd arrive home, he'd put $5 on the table and take the sack of burgers upstairs and pass them out to his brothers and sisters.

They were far from well off, but they never starved. Often his father would stop on his way home and pick up a chicken from the Polish butcher. Hand-me-downs were a way of life in the Cross household. "I think I had a brand-new pair of shoes just once in my childhood," he said.

By the time Irv was fifteen, it had become obvious that he was a very good athlete, but broadcasting was also on his mind. His younger brother Ray remembers seeing Irv talking into a tape recorder as a teenager, and wondering what he was doing.

"I asked my dad and he said, 'Just leave him alone,' Ray told the *Northwest Indiana Times*. "I still don't know how he got that recorder—someone must have given it to him. He just stood in front of a mirror like he was on TV or something, with his body language."

Ray, who was nicknamed Duff, finally asked his brother what he was up to. "Duff, I'm preparing for my future," Irv said. "You never know what kind of job I'll have in the future."

That same year (1954), Irv was invited to attend a regional baseball banquet in Chicago, just twenty-eight miles north of Hammond. He caught a ride with a few of his teammates and wound up on the long dais. To his shock and surprise, sitting just a few seats to his right was the one and only Jackie Robinson, in the flesh!

Irv was just seven years old in 1947 when Robinson broke the color barrier. He recalled that his family would crowd around the radio and listen to Dodgers games whenever Robinson played.

"I thought I was in a movie or dreaming," Irv wrote in his autobiography. "Jackie had that white hair and that great smile. My heart was pounding. Besides being courageous, Jackie was generous. He gave of his time. In all likelihood none of those kids that night would go on to become professional ballplayers. But he was willing to talk with us, a group of young, energetic impressionable kids who were thrilled to be in the same room with him."

After making his speech to the banquet crowd, Robinson shook hands with every kid who was there. "When he shook hands with me," said Irv, "he looked at me and said, 'Son, whatever you do in life, make your parents proud.' I will never forget what a deep impression Jackie Robinson's words had on me. Maybe it's because the great Jackie Robinson was saying it. Maybe it was because my mother died when I was ten, and I had missed her ever since. Either way, it definitely stuck with me."[3]

Irvin Acie Cross was the middle child, No. 8, of fifteen his parents had. He loved his parents very much, but he hated Fridays. That's when his dad got paid.

"He'd cash his paycheck, bring most of it home, then go to the tavern and get drunk," Irv said. "When he came home that's when he would beat Mom up."[4] The pain of that was still there more than sixty years later.

Irv would hide behind a chair while a couple of his brothers would try to get their dad to stop, but it was no use because he was too strong. But the day his mother died was the day his father stopped drinking.

By the time Irv graduated from high school in 1957, he was one of the best athletes in Indiana, excelling in all sports, and especially football and track. That year he was named "Male Athlete of the Year," and a couple of his teammates decided to take Irv out to dinner to celebrate.

The first restaurant they went to, which was right across the street from their high school, wouldn't let them in because Irv was Black. It's really hard to imagine there was that level of racism back then in a town just twenty-eight miles from Chicago.

"Of course we found somewhere else to eat," Irv recalled. "But along with the happy thoughts of that evening, not being able to eat there is something that still sticks in my mind."[5]

Cross excelled at football, playing both ways. He was a star wide receiver on offense and a great defensive back. He even played defensive end on occasion. Several schools were interested in a fine Black player with outstanding grades. Northwestern and its new coach, Ara Parseghian, won out.

"Ed Vennon was a Hammond High graduate who was a volunteer recruiter for Northwestern," Cross explained. "Ed spent an untold amount of time with me at my home and drove me to Evanston for my meeting with Coach Parseghian. I was impressed that Northwestern followed the rules when they recruited me."

Other schools were willing to cheat; one offered him $500 and another offered a car. "It was the University of Indiana that offered me a car," he said. "In those days there were incentives to offer student-athletes more than just a scholarship. My father was a hard-working laborer who worked his tail off all of his life. He believed in being fair and honest. He always said that your word was your bond, that if you shake somebody's hand that's the deal. The deal was that I would have a sponsor [at Indiana] to take care of whatever needs I might have. So they sent a '57 Ford Fairlane convertible and parked it in front of our house. What a neat car! My father and I talked about it, and he said, 'No,' and I said 'No.' That's the way it was."

In his meeting with Parseghian, the coach told Irv, "We can't offer you anything except a first-class education and an opportunity to play in the Big Ten."

"What I liked about Coach Parseghian was that he was a real sparkplug, a real driver," Irv recalled. "I loved playing for him. He was more than just a coach. He took a real interest in the kids' personal life and education was important to him. It was a great experience for me."

One team Cross distinctly remembers playing was the Irish of Notre Dame. Northwestern didn't have much depth, but Parseghian was great at getting the most out of his players. In fact, Northwestern defeated Notre Dame three consecutive years, from 1959 through '61. In his junior year, Cross caught a 78-yard touchdown pass that was the difference in a 30–24 victory over the Irish. At the time, it was the longest touchdown reception in Northwestern history. It's no wonder that a few years later, in 1964, Notre Dame hired Parseghian away from Northwestern. He rewarded them by winning national championships in 1966 and '73.

"You know," Irv said, "Brent [Musburger] and I were in the same [graduating] class at Northwestern. Except he never graduated and I did." Brent left early to take a job as a sportswriter.

After graduating, Irv became the seventh-round choice of the NFL defending-champion Philadelphia Eagles in 1961. He not only made the team, but wound up starting halfway through the season when Tom Brookshier sustained a broken leg, ending his playing career.

During training camp the rookies were given a written test to see if they knew their assignments. Irv was the last guy to finish, so they thought he might be having a problem. "But when I turned in my paper," Irv recalled, "the coach asked, 'What's this?' Instead of putting down my individual defensive assignment, I wrote the assignments for all twenty-two players. I told him, 'That's how we did it at Northwestern. That was our biggest edge.'" The coaches were so impressed that even though he was a rookie, they made him a co-captain and one of the Eagles' signal-callers.

"I'll never forget the first game we played [that season] was against the [Baltimore] Colts. I got into the [defensive] huddle and I look to my right and Chuck Bednarik is standing there. Holy smokes! There's the guy who was probably the greatest ever to play football in Philadelphia, and I'm telling him his assignment. He looked down at me [and in a gravelly voice] said, 'Come on, Rook, let's get the play.'"

Irv Cross died February 28, 2021, from heart disease after suffering from chronic traumatic encephalopathy (CTE) and early Alzheimer's. During our interview three months before he died, he sometimes was reaching for words but was in good spirits and laughed a lot reminiscing. During his first season with the Eagles, he endured so many concussions that his teammates started calling him "Paperhead." After being told that any further blow might be fatal, instead of quitting he had the trainers equip him with extra padding in his helmet.

"I just tried to keep my head out of the way while making tackles," Cross told the *Philadelphia Inquirer* on September 3, 2018. "But that's just the way it was. Most of the time, they gave you some smelling salts and you went back in. We didn't know."

The day after his passing, Brent Musburger talked about the early days working with Irv.

"Irv was such a gentleman," he told the NFL Network's Rich Eisen, "and he was a terrific football player. Looking back we know that Irv Cross was the first Black to host a sports studio show, and Phyllis was the first woman. But we didn't talk about it [at that time] and we didn't even think about it, to tell you the truth. I can't remember one discussion I had with Irv about race. We were friends. He deserved the position. He was my go-to guy. The one thing about Irv, with all the live fire we had, I could throw any question to him about football and I knew Irv would be able to handle it while I would regroup and get the next command from the producers. When things got stirred up, we always had the calmness of Irv to rely on."[6]

During his rookie year, Irv agreed to speak at nonprofit events for no fee, and wound up getting a lot of jobs. At Northwestern he had taken a number of public-speaking courses that improved his diction and approach to talking to groups. He worked hard at shaking a fear he had as a kid.

"When I was younger, I could be in a room for two hours, and you wouldn't know I was there. I wouldn't say a word."

Near the end of his playing career, Irv was speaking at a sports banquet when KYW-Radio and TV executive Bill Emerson heard him, and offered him a job. He became the first Black broadcasting live in Philadelphia. That was 1969.

"I think he was impressed that a football player could speak English," Cross said. "I got lucky. Nobody went into television in those days."[7] When contacted for this book, he added, "KYW was an NBC station and [local] sports was the last thing on the 11 o'clock news, so I wound up leading into Johnny Carson."

In the late '60s, NFL Films was still headquartered in Philadelphia, and Irv would go over there almost every day and take a look at the latest film and interviews that they had.

"I wanted to keep abreast of what was going on around the league," he said. "Because of that, I had tons of information on teams from all over the league. I also helped NFL Films edit some of their football footage. For example, I directed them to do freeze-frame plays [for the first time].

"NFL Films would ask me what the best way was to show the viewer what was happening when the ball is snapped and eleven defensive guys are going all over the place. I told them to use highlighted triangles, so I broke that down for them. The best way to do it is to stop the camera [freeze it] at an early point, have the broadcaster describe what the play is, then roll it in full motion. Then most people would say, 'Oh, that's how they did it.' I wanted to teach people how the game was played."

During the off-season he did analysis on Washington Redskins games, and that combined with the friends he made at NFL Films led to an offer from CBS Sports to do analysis on regional NFL games. Gil Brandt, the general manager of the Dallas Cowboys, also offered him a front-office job. Brandt would run into Cross when Cross was scouting the Big Ten Conference for the Eagles' draft. Instead, Irv chose the offer from CBS. "I have no doubt," Brandt wrote in the foreword of Irv's autobiography, *Bearing the Cross*, "that Irv Cross would have become the NFL's first Black general manager."

When he started for CBS, management felt he dressed too conservatively. Someone thought he should look like Don Cornelius, the host of *Soul Train*. "This guy took me to a department store and bought me a light-blue leisure suit, a loud, flowered shirt, and a big gold chain," Irv recalled. "I told him, 'I don't dress this way.' That wasn't my personality."

With the network he became the first Black to be employed full-time as a sports analyst on national television. He did analysis for four seasons, and then, with plenty of experience, he got the call in 1975 to join Brent Musburger and Phyllis George on *The NFL Today*.

Prior to that 1975 season, CBS invited Irv to a luncheon before the Super Bowl. "Bob Wussler came over and introduced himself and asked me what I thought about the game. I gave him a review he probably never heard before. I gave stats, strengths, weaknesses, what players were like, and the rest. What Wussler didn't know was that the night before I talked to some of the players. Wussler came back to me after the game and said, 'We're going to put this show together . . . ,' and that's how it all started."

Breaking another barrier, Irv was the first Black to co-anchor a live network sports show. Phyllis George was the first female to do the same.

"Early in that first season," Irv said, "we were invited to dinner at Phyllis's house in Denton when we were in town for a Cowboys game. At their house her mother pulled me aside, leaned over, and whispered to me, 'I want you to take care of Phyllis. I don't want any of those football players harassing her.' I told her, 'I'd be glad to do that.' There were just eight or nine of us there. It was a good chance to get to know each other a little bit, and her parents wanted a chance to meet everybody. Phyllis was a huge Cowboys fan. I enjoyed being with her because she worked hard to do her job."

Irv said that when he was working on *The NFL Today* that the spirit of Jackie Robinson was always with him. "I was going to work harder than anybody else. I was going to know more about pro football than anybody. If things didn't work out, it wouldn't be because I wasn't prepared."

"Brent was a smooth, polished guy who set everyone up," Irv said. "Phyllis was beautiful and smart. She attracted an entirely different audience, including women. Jimmy [The Greek] was a character, a gambler, who made us even more edgy." In describing everyone's roles to the Eagles' website, Irv explained: "Brent was going to do the news packages. Phyllis was going to do the personality profiles. And," Irv joked, "they kind of projected me to be the sex symbol."[8]

Irv knew the game inside out, and was determined not to fail. "I was getting an opportunity that was unique for that time," he said, "and my presence helped bring a more diverse audience. I don't refer to myself as a pioneer, but in 1975 the sports TV landscape was much different, much whiter. I never focused on that but I was keenly aware that if I failed, it might be a long time before another Black person got a similar opportunity. Every time I see James Brown or Greg Gumbel or Tom Jackson on TV, I take pride, knowing in some way I helped create an avenue for them.

"As it turned out, things worked out pretty well for me. On the air we had a chemistry that just clicked. We were all so different, yet it worked."[9]

According to the director, Bob Fishman, Irv fit right in. And when there were squabbles between other cast members, Irv was never involved.

"He was the steady hand, the steady guy on the show," said Fishman. "He was a perfect partner for a leader like Brent. He knew the game and people respected him. He was one of the sweetest, kindest guys. Just a solid guy."[10]

Just before the pregame show for Super Bowl X in Miami, the group got a call from their boss, Bob Wussler. At the time, they were all on a yacht on Biscayne Bay on their way to the Orange Bowl, the site of the game. That same day movie producers were also filming the thriller *Black Sunday*, and Wussler had a brief scene in the picture.

"I'll call back in thirty seconds," he told them. "Then Wussler called back," Irv recalled, "and said, 'Brent, Irv, Phyllis, we just received a bomb threat. Somebody wants to blow up our yacht.' We never found

The NFL Today cast and crew group photo, 1976. On the left side leaning in on desk is producer Mike Pearl; director Bob Fishman is on right side sitting next to Irv Cross. Brent Musburger and Phyllis George are at desk in center with CBS Sports head Barry Frank between them. (COURTESY CAROLE ACKERMAN COLEMAN)

out if he was kidding or not. Phyllis was standing next to me on the boat. We were all a little scared for a minute. She squeezed my hand and said, 'Then let's make this our best one.' It was great to hear that that she was all pumped and ready to go. She was a competitor. That was her natural response as a competitor."

Phyllis George once referred to herself, Brent, and Irv as "The Mod Squad." Years later, here's what she said about Cross: "Irv is the greatest. He is just a class person. Not only was he a great football player, he was a great on-air person. He was also just a great guy. Irv made me feel real comfortable."[11]

CHAPTER EIGHT

On the Road: Live! from Miami

AT ONE OF THE FIRST PRODUCTION MEETINGS FOR THE NEW *NFL TODAY* cast in 1975, they were discussing the opening whip-around for that coming Sunday's program, where they would show a quick live shot from three or four different stadiums. The director, Bob Fishman, mentioned to the group that he had a friend who bet on the games and his friend always wanted to know the weather.

Brent Musburger thought about it for a minute, and then jumped in and said, "I can say, 'You are looking live!'" Once he said it out loud, it was as if everyone had just seen the Mona Lisa for the first time. And for the next fifteen years, Musburger opened every show with that catchphrase, which became the signature of *The NFL Today*.

The new show was getting tremendous attention and publicity. Just the idea of such a popular Miss America as Phyllis George being part of it made *The NFL Today* appointment television. In the East and Midwest, churchgoers rushed home in time to see it. More attention meant more eyeballs watching, and higher ratings. Higher ratings translated immediately into more advertising dollars, and when Jimmy The Greek was added the following year, the ratings went even higher.

As the 1975 season of *The NFL Today* carried on, Phyllis became more and more confident in her role on the show, and the producers became more and more confident in her. "A surprisingly competent broadcaster," the *Baltimore Sun*'s television critic Bill Carter wrote. "Articulate and bright and clever enough to realize what she was hired for."

One of her first friends in New York was twenty-four-year-old production supervisor Janis Delson. They got to know each other when *The NFL Today* producer Mike Pearl invited everyone for drinks after the show each Sunday. They'd meet at the Holiday Inn, a block up the street on West 57th Street from the CBS Broadcast Center.

"It [the friendship] just sort of came about," said Delson. "We used to go out after the show quite a bit [as a group]. We'd go out for drinks, and I was also on the road with her. There was a lot of socializing then—in the beginning. We just got to talking about shopping, and how I had a shoe fetish, and it just sort of evolved that we would go shopping together. Sometimes on Sunday nights we'd segue over to dinner somewhere [as a group] on the East Side to a P.J. Clarke's or a Runyon's, or Peartrees or Jimmy Weston's. It was a very loose atmosphere, kind of blowing off steam. And of course we all smoked then."[1]

Phyllis and Janis would go to Bloomingdale's, just a few blocks away from Phyllis's apartment. "I remember she loved sweaters," said Delson. "She was always buying sweaters. If I would buy one sweater, she would buy four. Whatever she saw, whatever she liked, she bought. We never had appointments. We just walked in like any other customer would.

"Some people did not recognize her, and some people would say, 'Oh, you're on television, right?' but they'd mix up whether she was on local TV or network. When she explained it, they'd say, 'You're one of the first' and 'That's terrific' and 'Good luck.' She was always nice and kind with a smile. Never any 'Oh, leave me alone' kind of attitude. When she'd ask my opinion about whether to buy something, I'd say, 'I prefer this one, I don't prefer that one.' And sometimes she'd buy both."

Phyllis continued to excel in the interviews she did for *The NFL Today*. And she continued to get the players to relax and talk freely, like this 1975 interview with Dallas Cowboys quarterback Roger Staubach. Here's how one question went:

Phyllis: "You have an image as an All-American, a kind of a straight guy. Do you enjoy it or is it a burden?"

Staubach: "You interviewed Joe Namath. Everyone in the world compares me to Joe Namath. As far as off the field, he's single, a bachelor, swinging. I'm married with a family and he's having all the fun. You know I enjoy sex as much as Joe Namath [Phyllis laughs], only I do it with one girl, but it's still fun."[2]

Two years later (1977) she met, and soon after married, Hollywood producer Robert Evans, who became famous for producing films such as *The Godfather* and *Chinatown*, which were the saving grace for Paramount Studios. Evans, however, specialized in short-term marriages. Bob Wussler's daughter Rosemary remembers her father warning Phyllis against the marriage.

"He adored Phyllis," said Rosemary Wussler Boorman. "He was so brokenhearted when she married Bob Evans. He kept telling her, 'Please don't do that. Please don't do that. He's a bad guy.'"[3]

Evans was married seven times. He married his first wife in '61, divorcing in '62. He stayed with his second wife from '64 to '67. His third wife, actress Ali MacGraw, was officially married to Evans from '69 to '74, leaving him after falling in love with Steve McQueen while filming the aptly named picture *The Getaway*. After Phyllis, he married three more times.

Evans and George were married December 12, 1977, and divorced barely seven months later. CBS associate producer Yvonne Connors recalls it all.

"They were introduced by Jimmy The Greek," said Connors. "At the time I remember thinking, 'Phyllis, what are you doing?' After two months with Evans, she went home to her parents in Denton."[4]

A few years later, Phyllis was having lunch at the Polo Lounge in the Beverly Hills Hotel with a CBS producer, who preferred to remain anonymous. "She recalled what it was like to be married to Evans," he said, "and how he wanted another woman to join them in bed. That's when she mentally started packing for Denton."[5]

Regardless, she recovered without much damage. If anything, she grew even more popular, appearing on the cover of *People* magazine, among others. Soon after, *The Muppet Show* asked her to guest star. But there was a downside to the appearance: She got into a humorous "spat" with one of the stars of the show, Miss Piggy.

As part of the program, Phyllis was the host for the Muppet Awards. She announced, "There is no winner for best sketch of the year."

Miss Piggy: "What do you mean I didn't win? I'll cut you in two, George."

Phyllis: "I didn't decide. It was the decision of the blue-ribbon panel of judges."

Miss Piggy: "What are their names so we can put them on their tombstones?"

Phyllis: "Don't you think you ought to get ready for the next category?"

Miss Piggy: "No, why should I?"

Phyllis: "It's a big one, Performer of the Year, and you're nominated."

Miss Piggy: "Moi? Oh, then, well, Phyllis my sweet, I shall go get ready."

All friends again, Phyllis finished the show singing "There's No Business Like Show Business" with the whole cast. To the surprise of many, she had a terrific singing voice.

"We all realized what we had [in Phyllis]," said Mike Pearl, "when we took the show on the road for the playoffs and Super Bowl. Phyllis was the main attraction. When we all walked through an airport or down a street together, the public would go to Phyllis. They pretty much ignored Brent. There may have been some resentment there. And when we were out for dinner, Phyllis was the one being asked for autographs."[6]

Yvonne Connors would travel with Phyllis on the road and remembers one particular playoff game.

"When *The NFL Today* traveled to San Francisco," said Connors, "our set was out on the field. And when Phyllis walked out on the field, warm-ups stopped for a moment, all the players turned, and you should have heard the crowd! Talk about working a room—she knew how to work a stadium!"

By the time Super Bowl X rolled around—and it was CBS's turn to broadcast the game—all four panelists were outright stars. The public had grown to love them.

"*The NFL Today* was the harbinger of sports personality broadcasting," said George Schweitzer, who retired as chairman of CBS Marketing in 2020 after forty-eight years with the network. "It had people with a point of view, people with emotions who were not afraid to unleash them. It established those four as icons of broadcasting."[7]

When he realized that Super Bowl X would be played in Miami, Bob Wussler knew it would be the perfect location for CBS to broadcast the very first *live* Super Bowl pregame show. At the time, having a live pregame Super Bowl show at the site of the game was a very big deal—especially to the league.

"And he wanted it to be a gargantuan event," said his son, Rob Wussler. "He wanted it to be an entertainment spectacular. That's why he convinced CBS to have 'Super Night at the Super Bowl' [a prime-time special] the night before the game."[8]

And instead of just thirty minutes, the pregame show would be an hour and a half in length. It was perfect for Wussler because he had spent so much of 1972 in the cities of Miami and Miami Beach, shepherding his CBS News Special Events unit through both the Republican and Democratic conventions held that year at the Miami Beach Convention Center. He knew the sheriffs, the cops, the mayors, the best restaurants and bars for remote locations, and even the crossing guards. Even better, he was well-liked.

"Super Bowl X," said Bob Fishman, "was the first show that started the trend of multiple-hour pregame Super Bowl shows. That was all his [Wussler's] creation. He'd say, 'We'll have remotes here, we'll have remotes there. We have the perfect cast to do that. We're going to pick up celebrities on the Miami River on the way down to the Orange Bowl.' He was so inventive."[9]

Here's how they did it, according to Pearl and Fishman: The show opened at the ritzy Palm Bay Club, the home of the '70s glitterati, on the North Shore of Miami's Biscayne Bay. Mrs. Cornelia V. Dinkier, who owned the club, told reporters that she built it because "everything is always being done for the poor and nothing is ever done for the rich."

From there, Phyllis George, Irv Cross, Brent Musburger, and producer Mike Pearl got on a yacht, along with former Green Bay Packers star Paul Hornung, and they started sailing toward the Orange Bowl. Somewhere along the way they picked up Joe Namath, who was supposed to make his pick for the game at midfield while talking to Pat Summerall and Tom Brookshier.

The boat traversed into the Miami River near Little Havana, and eventually let everyone off at the Port of Miami, where they were all scheduled to get on a helicopter for a short ride to an area roped off just outside the stadium. Namath, however, decided not to get on the chopper. "He told me," said Pearl, "that he was not getting on a helicopter just to make a pick."

While Brent, Irv, and Phyllis were in the air, Summerall and Brookshier did a feature piece from the press box, and former Kansas City Chiefs coach Hank Stram did his strategy piece from the roof of the stadium. And all during the pregame they interspersed snippets of the nine feature pieces NFL Films had produced for the previous nine Super Bowls.

When Brent, Irv, and Phyllis landed, they were whisked into golf carts and were transported to the set on the field of the Orange Bowl. Despite Namath's last-minute departure, the plan worked magnificently.

"One really funny thing happened during rehearsal," recalled Fishman. "When Hank Stram was rehearsing his segment on the Orange Bowl roof, a gust of wind came up and almost blew his hairpiece off."

Stram had worked NFL games that season for CBS, mostly with Al Michaels as a partner. Near the end of the season they went to New Orleans, assigned to a Saints game. The night before the game, they were about to have dinner at Commander's Palace, a landmark Louisiana Creole restaurant in New Orleans.

"At about 6:30 Hank comes to my room," recalled Michaels, "and he says, 'Hey listen. John Mecom [owner of the Saints] called me. And he wants to have dinner with me.' I say, 'No problem,' and I know what this is all about because the Saints stunk in those years."

"The next morning," Michaels continued, "Hank and I were going to meet for breakfast about 8:30 and the game's scheduled to start at noon. We're at the Royal Sonesta Hotel. My phone rings in my room at 6:30 in the morning. It's Hank." Here's how the conversation went:

Stram: "I need to see you."

Michaels (after they met downstairs): "I know what it is. He wants you to coach his team, right?"

Stram: "Yep. [pause] Do you think I have a future in this [announcing] business?"

Michaels: "Hank, yes you do. You're very good right now. You're going to get better and better, but Hank, you want to coach. You have a chance to coach. You can't turn this down."[10]

Two days after Super Bowl X, Stram was named the new coach of the Saints.

After the Pittsburgh Steelers defeated the Cowboys in Super Bowl X, fourteen-year-old Rob Wussler walked from his seat in the Orange Bowl to a location under the stands where CBS Sports threw a makeshift party for its cast and crew.

"When I got there, I saw Phyllis and Brent hanging out," said Rob. "Hundreds of [production] people were there. What a time that was! And there was my dad, standing on top of one of the crates that brought the equipment in and out, and he was thanking everyone."

During the pregame and after the game, Al Michaels's assignment was to report from the Bowl Bar, a raunchy, wild place that was right across the street from the Orange Bowl. His partner on the remote was former player Alex Hawkins, a guy with a crazy sense of humor.

"I'm going to be there with wacky Alex Hawkins," said Michaels, "and we're going to interview fans. He was a character. We're sitting there about to have breakfast, the day of the game, and Alex orders 'runny eggs, limp bacon, and cold coffee.' The waitress laughs and says, 'I can't bring you that.' He says, 'Why not? You brought it to me yesterday.'

"Alex and I got along great. So we're at the Bowl Bar and we got a couple of [on-camera] hits and the place is raucous. So that's where I was. I never got inside the stadium. They decide they want to come to us after the game for another quick hit. Alex announces to the crowd, 'Calm down, they're coming to us again. I'll count you down and we want you to start to cheer and carry on.' In the meantime we hear in our earpiece that they don't have time for this. Alex got the crowd so loud, they're all riled up. And Alex is screaming [to no one in particular], 'Hey you motherfuckers,' but nobody can hear him. And that wraps up my year at CBS."

Michaels was pissed because he had worked nine or ten games for CBS in 1975, and he did it with five different partners. "There were only two guys who didn't get a postseason assignment," he said. "Don Criqui and me. Even Gary Bender got a game."

Regardless, Michaels did his job and did it well. If anyone at CBS was paying attention, he may never have left for ABC. But that certainly wasn't the focus of Bob Wussler after Super Bowl X. The first live Super Bowl pregame was a hit, and *The NFL Today* was about to get even bigger the following year, with the addition of Jimmy The Greek.

Super Bowl X itself was an exciting one, with Terry Bradshaw's Steelers outdueling Roger Staubach's Cowboys, 21–17. The broadcast of the game, directed by Tony Verna, received an Emmy for "Outstanding Live Sports Special." The broadcast included short interviews with comedians Jackie Gleason, Jonathan Winters, and Henny Youngman, and pictures from the Goodyear Blimp above the field. The television critic John J. O'Connor of the *New York Times* liked what he saw.

"Conceding that professional sports have become little more than elaborate television productions," O'Connor wrote on January 19, 1976. "CBS has deliberately moved toward transforming its presentations into 'entertainments.'" That was Wussler's touch. He definitely realized that the marriage of football and television was an important one.

"Football is an outlet," Wussler told the television history archivist Tom Weinberg. "It's a means of theater that attracts a large group of people in this country who might not be attracted to other forms of theater as we know them—variety, comedy and music. It's a game of the '50s,

'60s, and '70s that is presently building itself a tradition. It will be around for a long time to come. Football is attaining that tradition. But for today, football has been a better sport. It's action-packed, they don't play it every day. It's designed for the American appetite. It came along at a time when television was looking for something, and hand in glove, one didn't make the other, but they sure helped each other a lot."[11]

A couple years later, in January 1978, CBS had Super Bowl XII in New Orleans, between Dallas and Denver. In the two years that had passed, Wussler had been promoted to president of the network, but in a 1977 reorganization, he came back as the president of the CBS Sports division. And getting a chance to produce another Super Bowl and live pregame show was perfect for him.

One of the traditions Wussler liked was the camaraderie the CBS Sports group had during Super Bowl week. On the day before the game, executives, crew, and broadcasters chose up sides for a touch football game. They called it Super Bowl 11½. Former CBS salesman Dick Robertson recalled one play in particular from that game.

"We were in the huddle and Hank Stram says, 'Okay, on three Pat [Summerall] cut over that way and I'll hit you with the pass.' Well, one of our linemen was Gene Jankowski, the head of the entire CBS Broadcast Group—the boss of bosses. Stram hollers 'hut one, hut two' and on three the ball gets snapped and from out of nowhere Tom Brookshier, who was known as one of the hardest-hitting defensive backs when he played, comes flying and flattens Jankowski. Everyone stopped. Slowly Jankowski got up. No one said a word. I always wondered if that hit had anything to do with Brookie being removed from the No. 1 broadcast team a few years later."[12]

That year CBS again planned for a ninety-minute live pregame show, which was named *The Super Bowl Today*. The Phoenix Open golf tournament was scheduled to lead into it, which would help boost the ratings some. But a problem developed because it was raining that January Sunday in Phoenix, and they had stopped playing golf, hoping the rain would pass. The usually stoic Mike Pearl started getting upset.

"Nothing ever bothered him," said Pearl's close friend Hank Goldberg. "Except once, when the Phoenix Open kept delaying the start of

Scene from CBS Sports' company touch football game during the week before Super Bowl XII in New Orleans. From left, Paul Hornung, unknown presenter, Hank Stram, producer Bob Stenner, Kevin O'Malley, Tommy O'Neill, sales exec Dick Robertson, Bob Wussler, and Phyllis George. Network president Jim Rosenfeld is below Phyllis. (COURTESY DICK ROBERTSON)

Phyllis George in cap and sweatshirt getting ready to catch a pass during the CBS Sports touch football game in New Orleans in January of 1978. (COURTESY OF PAMELA BROWN)

his pregame show. I was sitting in the truck, and I saw him pick up the show's playbook and throw it up against the wall. That was the only time I ever saw him show emotion."[13]

Frank Chirkinian was producing the Phoenix Open and he stalled as long as he could, having his broadcasters analyze everything from the wet greens to the weather. They had golfers doing card tricks in the clubhouse. There was another forty minutes before the scheduled start of Wussler's live pregame show. He had remotes set up all over New Orleans. In normal conditions Chirkinian would give the time back to the local stations until the scheduled start of *The Super Bowl Today*. But these were not normal conditions. Wussler wasn't about to let the local stations get the time back. He had to fill, but how?

"They were obviously running out of things to fill with," said Bob Fishman. "So Wussler said to the crew, 'We can do a pre-preshow. He alerted Mike [Pearl], myself, our T.D. [technical director], and he said, 'We're going on the air in twenty minutes. Can you get everybody assembled?' And our reaction was, 'Huh? What are you talking about?'

"And he said, 'We're going to have our producers at the various remotes as the talent [announcers], and they're going to interview our real talent. So we're going to go to Sid Kaufman, and Sid, you're going to interview Brent, Phyllis, and Irv as they're getting into the carriage to make their way up Bourbon Street. And Kevin O'Malley, you're going to do this segment from the press box'—and he's manipulating all this as we're going."

A few minutes later they come on the air, and the opening was Wussler on camera: "Hi everybody, I'm Bob Wussler and a funny thing happened on the way to the Phoenix Open—it rained—so we're going to do a little tour of how we do a pregame show."

"And with his mic in hand," Fishman said, "he actually walked across and down the [production] aisle. He stopped and talked to Mike, and said, 'Okay, Mike Pearl, our line producer, what do you have in store for us?' Mike says we're going to do this and we're going to do that. Then he walks past Mike to me and says, 'Well, Bob, you're directing, what does a director do and how are you going to make this all come together?' Then he walks down the aisle and asks our A.D. [associate director], Peter

Bleckner, 'What is your job?' And then he walks over to Bobby Brown, our technical director, and Bobby was British and had that wonderful accent. Bobby says, 'I am the man who puts on the pictures that our director calls for.' And with tongue-in-cheek he [Brown] said, 'Well, Robert, this row of buttons is the switcher, and with this talented hand [they push in for a close-up of Bobby's hand], we move from this position on the swisher to the other position.' Well, it was hysterical."

"We gave everybody a great inside look," Fishman continued, "then we'd throw it out to the remotes and they would do their thing and then he'd wrap it up and say, 'All right, we're going to go over to golf now, and we'll see you in a half hour for the real pregame show.' That was his brilliance. That was Wussler in a nutshell, because he had the experience of doing moon shots and elections and conventions. I'll never forget that. It was remarkable."

Unfortunately, barely a year later Wussler resigned. "The FCC ruled that the network had blurred the line," wrote *Sports Illustrated*, "between sports and showbiz by misleading the public in promos for a series of 'winner-take-all' tennis matches when, in fact, all contestants were paid lavishly."[14] Wussler had denied any knowledge of it. It didn't matter.

"There were some people in Washington, with the F.C.C., who wanted to get at CBS," Wussler told United Press International in 1986. "And there I was, caught in the middle. So I was the fall guy."

However, he resurfaced in 1980 at TBS, where for the next decade he helped Ted Turner take his new cable channel to international heights, including his work getting the Goodwill Games off the ground.

"I had twenty-one marvelous years at CBS," Wussler told the archivist Tom Weinberg. "I went there when I was twenty years old and left when I was forty-one. As far as I was concerned I thought I'd be there for forty-five years and I'd retire at sixty-five. Fate and the way the cards got dealt are not always the way you'd like them to be. In my case it didn't happen the way I'd have liked them to be."[15]

CBS's Schweitzer, who retired as the network's marketing chairman after forty-eight years there, understood the importance of Bob Wussler's contribution. "What he did in his time was revolutionary and hugely successful," said Schweitzer. "And this paved the way for Personality Sports Television. He saw this as the game before the game, and he knew that people would have an appetite for this. He was a classic television showman."

Van Gordon Sauter, who was plucked by Wussler from radio news to become the news director of CBS-owned WBBM-TV in Chicago, and would go from there to various higher levels at CBS, including president of the CBS Television Network, recognized Wussler's brilliance and mourned his loss.

"The tragedy to Wussler's life," said Sauter, "was that he ended up becoming an executive, and never got his hands on anything to produce again."[16]

Even though Wussler bid CBS Sports good-bye, the show he created, *The NFL Today*, had become a steamroller against the competition. It looked like nothing could stop it—until Phyllis George announced she was leaving the show.

CHAPTER NINE

Jayne Kennedy: The Greatest Talent Hunt Since Scarlett O'Hara

By 1970, THE COUNTRY HAD BEGUN TO HEAL FROM THE RACE RIOTS OF the '60s and the murders of Robert Kennedy and Martin Luther King Jr. in 1968. For a young Black woman like Jane Harrison, growing up in the Cleveland, Ohio, suburb of Wickliffe may have been a little easier than growing up in Selma, Alabama, but prejudice still existed everywhere.

In ninth grade she changed the spelling of her first name to Jayne. "I was tired of hearing *Fun with Dick and Jane* and the Tarzan jokes," she said when contacted for this book. "Jayne made that stop."[1]

In 1970 life seemed pretty good for Jayne. She was in her senior year in high school, and she had a job modeling clothes for the May Company, the department store chain. On Sundays she'd follow the fortunes of the Cleveland Browns with her dad. Tall and strikingly attractive, someone asked her to run for Miss Cleveland, which she won, sending her to the Miss Ohio contest, where the winner would compete for Miss USA.

"The Miss Ohio pageant was held at Mentor Mall," Jayne recalled. (Mentor is a suburb of Cleveland.) "It was the same place I worked weekends as a model for the May Company department stores teen fashion brand. Some of my high school girlfriends and some May Company employees showed up to lend their support. I had no idea that there was even a chance that I would win."

But she did win, becoming the first Black woman named Miss Ohio. The contest, however, did not provide any prizes or scholarships. Upon hearing this, the wife of Cleveland's first Black mayor, Carl B. Stokes, went out shopping to gather prizes of her own for Jayne. Then it was off to Miami for Miss USA.

In Miami there was a lot of talk about "the Black contestant." "You could hear the whispers," Jayne said. "'The Black girl isn't gonna win.' But I still placed in the top 10 in the swimsuit competition and became a semifinalist [top 15] overall."

When she got back, some proud neighbors in her hometown of Wickliffe installed a sign that read "Welcome to Wickliffe, the Home of Miss Ohio, Jane [sic] Harrison." The sign was torn down three times and put back up each time. "After the third time," Jayne recalled, "they just gave up. Many people were just not ready for a Black Miss Ohio."

Shortly after graduating high school, she met Leon Kennedy, a disc jockey with a talent for writing and acting. They were married in 1971, with Motown's Bill "Smokey" Robinson serving as the best man. They moved to Los Angeles, where Jayne found it a little easier to get work than Leon.

She appeared for a time as one of the Dingaling Sisters on *The Dean Martin Show* in the early '70s and also on the popular TV show *Laugh-In*. She did episodic work on TV shows like *Ironside*, *Banacek*, *Sanford and Son*, *The Six-Million-Dollar Man*, and *The Rockford Files*. And in 1977 she also appeared in an episode of *Wonder Woman*. As Leon started to write and produce, Leon and Jayne became a power couple in Black circles, and grew close with people like former Cleveland Browns star Jim Brown and heavyweight boxing champion Muhammad Ali.

Back in New York, Phyllis George surprised everyone when she notified the brass in early 1978 that she wanted off the show. She had just married Robert Evans on December 12, and the marriage was not going well. By March she was living back home with her parents, and she needed time to recover.

CBS didn't know if this was going to be temporary or permanent, but they had to find a suitable replacement fast. The network sent the word out to all the top talent agencies to submit the names of their best women to replace Phyllis.

CBS Sports publicist Carroll "Beano" Cook, who was the master of the one-liner, said, "It was the greatest talent hunt since Scarlett O'Hara."[2]

"I heard *The NFL Today* was looking for a replacement," Jayne recalled. "I loved football. I grew up watching Jim Brown. He was my superhero. When I heard about the opening, I knew that was perfect. I knew I could put my heart into it. I asked my manager at ICM [International Creative Management] about it. They were asked to submit a list [to CBS] of ten clients [for auditions], but they said no [to me]. They told me that CBS was looking for journalists, and they're not looking for a Black [woman]. But I said, 'I can do this,' and again they said no."

ICM's list was rejected by CBS, so it submitted a second list and a third list and each time still refused to put Jayne on it. She practically pleaded with them, but ICM kept saying no. It was at that point that Jayne and Leon decided to find another way to get Jayne in front of the CBS execs.

"I called Jim Brown," Jayne said, "who had become a friend since I had come to California in 1971. He put me in touch with [CBS Sports producer] Bob Stenner. He put me in touch with George Wallach, who was Bruce Jenner's manager at the time. Jenner had just won the gold medal in the decathlon at the 1976 Olympic Games."

George Wallach managed Jenner's slew of offers. "Wallach is a man that explodes with marketable ideas that elude you or me," wrote *Sports Illustrated* in its September 26, 1977, issue.

"George Wallach thought I would be a great option," Jayne continued, "and he knew Linda Sutter, the head of talent for CBS Sports. He said she was coming to Los Angeles the very next week, so 'let me introduce you to Linda, because she's the one who's going to be hiring the talent.'"

Truth be told, Linda Sutter was the talent coordinator at CBS Sports, but not an executive who made talent decisions. She got the job because she was a "special friend" of Barry Frank, who replaced Bob Wussler as head of the division.

"She was a total fraud," said director of operations Janis Delson. "She lied about where she went to school, where she lived, and we weren't even sure her name was actually Linda Sutter."[3]

Carole Ackerman Coleman was the executive secretary for Frank and sat directly across from Sutter, outside Frank's office. "What a nut job she was," said Coleman when reached for this book. "After Barry discontinued their relationship, Linda would call a florist regularly and order flowers for herself. When they arrived she'd say, loud enough for everyone to hear, 'I wonder who sent these?' I guess she was trying to make him jealous. She was off her rocker."[4]

Shortly thereafter, Frank resigned, and Sutter was soon to follow. But at that moment in history, Linda Sutter actually did play an important role in the selection of Phyllis George's replacement.

Wallach had arranged a lunch meeting for Sutter to meet Jayne at Century City. "She thought I was perfect," Jayne recalled. "She said, 'You've got to come to New York for the interview. I'll make sure you get on the list. I will bring you in.'"

And true to her word, Jayne was one of sixteen women who auditioned for the job on a July weekend in 1978. Cyndy Garvey, wife of Los Angeles Dodgers star Steve Garvey, was an early favorite for the job. No one is positive if she was actually one of the sixteen who auditioned in New York, but she certainly expressed interest. She was already signed on to be cohost with Regis Philbin on KABC's morning talk show, *A.M. Los Angeles*. One actress who definitely was part of the audition that day was Jo Ann Pflug, one of the stars of the 1970 film *M*A*S*H*.

There were three parts to the live audition. The first part was five minutes of repartee with Brent Musburger, who came into Manhattan for the long round of auditions. The second part was five minutes reading material off the TelePrompTer. The third part was a live five-minute interview with a New York Giant football player, whose identity was withheld from those auditioning until right before the session. *The NFL Today* producer Michael Pearl ran the auditions. CBS actually brought in three players to interview.

"In the makeup room a lot of the girls were clamoring around the athletes they brought in, trying to get notes to use," said Jayne. "There was a backgammon game in the corner of the room, and while I waited for my turn, I asked this guy I was going to interview if he wanted to play. He did, and by the time I got to the set, we were old friends.

"There were sixteen of us [auditioning] and I was maybe number fourteen. So I did my thing with Brent on camera and the five-minute athlete interview, and after I was done Brent stood up and said, 'That's it. It's either Jayne or nobody.' He didn't even stay to interview the other two girls. He just left the studio."

Everyone—director Bob Fishman, Mike Pearl, Kevin O'Malley, and Frank Smith, who replaced Barry Frank as the head of the division—agreed that Jayne was their choice. "It was unanimous," said O'Malley, "and I remember Fishman saying, 'You couldn't make her look any less gorgeous if you tried.'" That night they took her to Quo Vadis, where Jacqueline Kennedy and other celebrities often dined. It was commonly referred to as one of the last bastions of *grande luxe* dining in New York.

"Jayne was wearing a clinging silver lamé pants suit and looked beyond stunning," recalled O'Malley. "When we walked into the dining room, conversation stopped everywhere, and every man in the room dropped his jaw."[5]

She thought the job was hers. Then she was told she had to wait for one final approval.

"They couldn't hire me," Jayne said, still dealing with racism, "for fear of the Southern affiliates walking. They sent my audition tape to the Southern affiliates and asked what they thought. CBS was afraid it would be a problem because now they would have two Blacks and one white on the set. That's when they decided to put Jimmy The Greek on the set too. That way they had two Blacks and two whites [to satisfy the Southern affiliates]."

Van Gordon Sauter, who succeeded Frank Smith as president of CBS Sports two years later in 1980, was asked if he knew about this. Here is his email response:

A Frank Smith poll of Southern affiliate sentiment is new to me. However, it would hardly surprise me that 42 years ago a confidential polling of southern affiliates, or confidential polling within the CBS Broadcast Group on West 52d Street, would reflect a general resistance to a 2-1 Black/white talent ratio. When I was veep/general manager of the CBS company-owned TV station in Los Angeles during the late 70s, our primary talents [announcers] were a white male anchor, a female Asian anchor, a black sports person and a Hispanic weather person. Race was an issue in the urban markets. Representation was critical. And that could be arcane. But I think a strong case could be made at that time, in Sports, for a Black male anchor, a Black female co-anchor and a white co-anchor. I don't recall how that matter was resolved. Also, I don't recall any formal sampling of Southern affiliates about racial/programming issues. The only regional episode I can recall is when we, in the most casual manner, mentioned to a routine meeting of southern affiliates the possibility of broadcasting some soccer matches. It was met with outrage. One affiliate said something to the effect that, "you [the network] can stuff that soccer ball up your ass." And was applauded.[6]

After overcoming ICM not putting her on their submission list three different times, doing her own networking to get a meeting, and then finally getting an audition and winning the job, she still didn't have it until the Southern affiliates said, "Okay." It had to be agonizing.

"Absolutely," she said. "And then they only gave me a six-week contract. I had to prove myself all over again in the studio. My second weekend I was in the studio on Friday and I overheard them talking. They had to get an interview with [Muhammad] Ali for *CBS Sports Spectacular* the day after his fight that Friday night in New Orleans with Leon Spinks [September 15, 1978], but Ali's lawyers were giving them a hard time. I jumped in and said, 'Hey, I can get you the interview.' I don't know why they believed me. I had only been there two weeks.

"I had been a friend of Ali since 1973–74. Leon and I were with him in Manila for the Thrilla in Manila [vs. Joe Frazier, October 1, 1975]. We had become very good friends. I said, 'If you get me a private plane and a crew, I will get the interview, and I will bring it back.' So they did it. I called Ali and told him what I needed. He said, 'I'll leave a key to my suite for you at the front desk. After the fight I need you to go straight to the room and get set up, because I have to be at ABC for a post-fight after this.'

"The crew was set up when he walked in the door. He still had his robe on. His hands were still bandaged. He said, 'I'd only do this for my friend Jayne.' So I got the interview. I jumped on a plane and went back to New York. They put a part of it on *Sports Spectacular* on Saturday and gave me a feature piece to do Sunday morning on *The NFL Today*.

"Monday morning I got a call that CBS had picked up my contract for the whole year."

There was a very good reason that Muhammad Ali, the most famous athlete in the world, would take Jayne Kennedy's call. In September of 1978, a month shy of her twenty-seventh birthday, she was a stunningly beautiful woman, yet her softness came through the camera. When she was officially announced as a cast member for *The NFL Today*, many media outlets latched on to the fact that in 1970 she became the first Black woman named Miss Ohio. But that was eight years back in her rearview mirror. Since then she had worked seven years as an actress, singer, dancer, model, and TV host. She had also traveled the world. "So when it came down to it," she said, "winning Miss Ohio had nothing to do with it. And it certainly wasn't on my résumé."

When she went on the air, she became an instant inspiration for other Black Americans looking for a career in television. One of them was Oprah Winfrey. "Here's what Oprah later told me," Jayne said. Oprah: "Gayle King and I used to sit on the floor, and every time you came on the show we'd jump up and down screaming, 'Colored people on TV, colored people on TV.' Because you did it Jayne, it made me believe that I could."

No one was happier that Jayne had joined the show than Irv Cross. "Jayne is a beautiful woman," he said in his autobiography, *Bearing the Cross*, written with Clifton Brown. "She's as beautiful on the inside as she was on the outside. Thank goodness CBS decided that two blacks [on the show] weren't one too many. She didn't miss a beat."[7] When she was reminded of what Irv had written about her, she responded, "Irv was my rock."

But despite all the episodic TV work she had done, she was a neophyte when it came to live television. In Studio 43, from where *The NFL Today* was broadcast, there were multiple cameras, a score of monitors, and action everywhere she looked.

"I begged them to give me some training," she recalled. "I would come into the studio every day, if need be [to practice], and they said no.

This 1978 *NFL Today* cast photo shows Jayne Kennedy between Irv Cross and Brent Musburger, with Jimmy The Greek and Jack Whitaker behind. (COURTESY CBS SPORTS)

I begged them to give me some experience on camera before I had to do it live, and they said no. They just wanted to throw me in the pool and see if I could swim. Linda Sutter was the intermediary [for my request], and whoever she asked said no. I just wanted to show people who I was. I just wanted to be myself."

Still, Jayne's debut on the program drew an enormous amount of publicity. She was on the cover of the glamorous Black magazines *Ebony* and *Jet*. There were numerous requests for interviews. Despite being a little unsure of herself in the beginning, her popularity grew. Then one Sunday Brent purposely threw her a curve ball that nearly ruined her career. *The NFL Today* director Bob Fishman remembers it this way:

"Jayne was something else. She was great," Fishman said, "but Brent was really cruel to her on one particular show. For some reason he was ticked off at everybody on that particular day—maybe it was because of all the notoriety she was getting, I don't know. We came up to halftime and I remember this clearly. Brent would do the score rundowns and then he and Irv would do the highlights. And this halftime Brent said something like, 'We're back live at *The NFL Today* studios in New York, and Jayne, why don't you take us around the league [and report the scores of the games]?' She looked like a deer in the headlights. It was awful. I remember hitting his headset and saying, 'That was a real son-of-a-bitch move.' But Brent just ignored the comment.

"He threw her a curve ball. She wasn't prepared for it. She didn't know what team was leading what, and it was just awful. She'd read the team that was losing first. Why would Brent do that? So cruel."[8]

As she attempted to read the scores, she was shaking. They were too scared of Brent at that point to reprimand him. Fishman's comment in his earpiece was as tough as it got. They knew Brent controlled everything on the show, and they didn't want to ruffle his feathers. Producer Mike Pearl did approach Brent about it, however.

"I told Brent that it was wrong," said Pearl. "He said he was just trying to have fun with it. There were no repercussions. I apologized to Jayne, who as I remember, took it in stride. Second-guessing myself, if we were just doing a score segment, we should have had just Brent and Irv on the set."[9]

It turned out that Jayne was not fine with it and did not take it in stride.

Said Jayne of the incident: "I don't know why Brent did it. And that was one of the reasons I asked CBS to give me studio [practice] time—to work with me so I wouldn't have anything like that facing me. Brent didn't tell me he was going to do that. It was completely unfair. It was a problem and continued to be a problem. People would say, 'She's a girl. She didn't do it like guys do it.' Probably every male reporter in the country that hated female sportscasters tried to make me look bad. There's a tie to gambling, because if you read the score with losing score first, their ear is tuned to hear the winning score first, and they don't actually listen to what you're saying. Because all I did was to read the losing score before the winning score. Over the years I've seen guys doing the exact same thing, but because it was a woman doing it, they made a big to-do over it."

"It was a nightmare to do live television," she continued. "Nobody understood what it was like to be in the studio. In the 1 o'clock shows, you have three of those, and then your 2 o'clock shows and you're coming up on your halftimes for the 1 o'clock games, then halftime for your 2s, then you've got your postgame—it was crazy. In the studio, with all those monitors, it wasn't like it is today with everything being so easy. People were handing you notes behind the desk and under the set. You've got two different people on your headset, and you're on a show that's basically unscripted, and you've got to figure it out. Well, how do I chatter, in between their chatter? It was a nightmare and they should have given me training."

Despite all that, she made it through the first season fine. Somehow Jayne and Brent got past the incident. She even worked easily alongside Jimmy, who she described as "a big, angry teddy bear." She also loved working with Pearl and Fishman. "You couldn't have had a better team," she said.

The first week of the playoffs that 1978 season, the show traveled to Tampa, where the Tampa Bay Buccaneers were hosting the Philadelphia Eagles. At the end of the pregame show, Brent asked Irv and The Greek who they liked. They each said Philadelphia. Then offhand Brent said, "Jayne, who do you think will win?"

"I had spent time that week with some of the Tampa players," Jayne said, "because I had done an interview earlier that year with Doug Williams. So I said I'd cook for them at Doug's house. When Brent asked me, I gave my two cents worth on why I thought Tampa was going to win, and when I said Tampa, Jimmy's jaw dropped. After the game [which Tampa won] Doug caught up with me at the airport and said, 'Thank you for believing in us.' The next week we came back to Tampa, and the driver took me through the city. He wanted to show me that there were signs up all over that read 'To hell with Cosell, we've got Jayne.'"

Jayne's second year with *The NFL Today* went smoothly enough, but as the show arrived in Los Angeles in January of 1980 for Super Bowl XIV, management seemed aloof toward her.

This was because Phyllis George's agent, Los Angeles attorney Ed Hookstratten, who had Johnny Carson and Elvis Presley as clients, had notified CBS that Phyllis would consider returning if there was an

In 1980 when *The NFL Today* went to Hollywood for Super Bowl XIV, celebrities like Warren Beatty welcomed them. That's Beatty on the right with producer Mike Pearl and Jayne Kennedy, with director Bob Fishman leaning in from behind.
(COURTESY JAYNE KENNEDY)

expanded role for her at CBS. In fact, a handshake deal had already been agreed to before CBS landed in L.A. Jayne, through no fault of her own, was out. Unfortunately, no one told Jayne.

Ted Shaker, who became the producer of *The NFL Today* the following year, confirmed this. "We [Shaker and new division head] went to see Phyllis at the [governor's] mansion in the spring," Shaker said. (By then she had married John Y. Brown, who became governor of Kentucky.) "Prior to that, the groundwork was laid for her return with her agent, Ed Hookstratten."[10]

Phyllis first met John Y. Brown, owner of the Kentucky Fried Chicken empire, in L.A., where he was hosting Muhammad Ali at the Beverly Wilshire Hotel. That was 1977. They didn't meet again for nearly two years, after she had married and divorced Robert Evans. This time it worked. They were married March 17, 1979. The pair campaigned together after Brown announced he was running for governor, and when he was elected that November, she settled into a life as a governor's wife.

"I was doing the Super Bowl XIV pregame show from the Rose Bowl," Jayne recalled. "They had given me an assignment to do the pregame from a helicopter. Just before I was about to go on, I got bumped, and they'd go to, 'Here's Phyllis George at the Ginger Man [restaurant] in Beverly Hills with her husband, Kentucky governor John Y. Brown.' It happened more than once, and I didn't know at the time that they were going to be bringing Phyllis back on the show until way later. I was upset and got off the helicopter, and Irv [Cross] grabbed me and said, 'Jayne, there's nothing you can do. Nothing you can do. It's done.' I said, 'What's done?' It was months later that I found out I'd been fired.

"They sent me a telex," she said. "I was on my way to the airport to fly to Seoul, Korea, to host the Miss Universe show [for CBS]. It was my fourth time cohosting for CBS. The telex arrived at the exact moment I was headed for the airport. CBS knew my schedule, and they knew there was nothing I could do. There was no one I could call. No cell phones in those days. I just had to think about it the whole flight. Then when I got to Korea, one of the cue-card guys grabbed me aside and said, 'Jayne, we've been told to edit you out of the show as much as possible.' They said I had breached my contract because I had signed on to do a show for NBC called *Speak Up America*. NBC even gave them first call on my services."

She had told CBS Sports head Frank Smith about the NBC offer. "That would be amazing," she said he told her, adding, "That would give us great prime-time exposure." He also put it in writing permitting her to do the NBC show.

"Since Brent was working during weekdays in L.A., I thought it was a double standard," she said. Brent was the weeknight newscaster, Monday through Thursday, at the CBS-owned-and-operated KNXT-TV, a station run by his former boss in Chicago, Van Sauter.

"I never wanted to leave *The NFL Today*," she said. "Never! *The NFL Today* was my dream job. When I showed them the letter from Frank Smith, they had to hire me back."

But that lasted only as long as the CBS lawyers could figure out another way to cut her loose. So this time she hired the now-famous women's attorney Gloria Allred, who was not as well known then. CBS hired Jayne back again until they found another way to release her. "They wound up paying me for the year," Jayne said, "and that was it. It was devastating when they fired me. It was very emotional."

CBS came out of this with blood on its hands. It was shameful how they treated Jayne Kennedy in the end. They certainly could have kept her on doing anthology events for *CBS Sports Spectacular* and interviews for other live events like football and basketball. But CBS did not want to spoil Phyllis's return with Jayne still around to remind people what they had done.

Regarding Jayne's departure from CBS, producer Ted Shaker said, "She was a wonderful person, I thought. Totally lovely. She tried hard. She just wasn't Phyllis."

By the following September, everyone had moved on. The media, excited by Phyllis's return, pumped up *The NFL Today* even more. Even Jayne got over it. She moved on and in 1982 became the only female host of the syndicated series *Greatest Sports Legends*, which she hosted for six seasons, including the program's 30th anniversary show in which every one of the living sports legends they had saluted came back. "It was one of the greatest moments of my career," she said.

CHAPTER TEN

The Fight at Peartrees

WHEN TED SHAKER GOT HIS ENTRY-LEVEL JOB AT CBS, HE MAY HAVE had an advantage getting the interview. His father, Theodore F. Shaker, was a former executive at the CBS Television Network and a group vice president at ABC. But once Ted got his foot in the door, he earned every advancement along the way.

In 1973 he began literally as low as you can go at CBS, working in the videotape vault in the basement of the CBS Broadcast Center. After several months he graduated up to shipping clerk and then got a job working on the kids show *In the News*, eventually becoming associate producer there.

"I then tried for CBS Sports," Shaker said, "and eventually in '77 I met with Bob Wussler, who by then had become president of the network."[1] Wussler most likely recommended him to Barry Frank, who Wussler had handpicked as his successor to run CBS Sports.

"Eventually I had a conversation with Barry," Shaker said. "He gave me his test to see your expertise in sports. I think I answered them all wrong. It turns out that he decided to hire me as an associate producer anyway. I came in as a postproduction storytelling guy, and they didn't have many there like that."

One of his first assignments was working on a feature for the Belmont Stakes with director Tony Verna, credited as the first director to use instant replay. Verna was one of CBS Sports' best-known directors, and was very self-promotional. On their walk through the Belmont backstretch, Verna turned to Shaker and said, "You're going to be so fortunate to be working with me."

"I was thinking," said Shaker, "who the fuck is this guy?"

His next job was to babysit Jimmy The Greek. "I was the Greek-keeper," he said. "Eventually our information guys like Frank Ross and Mike Francesa became the Greek-keepers. As Greek-keeper I tried to remind him what we were doing the next day and to keep him out of trouble."

They'd go to Elmer's steakhouse on East 54th Street, which was one of Jimmy's favorite restaurants. Elmer's was the back half of what once was the famous El Morocco nightclub in the 1950s. El Morocco first opened as a speakeasy and eventually drew celebrities like Joe DiMaggio and Marilyn Monroe to its zebra-striped motif. By the late '70s Elmer's still attracted high-profile clientele like The Greek and his pal John Madden. The restaurant, however, never adapted for cable TV, but on Monday nights The Greek had the manager set up a small TV with rabbit ears so he and his pals could watch the Monday night football game.

"My job was my life," Shaker continued, "so spending that time with Jimmy was okay. He had tremendous instincts. He could read the room; he could read an individual. He'd get a call and they'd bring the phone to his table and it would be Al Davis. He was always on the phone and he worked hard at it. As time went on he became a little less able to retain all that stuff, but he was a force of nature then."

During the next two years Shaker learned quickly, and as associate producer of *The NFL Today*, he was as qualified as anyone when Mike Pearl decided to leave. In February of 1980, Pearl had a tremendous success producing the Daytona 500 live. He had been looking for other challenges outside of the studio, so a few days later when Roone Arledge invited him to join ABC Sports, Pearl accepted. In his place, Ted Shaker was promoted to the unenviable job as producer of *The NFL Today*.

"In my first season producing, [Bob] Fishman came back in to direct and to help guide me," Shaker said. "It became this wonderful seven-day-a-week event—always thinking about it."

Brent Musburger lived in Weston, Connecticut, then and Shaker in nearby New Canaan. They'd drive into the studio together Sunday mornings and then drive home together Sunday nights.

"On the way home," said Shaker, "we'd stop at a deli and buy a six-pack of beer and drink them on the way." When they'd get to the tollbooth on Interstate 95 at the New York/Connecticut line, there would always be a long line to pay. This was before E-ZPass. That's when the mischievous boy in both of them would come out.

"We were crazy," Shaker said. "We'd run the tollbooth [going through an unmanned lane]. We were bulletproof and what could go wrong?"

"On the way in on Sunday mornings we'd talk about what we were going to do that day," he continued. "On the way home it was what stories there were and what to look forward to the next week, and we gossiped about who screwed this or that up.

"It was a heady time. We were on top of the world. The show was a great big hit."

In essence, Shaker, a very talented producer, needed Brent's cooperation and help even more than Fishman's. He obviously recognized that *The NFL Today* could easily fall apart without Brent's unique gifts, and he sorely depended on them. He needed to stay on Brent's good side, and keep his favor.

"Brent was the most gifted, proficient, technical broadcaster I have ever worked with or have ever seen," said Shaker. "He'd remember everything. If you said in his earpiece that you have thirty seconds, he would hit it on the nose. If I'd whisper 'We're going to bring in another city's audience now' as he was talking, he would do it. And at the same time he'd be juggling these high-profile personalities around him. He was just a remarkable talent."

Kevin O'Malley was always one of the smartest executives at CBS Sports. In 1978 O'Malley may have felt a bit slighted when Frank Smith hired independent producer Eddie Einhorn to be Executive Producer of CBS Sports Spectacular. Einhorn was a dealmaker but a man with no network experience, which sometimes showed.

At a staff programming meeting late in October of '78, Einhorn announced a last-minute change for the first Saturday in November. It was a change that would disrupt scheduling for the series. When asked why the sudden change, Einhorn referred to one of two annual advertiser rating months known as "sweeps."

"Because of November sweeps," he naively said.

"Funny thing about November sweeps," O'Malley deadpanned. "They always fall in November."

By 1980 Van Gordon Sauter had replaced Frank Smith as president of CBS Sports. Smith, a veteran sales executive, was a stopgap after Wussler's abrupt departure. Sauter became the fifth head of the division in five years: Wussler twice, Barry Frank, Frank Smith, and now Sauter, who came directly from Los Angeles where he had been running KNXT-TV, the company's owned-and-operated station.

"Van was, in most ways, the antithesis of a network executive," said executive Kevin O'Malley. "He had a tie that was not fussy, he had shaggy hair and a shaggy full beard, and he was often rumpled, but he was as articulate as could be, and he had a voice like Moses on the Mount."[2]

Sauter was also the man who first brought Musburger to broadcasting—first to radio at WBBM in Chicago, and then to TV. He was a worldly, interesting man with ideas to bring CBS Sports "out of the country club days." He also happened to be married to Kathleen Brown, sister of California governor Jerry Brown.

In the two years Sauter was president of CBS Sports, he helped the network obtain NCAA football and basketball rights, and brought some journalism back to its anthology show, *CBS Sports Spectacular*, by hiring Pat O'Brien and John Tesh. There's no doubt, however, that he recognized how important *The NFL Today* was as a lead-in to the network's live NFL football broadcasts.

In 1980 nothing seemed easy in the world. The Iranian hostage situation had no end in sight, and inflation was running rampant in the United States, averaging 13.6 percent. That year John Lennon was shot in New York, and a bunch of college hockey players defeated the Russians at the Lake Placid Olympics in what has become known as the "Miracle on Ice." The Dow Jones was under 1,000, and the Swedish singing group ABBA had a new hit song called "The Winner Takes It All." For a diversion, American television viewers worried all summer about "Who shot J.R.?" on *Dallas*, a huge hit show for CBS.

In the spring of that year, Sauter and Shaker took CBS's private plane to Lexington, Kentucky, to meet with Phyllis George, now married to governor John Y. Brown. The meeting took place at Brown's Cave Hill estate in Lexington, which had been set up as a temporary governor's headquarters while the Governor's Mansion in Frankfort was being repaired. The purpose of the meeting was to wrap up the final details for Phyllis's return to the show. If Phyllis returned, her popularity would give the show an immediate ratings bump.

When they arrived, they walked through a large entranceway with huge pillars into the governor's residence, according to Shaker. They were then ushered into a large sitting room that was classically decorated with a thick carpet and soft couches and chairs in a red motif.

"She couldn't have been any more charming or nice," Shaker said. "She was interested and wanted to make sure she could do some of the things she wanted to do on the show." In other words, she wanted more airtime and, of course, Shaker and Sauter obliged.

"So she was back! She could light up the room," Shaker said with glee. "She was unique. That personality, the smile, the Southern charm, all made her a star. What a positive it was to have her back! We went from there. It was a hit show, and she was one of the mainstays of making that happen."

With Phyllis back, she demanded more attention than Jayne Kennedy had and definitely more airtime. With just twenty-two minutes available in the show, the one who was going to get squeezed for airtime was Jimmy The Greek. It seemed that more and more when Brent had an extra thirty seconds he'd go in Phyllis's direction with a question rather than Irv Cross's or The Greek's. Irv never complained, but Jimmy felt he was just as much the star of the show as anyone else. He certainly was recognized and well liked by the public. Producer Chuck Milton recalls a specific instance.

"I thought Jimmy was our most popular broadcaster," Milton said. "He was living in the Park Hotel on Seventh Avenue at 56th Street. Every now and then he and I would walk back to the CBS building [known as Black Rock] a few blocks away. Cab drivers would yell at him. All sorts of guys walking the street would say something. 'Hey Greek, who'd you like?' Everyone felt his picks on the games were lousy, but nobody missed watching them. They felt Jimmy understood their situation. They had a rapport with him. He was good company."[3]

By October 26, 1980, it was Jimmy's fifth season on the show, and it's possible Brent was growing tired of Snyder's so-called inside information that they discussed on the segment known as "The Greek's Grapevine." On this day, however, Snyder had a legitimate piece of news. He was about to report that Notre Dame was going to hire Gerry Faust, a high school football coach from Akron, Ohio, to replace its current coach, Dan Devine, at the season's end.

This was huge news. The great, almighty Notre Dame hiring a high school football coach, no less! And nobody else had it. Remarkably, The Greek found out with still a month to go in the schedule. But as Brent led into the piece, instead of saying something like, "What have you got for us today, Greek?" Brent blurted out Jimmy's exclusive news himself, leaving Snyder tongue-tied with nothing to say. What should have been Jimmy's greatest moment in his five years with the show turned into one of his most embarrassing.

"Brent hung him out to dry," said Mike Pearl, who was watching from home.[4] In fact, it was well accepted in the control room that Brent would often steal someone else's headline. According to Pearl, Musburger sometimes listened in while Pat Summerall and Tom Brookshier rehearsed their spot for the show's opening in the whip-around, then Brent would mention their news as he threw it to them, live on the air. Summerall and Brookshier became infuriated with Musburger because it happened more than once.

"Before the playoffs our first year," Pearl said, "we had a production meeting including the studio people and the game people together. Brent and Pat sort of stared each other down. You could tell it was boiling. I knew at that point we weren't going to have dinner at the same restaurant."

According to the *New York Times*, Phyllis also complained to her daughter Pamela that "during commercial breaks she'd have an idea and one of the guys would steal it as if it were his.[5]

"Irv would never do that," said one former CBS producer, "and The Greek wasn't that clever. She was obviously talking about Brent."

The Greek steamed all that day, and when the day was over he left to meet his friend Hank Goldberg at Peartrees. Goldberg, a radio and TV sports celebrity in Miami, had known Snyder for years and sometimes had ghostwritten his odds column.

Peartrees was a favorite weekend restaurant hangout of the CBS crowd. It was owned by Michael "Buzzy" O'Keefe and located on the ground floor of One Beekman Place on the East Side of Manhattan near the United Nations. The apartments at Beekman Place were built in 1929 and had society folks living there over the years, including several Rockefellers. In fact, Truman Capote would usually have his nightcap in the corner of the bar every Saturday night.

The CBS Sports crowd usually congregated at the long bar, where John "Shirts" Hughes was serving them up, or they'd sit at one of several tables across from the bar. O'Keefe, the owner, was rarely seen those days, after he opened his dream restaurant, the River Café, a few years earlier under the Brooklyn Bridge, with spectacular views of Wall Street's financial center across the East River.

Snyder and Goldberg grabbed a table across from the bar, along with a few other CBS staffers. Soon, Musburger, his brother Todd, and Ted Shaker came in and joined them. It didn't take Jimmy long before he started to complain about what happened.

Here's how several different people who were there saw it:

Hank Goldberg: Jimmy was fuming. When Brent broke The Greek's news, Jimmy was tongue-tied. He didn't know what to say. So he just said "homina, homina" like Ralph Kramden used to say on *The Honeymooners*. And as the day grew on he continued to fume. That night he came over to Peartrees because he knew a few of us would be there.

I was at the bar at the time with [CBS Sports executive] Kevin O'Malley and researcher Frank Ross. Soon after Brent arrived, Jimmy came in and started complaining to Brent about what happened. Brent said, "Jimmy, I can kill you any time I feel like it." And Jimmy leaned over and slapped him. Brent came out of his chair and Frank Ross leaned over and grabbed Jimmy. Todd had Brent, and Ross had Jimmy. Then Todd yelled to Jimmy, "Go on, Greek! Show us how you used to do it when you were a gangster." Jimmy was really pissed. Ross and I got Jimmy out of there and got him into a taxi. Jimmy never had any affiliation with the Mob of any kind.[6]

Ted Shaker: I don't remember the Gerry Faust thing. Here's my recollection. Jimmy didn't feel he was getting enough airtime, and he fumed about that. After the first pregame show aired that day, he was livid. We heard it before. On this day he was particularly pissed.

That Sunday night I don't know why we went over to this bar [Peartrees]. I don't know why we went. Todd was at our table and Jimmy began his grievances about how Brent was unfair and he's not going to take it anymore. Everybody's had something to drink—many things to drink—and the bar is full. At a certain point what begins as a discussion becomes an argument then a yelling match.

Then Brent stood up and walked toward Jimmy and Jimmy stood up. Brent then said something that so infuriated Jimmy. I'm paraphrasing, but this was what he said: "I can make you disappear [on this show] if I want to, so be careful what you say." Then Brent came back with something else, and then Jimmy hit him. It wasn't a slap but a punch to Brent's face. I grabbed Jimmy, and Todd grabbed Brent. It became a cause célèbre.

Kevin O'Malley: Brent is a very smart guy, but he has an ego and he can suck the air out of the room. Brent could do the studio show with games from eight sites, and he'd always know where he was and he always knew whom he was talking to. He was an enormous asset. The Greek, another big ego, resented Brent's dominance in decision-making. Brent was maybe five times as smart as him, but Brent resented it that night at Peartrees. I was at the bar, and I quickly got in the middle when we were separating people. It didn't last very long—it was kind of a one-punch nothing-burger—but John Walsh [editor of *Inside Sports* magazine] told a friend of his at the *Washington Post* and that guy put an item in the *Post* and from there it became a story.

From there on, The Greek and Musburger clearly avoided each other. They managed to get it done together somehow. The Greek was sly and he was a clever guy about his own survival. When he sat down and thought about it, he said to himself, "I'm not going to get along here by fighting with Musburger." But The Greek always misbehaved. When you work for a company that has a self-image like CBS, if you're criticized a lot in the right publications, it makes people uncomfortable. I think ultimately that that as much as anything else led to his final good-bye.

The next day, Monday morning, they had a meeting in Van Sauter's office. It was, "How do we keep this thing quiet?" Of course, Ben Franklin was right when he said, "Three people can keep a secret only if two are dead." It was too late. The *Washington Post* had a note on it, and by Tuesday it was a front-page story in the New York papers. Wednesday's *Washington Post* (October 29, 1980) featured a story by TV columnist John Carmody.

"Fortunately for my jaw," Musburger told Carmody, "the Greek's punch is as accurate as his handicapping has been lately . . . wide to the left." He then added, "We're all good friends on the show, but sometimes the pressures kind of build up over the afternoon. It happens."

When Carmody reached The Greek, he said something very similar: "After five years together, there's nothing to it. It was just a long day."

Shaker had his own idea on how the story got out. "I think Van leaked it to the press," he said. "It became a really big story. So we spent the week trying to make it work."

The following Sunday, *The NFL Today* opened with boxing gloves in front of Brent and Jimmy, and Phyllis ringing a bell and proclaiming, "Round One." They had fun with it, and by then they all were dedicated to making the show work. There was too much at stake. "Everyone knew it was a good thing," said Shaker. "I was proud that we were able to work it out and act like professionals."

Van Sauter didn't panic when he found out about the altercation the next day. In fact, he saw it as a possible ratings bonanza. No suspensions or penalties were handed out. It was a sort of "no harm, no foul" kind of thing for him.

"Jimmy was electric. He could just spark," Sauter said. "My attitude was that the story is going to get out. The sports people are blabbermouths—far more than the CBS News people, which is just amazing. I knew it was going to get out, so whenever these two [Brent and Jimmy] come back together, there will be a hell of an audience for it. And in the meantime, everybody who cares about sports will be talking about this event—those two guys—and so forth. And it ended up being an asset.

"There was, I think, after that an apprehension about The Greek. I think it damaged him. I don't think it had any impact on Musburger. Jimmy was difficult. Musburger would talk back to you—'This is dumb, it's a bad idea,' he might say, or, 'I don't know why you want me to do this,' etc. At the end of it all, Musburger knew he was an employee and he would go do what employees did, in spite of all his clout. Jimmy didn't have any depth. Jimmy was a force of nature. There weren't a lot of rational things you could say to Jimmy that were going to change his mind. I liked him immensely. I thought he was an asset. I'm not convinced we always used him well. But he was a hell of an asset."[7]

This wasn't the first time there was tension and shouting between Brent and Phyllis and The Greek. "One of the reasons for friction between Brent and The Greek," said Mike Pearl, "was Jimmy's close friendship with Oakland Raiders owner Al Davis. Jimmy used to openly root for the Raiders on the set while we were on the air, distracting Brent."

About three-quarters of the way through Jimmy's first season on the show (1976), Pearl had to rein everyone back in the night before the broadcast. "I had told them," Pearl explained, "that Brent was editorially in charge out there when I'm doing something else in the control room. But the bickering didn't stop. Then 5 o'clock on Saturday night before the next Sunday show, I got them all in a room and I said, 'Everyone in this room has bitched about every other person in this room. I'm tired listening to all the bitching. So why don't we just go around the room and have everybody bitch to each other about everybody else and get it out in the open, so when we walk out of here we can be clean and start fresh.' No one said a word, and that was that."

Yes, that might have been that, until October 26, 1980.

Brent didn't exactly come out of the affair with The Greek unscathed. His habit of stealing the headline and the limelight had been no secret among the production crew. "There were certainly times when Brent would do that," said the show's director, Bob Fishman.[8]

Summerall and Brookshier never forgave him and continued to hold a grudge. Janis Delson, the control room director of production, recalled the time she was worried Brookshier might go too far.

"Brookshier was traveling home from the Sun Bowl, in El Paso, through Dallas to Philadelphia," Delson said. "The Sun Bowl people would always over-serve the CBS guys, and Brookie had been over-served. The only problem was that Tom had a gun with him. It was a relic, and instead of getting arrested, he just had to give it to the pilot to hold. But instead of flying straight through to Philly, Tom decided he'd stay over a night in Dallas.

"We were in Dallas with the pregame talent for a playoff game, and we were all afraid that the combination of Brookshier and alcohol and the gun and Musburger being near was . . . Well, we were afraid of what we were going to get. We called Pearl from the airport and we warned him to keep Musburger away. Thank God nothing happened, but with Brookshier you never were certain."[9]

After patching things up, *The NFL Today* kept sailing right along at No. 1 in the ratings. But neither Musburger nor Snyder was happy. They both secretly fostered resentment toward the other, which came out the following January, according to Kevin O'Malley.

Brent's suggestion for the 1980 Super Bowl pregame show in Los Angeles, said O'Malley, was to send The Greek to Delphi, Greece. He wanted Jimmy ostracized—not in L.A., not in New York, but in Delphi, as far away as possible. "The Greek found out, and that became the final rupture," O'Malley concluded. "From there the coldness just culminated. There was a lot of resentment from The Greek too. He could tell that Brent wasn't taking him seriously, wasn't treating him like a serious human being. And Brent could be pretty outlandish."

Seven years later, in December of 1987, Snyder appeared on *Late Night with David Letterman*, ostensibly to promote *The NFL Today*. After some banter about the presidential election, Letterman kidded The Greek about the fight.

"How are you and Brent gettin' along?" Letterman asked with a giggle.

"Listen," Jimmy replied, "we've been together almost thirteen years. We're entitled to one argument. I mean you have that many arguments with your wife every week. He and I are the closest of friends."

"But somebody did get punched out, right?" Letterman asked, getting a roar from the audience.

"It was about even," Jimmy said sheepishly.

"All right! A little punch-out! Did you hear that, Paul?" Letterman said to his bandleader Paul Shaffer. "We're entitled to one punch-out!"

For that moment everybody laughed, but a few months later The Greek wasn't laughing when CBS fired him for some controversial comments he made. And no, he and Brent, it turned out, weren't the closest of friends after all.

CHAPTER ELEVEN

Al Michaels's Wild and Crazy Year at CBS

AL MICHAELS, PERHAPS THE GREATEST NFL PLAY-BY-PLAY ANNOUNCER in broadcasting history, started his career at age twenty-two, working for the Los Angeles Lakers, sitting alongside the great Chick Hearn. Unfortunately, Hearn didn't let him do much more than sit.

Michaels knew he was going to be a play-by-play announcer when he was ten years old in Brooklyn. He'd go to bed each night listening to Major League games from stations in Boston, Chicago, and St. Louis. When his parents moved the family to Los Angeles, Al went to Arizona State University, where he called more than 300 baseball, basketball, and football games for the campus radio station, KASN. "You could only pick up the signal in the boiler room of the girls' dorm," Michaels told *Sports Illustrated* in a February 15, 1988, article.

After graduating in 1966, he put together an audition tape and sent it to the Los Angeles Kings. Alan Rothenberg, who was vice president of both the Kings and the L.A. Lakers, was the first to listen to it. "He sounded like a mini-Vin Scully," Rothenberg said in the *S.I.* article, so he hired Michaels to be the radio color analyst, alongside the one-and-only Chick Hearn. Hearn, though, preferred to call games alone, which he had been doing since the Lakers came West from Minneapolis in 1960.

Michaels barely got on the air. The only on-air time he got was at halftime when he gave the stats and other scores from around the league. After four games the team was about to leave on a road trip when Hearn told Rothenberg, "If the kid gets on the plane, I don't." Michaels got the bad news that he was fired and was completely devastated.

While he waited for his next broadcasting job, he was a contest coordinator for Chuck Barris's *The Dating Game*, helping to pick bachelorettes for the show. His father, Jay Michaels, was one of the top agents for Mark McCormack's International Management Group (IMG)—the first blockbuster sports agency. When Jay headed to Hawaii on business, he took Al with him, and while there, Al landed the play-by-play job calling all 147 Hawaii Islanders baseball games.

Some things are meant to happen. Had he remained an analyst alongside Hearn, who never gave Michaels a chance to talk, he might have never gotten the offer to be the new play-by-play broadcaster for the Cincinnati Reds in 1971. He was all of twenty-five in 1972 when the Big Red Machine won the pennant and Michaels had a chance to call some of the World Series on NBC. Then in 1974 he left the Reds when he was offered a hefty raise to be the No. 1 guy for the San Francisco Giants.

"It was [NBC Sports head] Chet Simmons who recommended me to the Reds," Michaels said when contacted for this book. "And I wound up doing two NFL games for NBC later that year. The first game I did was Buffalo at Minnesota. It was only going on a point-to-point basis, back to Buffalo. My partner was [former Chicago Bears running back] Johnny Morris. A week or two later they sent me to Shea [Stadium] to do Buffalo at the [New York] Jets [which was only televised in the New York City market]."[1]

It was a start. Those two games were the only two NFL games he did until 1974, when he moved to San Francisco and NBC hired him to call seven or eight regional games.

Growing up, Al loved listening to Ray Scott call NFL games for CBS. Scott was known for his economic use of words doing Green Bay Packers games: "Starr to Taylor. [dramatic pause] Touchdown!"

"I remember the Ray Scott years," Michaels said. "It was almost like being in church on Sundays, the way Ray would do the games. Ray was the right guy for that time."

When it was time for Michaels to do a new deal for 1975, he and NBC got in a bit of a contract dispute. "I was getting about $700 a game and I wanted a thousand," Michaels said, "and they didn't want to give it to me. I had heard that CBS was interested, so I went to CBS for like $1,250 a game."

The Giants allowed him to miss some games at the end of the year to do football, which the Reds never allowed him to do. It turned out to be quite a season for Al Michaels at CBS.

"You could write a book about this season," Michaels said, laughing. "In 1975 my first game was Atlanta at St. Louis and my partner was going to be Wayne Walker. He was the former [Detroit] Lions linebacker who was living in the Bay area, as I was. Wayne was also the local CBS Sports anchor on KPIX-TV in San Francisco. So Wayne and I wind up doing that game and I think two others. The producer was Hal Uplinger, and the director was Tony Verna."

"Now we get to Week Six, it's about mid-October," Michaels continued. "Wayne had married a very beautiful divorcee he knew in Detroit, and they had a beautiful, beautiful mansion in Tiburon, overlooking San Francisco. She was a multimillionaire with a couple of kids. So we are assigned to a game in Los Angeles with the Rams. About five days before the game, we get a call from CBS saying, 'We're taking you guys off that game and sending you to do San Francisco at New England.'"

That bit of news didn't sit well with Walker, who had made plans for L.A. Here's what followed:

Walker: "Oh no, oh no! We already have our plans for Disneyland and dinners all week there."
CBS Sports caller: "Either you're going to go to New England or you're not going to do any more games for us."
Walker: "Okay, I'm not doing any games for you."

"That ended Wayne's career doing football on CBS," Michaels said, hardly believing what happened. "So I go to New England, and I wind up doing the game with a guy named Tim Van Galder, who was a journeyman quarterback for the St. Louis Cardinals. They brought him in as a stopgap."

Van Galder, who at that time was the sports director at KMOX-TV in St. Louis, arrived in Buffalo just in time. He didn't even meet Michaels until he got to the stadium. The producer for the game was Tommy O'Neill, who thought he'd have a little fun with the fact that Van Galder was an unknown to most of the fans watching from Buffalo and San Francisco.

"In the opening of the show," O'Neill said with a laugh, "Al opens by saying, 'Hi everybody. I'm Al Michaels and you all know who this is [motioning toward Van Galder].' Under Al [on the TV screen] there's a chyron that has Al's name, and under Tim is a chyron with a great big question mark."[2]

Somehow they managed to get through it, and Michaels was able to move on to a third partner. The following year Van Galder worked four games with Bob Costas for CBS. Costas had been calling pro basketball games for the Spirits of St. Louis, and he and Van Galder had become friends. Van Galder also realized how lucky he was to be doing games at all.

"My deal was that I wasn't such a big name," Van Galder told Iowa State University's *Cyclone Sidebar* on January 5, 2015, "and I probably wasn't that great at it either. But, all you are doing is telling folks what they just saw. It's not science, but it was fun."

And he may go down in history as the only guy to have worked alongside both Al Michaels and Bob Costas.

"Now I was partner-less," said Michaels. "My next partner is none other than Johnny Morris. I'm halfway through the season, and I've already had my third partner. After Johnny I'm assigned to New Orleans at Oakland, and my partner is going to be Johnny Unitas [his fourth]. On the Friday before the game, I drive across the Bay to Oakland to talk with John Madden, who was the Raiders' coach. It was the first time I'm meeting Madden, and it turns out he was a big baseball fan and we wind up talking in his office for forty-five minutes. He tells me how one day he wants to buy an RV and drive across the country like *Travels with Charley*. That was my first interaction with John Madden, and right off the bat we clicked. Thirty years later [at NBC] it was fantastic!"

Week Nine of the 1975 season was coming up, and once more Al Michaels had no idea who his partner was going to be. Nobody at CBS knew when they told him he was going to Atlanta. It's a Friday night, and he took a taxi from the Hartsfield-Jackson Atlanta International Airport to the downtown Marriott.

"There are two lines to check in, and I look over to my right and I see [former Kansas City Chiefs coach] Hank Stram, whom I've never met, but I recognize him. I go over and say, 'Hank, I'm Al Michaels, are you doing the game for CBS?' And that's how I wind up doing games with Hank for the rest of the season. He was my fifth partner."

They did the game in Atlanta, and everything worked well. The next week they were assigned to Detroit at Kansas City, which was a little awkward for Stram since the Chiefs had just fired him the year before. And it was especially awkward since Stram's former assistant, Paul Wiggin, was now the head coach.

"We go to Kansas City," said Michaels, "and it's the day before the game. Normally we would go over and meet with the home-team coach. Hank does not want to go over to meet with Paul Wiggin. And irony of ironies, when Wiggin had been [coaching] at Stanford, he was my neighbor, so I knew Paul. So I get in the car and go out to Arrowhead Stadium alone and meet with Wiggin. He wanted to know where Hank was. I said he was under the weather."

"I drive back and pick up Hank at the hotel," Michaels continued. "We were going to dinner, but as soon as Hank gets in the car the first thing he asks me about is the furniture in Wiggin's office. He wanted to know where the couch was; he wanted to know where the Tiffany lamp was. He wanted to know everything. And the fact that Hank was returning to do the game for CBS was a big deal [in the local papers] there. Photographers took pictures of him in the booth, and it was on the front page of the *Kansas City Star*."

As Michaels recounted in chapter 8, the following week he and Stram were assigned to a game in New Orleans. Just before they were to meet for dinner, Stram told Al that New Orleans Saints owner John Mecom requested Stram meet him for a private dinner. During the meal, they discussed Stram becoming the new Saints coach. Stram revealed it all the following morning when he woke Michaels at 6:30 a.m. Al was not surprised at all that they wanted Stram, he said, "because the Saints stunk in those years."

Stram, in fact, was announced as the new Saints head coach two days after Super Bowl X. He lasted just two seasons in New Orleans. In 1978, he was back at CBS paired with Gary Bender.

Even though Michaels was way down in the CBS hierarchy of NFL play-by-play announcers in 1975, he was still terribly disappointed that he didn't receive a postseason play-by-play assignment.

That disappointment stayed with Michaels the following year, when it was time to decide which network he wanted to work for. Instead of taking CBS's offer, he jumped over to ABC Sports in 1976, where he worked on mostly taped events for their anthology show, *Wide World of Sports*, like motorcycles on ice, cliff diving, and barrel jumping. Even though one of those events led to him calling the "Miracle on Ice" at the 1980 Winter Olympics in Lake Placid, it wasn't until 1983 that Al got to do play-by-play at ABC on a regular basis. "The frustration came in," he said. "I didn't want those [*Wide World*] events to become my legacy."

In 1975 no one at CBS was paying enough attention to realize just how good Al Michaels was. They were too worried about having the games covered with whomever they could get, be it Tim Van Galder or anyone else. The same thing happened the following year. In 1976 Bob Costas, another brilliant young announcer, called four NFL games for CBS, and in '77 he called a full slate. He had similar assignments the next two years, although the games were not that attractive. No one at CBS was listening. No one was paying attention. Jay Rosenstein, who was in the Communications area, might have been the only one who recognized Costas's talent.

"We had what amounted to the Costas for Curt Gowdy trade," Rosenstein said when contacted for this book. "Carl Lindemann came over [from NBC] to run programming [at CBS Sports], and Carl said we have a chance to get [veteran play-by-play announcer] Gowdy. That meant that Bob Costas, who was working the sixth or seventh [best] game every weekend, had to go. When they brought Gowdy over, they didn't have any room for Costas. He was really good back then."[3]

The only problem was that no one asked Rosenstein his opinion. Gowdy was on the tail end of his career, and Costas was on the way up. When his contract was up for renewal, they let him walk across the street to NBC in 1980, where Costas became a superstar for the next thirty years.

Al Michaels, Bob Costas, Pat Summerall, and John Madden—what a killer lineup CBS could have had. Could have, if only someone there could recognize greatness. Bob Wussler, the only one there who seemed to have that gift, was gone.

CHAPTER TWELVE

Phyllis Gets Married . . . Again

ONE SUMMER WHILE IN HIGH SCHOOL, JOHN Y. BROWN JR. DECIDED TO sell vacuum cleaners instead of taking a construction job with his football teammates. He earned $1,000 a month selling those vacuums, but his father, John Y. Brown Sr., a sitting congressman from Kentucky, chastised him for not working with his friends.

"Someday," the boy vowed, "I won't be known as your son. You'll be known as my father."[1]

John Y. Jr. graduated from the University of Kentucky in 1957, and during his free time he earned a whopping $25,000 selling the *Encyclopedia Britannica* door to door. In those days of no Internet, no Google, no twenty-four-hour cable news, if you wanted to find something out, you either went to the library or opened the encyclopedia.

After graduating and while working at his father's law firm in 1963, he met Colonel Harland Sanders at a breakfast meeting. Sanders was a local legend for his fried chicken. He had a great recipe for frying chicken and a successful dine-in restaurant, serving it up. After Brown's wife became involved with a local barbecue place called Porky Pig's, John Y. became fascinated with the idea of a fast-food chicken restaurant that could be franchised. He talked Sanders, who was seventy-five, into selling him the business for $2 million, and he kept the Colonel on as the face of the company.

By 1970 the Kentucky Fried Chicken chain had grown to over 4,500 stores internationally, and nearly $1 billion in sales. The next year, looking for a new challenge, John Y. Brown Jr. sold KFC for $245 million (nearly $2 billion in today's money).

"I don't like some of the things John Y. done to me," Sanders told the *Washington Post* in 1979, without being specific. "Let the record speak for itself. He over-persuaded me to get out."[2] The Colonel may have been right, but the expansion of a chicken recipe into an international business was all John Y's ingenuity.

In the mid-'70s Brown dabbled in basketball franchises, owning and either trading or selling the Kentucky Colonels of the American Basketball Association (ABA) and the Buffalo Braves and Boston Celtics, both of the National Basketball Association (NBA). In 1976 the ABA and the NBA were about to merge. The NBA agreed to take four ABA teams. If Brown wanted to be one of the four, he would have to pay a $3 million fee. On the other hand, if he'd agree to fold his team, he'd be paid $3 million. Brown decided to fold, a mistake that cost him dearly, with most NBA teams today valued at a minimum of $500 million. His wife divorced him shortly after that, possibly because she had been the president of the Kentucky Colonels and disagreed with his decision.

On the day his divorce became final in 1977, Brown saw Phyllis George on TV and decided, "I sure do like her, and I think I'll go out with her."[3] After friends introduced them at the Beverly Wilshire Hotel, Howard Cosell hijacked their first date by forcing them to sit at his table in the hotel's famous Hernando's lounge. Soon Warren Beatty, who was living at the hotel, joined them. They never had a chance to get to know each other. Instead, she met and married Robert Evans.

"After traveling for seven years I was exhausted," Phyllis told the *Washington Post*. "I just wanted a closet to hang my clothes in, instead of a suitcase. I met Bob [Evans] and after I had been interviewing athletes—they're good old guys—well, with Bob I could talk about the theater, about the world. I had been Cinderella and I wanted to try that Hollywood life I'd always read about. It was not what I thought it was. Oh, everybody's nice—don't misunderstand me. But, well, I like to go to church on Sundays."[4]

In 1978 Phyllis was taking time off from *The NFL Today* to recover from her disastrous marriage to Evans. "When you do something that is not right for you," she later said, "you know it almost immediately."[5]

Two years after they first met, Phyllis was leaving a party when she ran into John Y. on the stairway. It was a fateful meeting.

"Here was this wonderful man, the kind that mother told me about, and he was interested in me," she told *People* in 1979. "I hadn't recognized it before because he was so low-key."[6]

Brown learned a lot about himself when he was selling encyclopedias in the Kentucky mountains. "It taught me to talk, to look someone square in the eye," he told the *Washington Post* during the campaign. "Taught me timing and feel, and how to close. A lot of people can sell, but they don't know how to close."[7]

Brown closed the deal with Phyllis. Two months later he proposed, and she said yes.

The Reverend Dr. Norman Vincent Peale married them on November 17, 1979. A family friend of Phyllis's, Dr. Peale had become famous for writing the best seller *The Power of Positive Thinking*. The night before the New York wedding they celebrated at Studio 54. Wedding guests included Bert Parks, Paul Hornung, Eunice Shriver, Walter Cronkite, and Andy Williams, who sang "Just the Way You Are."[8]

Just a few days into their honeymoon, Brown told Phyllis he wanted to run for governor of Kentucky. She was all for it, so only ten days after their wedding, he announced his candidacy.

Campaigning with Brown was easy for Phyllis. It was much easier for her to say hello to strangers than for him. While campaigning they were known as "kissing cousins," smooching every chance they got. The *Washington Post* reported that one voter from Paducah said, "Ya'll look like you're on a damn honeymoon," to which Phyllis responded, "We are."[9]

"When we were campaigning up in the mountains of Kentucky," Phyllis said, "a man asked me my name. I said, 'I'm Phyllis George.' And he said, 'In these parts of the woods you're Mrs. Brown.' So from that moment on I was Mrs. Phyllis George Brown."[10]

Brown won a close Democratic primary, then won the general election by almost 200,000 votes. Before moving into the Governor's Mansion in Frankfort, Kentucky, they discovered the building was in terrible disrepair and was a virtual firetrap. Instead, they made Brown's Cave Hill estate in Lexington a temporary governor's quarters.

When it was discovered that there were no state or national funds available to pay for the modernization of the Governor's Mansion, which was originally built in 1798, Phyllis started a "Save the Mansion" fund, soliciting private donors to pitch in for the repairs. Brown even gave up his salary for his term. But after overseeing renovations and later getting involved in Kentucky craft shows, Phyllis began to miss the action of *The NFL Today*.

As the decade turned to 1980, Phyllis reached out to her agent, Ed Hookstratten, to see if CBS would want her back. An agreement in principle was made, and in January of '80, without any formal announcement being made, Phyllis and John Y. made a few celebrity appearances during CBS's Super Bowl pregame show from Los Angeles. A few months later, Ted Shaker, who would take over for Mike Pearl producing, and new CBS president Van Gordon Sauter flew to Lexington to officially welcome her.

"We went to a country house," Sauter emailed. "Sumptuous. Comfortable. In no way was it ostentatious. They were gracious. As I recall, there were no complexities and the conversation was more social than professional. At the end of the visit, the governor asked if we wanted to take a chopper trip for an aerial view of the horse country. He called up a chopper and we did a lovely trip . . . terrifying, I think, [looking down at] some very high-priced and fragile Thoroughbreds."[11]

The bottom line for Shaker, though, was that Phyllis George was back!

The public recognized greatness. The four stars of *The NFL Today* were becoming icons. They were now celebrities, whose popularity drew attention from the political world, Hollywood, Broadway, and comedians like Johnny Carson. They walked with ease into the Polo Lounge, with all eyes on them, and invitations to the best restaurants and private clubs were plentiful. One married a governor, apparently with the approval of Howard Cosell and Warren Beatty, and a famous actor threatened another for picking the wrong teams. But there were peaceful recitals and laughs too.

Super Bowl XIV, for all practical purposes, was in Los Angeles that third week of January in 1980. Many of the CBS Sports staff stayed at the

Beverly Wilshire Hotel on Wilshire Avenue, in Beverly Hills, just around the corner from Rodeo Drive. It is the hotel where the characters played by Julia Roberts and Richard Gere were staying in the film *Pretty Woman*.

"It was like we were the celebrity sports show coming to Hollywood," said *The NFL Today* director Bob Fishman. "We'd be invited to the Playboy Mansion, or Phyllis would be asked to visit with Warren Beatty. We were *the* talked about show."[12]

That week Beatty met with Jimmy The Greek to discuss the possibility of Beatty directing a film based on Jimmy's life. And that week several of those working on *The NFL Today* were invited to the Playboy Mansion. When they walked in, something completely bizarre happened.

"I recall Mike Pearl and Jimmy and myself," said Fishman, "and a few others walking into the mansion. There are beautiful Playboy bunnies everywhere. As we approached the stairway leading up to the bedrooms, there were several more bunnies there. Then we see the actor James Caan, who played Sonny in *The Godfather*, making his way down the stairs. He had a drink in his hand.

"All of a sudden Caan spots The Greek and goes right up to him and starts yelling about the picks he made. The Greek, not one to take criticism lightly, yelled right back. They went at it for a few minutes, actually screaming at each other, before we had to break it up. In retrospect, it's still kind of funny."

That Super Bowl week Phyllis was in L.A. to make an appearance on *The Tonight Show Starring Johnny Carson*. The show wanted her because during that second week of January 1980, the Miss America powers decided it was time to part ways with perennial host Bert Parks after twenty-five years. Carson was having a field day poking fun at the pageant people for the decision. Several nights in a row he read letters written by former Miss America winners protesting the decision. On the evening of January 10, he had Phyllis on the show to discuss it.

"I won for the year 1971," Phyllis told Carson, "and cohosted with him [Bert] every year after for the next nine years. When I found out how it [the firing] was done, I was hurt. How could you have a Miss America pageant without Bert singing, 'There she is . . .'?"

Carson, with tongue in cheek, responded, "I tear up every time he sings that." Phyllis was not going to play along with Johnny. She was there to defend her friend.

"We have more serious things going on in the world than this," she said sternly, "but Bert is an institution. Every year, just one night, everybody's watching. I'm a small-town girl from Denton, Texas. I was sheltered. I went to Atlantic City and I didn't even know that the Boardwalk was made out of boards. And that man [Parks] was my friend. He was always friendly and warm and that gave me confidence."[13]

Carson listened, then smirked and went to commercial.

If you were working for CBS Sports that week, during the day there were trips to the Rose Bowl in Pasadena to rehearse, and on the way back, if you were lucky, you'd be driving with Jack Whitaker and listening to him describe all the great nightclubs that existed in the '50s on the Sunset Strip. Nightclubs like Ciro's, which was a hangout for film stars, or the Mocambo, where Marilyn Monroe promised the owners that she'd sit ringside for a week if they'd hire Ella Fitzgerald, or the Crescendo Club, where jazz greats like Billie Holiday, Louis Armstrong, and Dizzy Gillespie performed.

Evenings were often spent either dining or drinking at the Ginger Man, the celebrity restaurant owned by actors Patrick O'Neal and Carroll O'Connor. The latter won praise for his portrayal of Archie Bunker on *All in the Family*. O'Neal, not nearly as famous for his acting, said, "My restaurants have had longer runs than some of the plays I've been in."[14]

The Beverly Hills Ginger Man was a copy of O'Neal's original in Manhattan across from Lincoln Center. Both were saloons that celebrities frequently enjoyed. When you walked in the front door in Beverly Hills, a celebrity table was on your left, and it wouldn't be unusual that Super Bowl week to see *Sports Illustrated*'s Dan Jenkins at that table with his buddies, being entertained by comedian Robin Williams. Looking past that table, the bar was directly in front of you, where jovial, curly-haired Marvin Cohen always greeted you. There was an upright piano in the corner and occasionally Carroll O'Connor would be holding court there, playing a few tunes as he did on *All in the Family*. If you worked for CBS that week in January of 1980, those were the days.

Two years later, CBS had Super Bowl XVI in Detroit, in an effort to placate the automobile manufacturers who bought millions of dollars of advertising each year. The game was played at the Silverdome in Pontiac, a short ride away. The fear was that they'd encounter some terrible winter weather. It turned out to be even worse than the worst fears. The buses taking most of the press didn't make it through the snow and the ice until after the game had begun.

Phyllis, who wasn't part of *The NFL Today* for the previous Super Bowl, arrived in Detroit on a private plane. Yvonne Connors met her at the airport for CBS to make sure the arrival went smoothly.

"She came with her baby [Lincoln], the nanny, Choo Choo Charlie their dog, and the Kentucky State Secret Service," said Connors. "At the hotel we usually had a cul-de-sac where she had her suite. I was next door and the head of the Secret Service detail, Joe Leyton, was across the hall."

"She traveled with a lot of jewelry," Connors continued, "and when I asked her about it, she said, 'Oh, they're only stones.' But she took very seriously what she did. They were long days. Sometimes 7 a.m. until 8 p.m. Most of the athletes liked talking to her and talking about their families and what they like to do when they weren't playing football."

At a certain point Phyllis realized how important it was that she broke the barrier of being the first woman on a live sports show. "I'll lead," she told Yvonne, "and the path will be open for other women after me."[15]

After Phyllis returned, *The NFL Today* kept sailing right along, with Brent making it all look easy. In 1982 Duke Struck, the show's new director, told the *New York Times* on December 7, 1982, "Our broadcast flows through Brent. The whole place could be coming down, but from the viewer's perspective, he's solid."

Struck, a veteran studio director, took over directing *The NFL Today* after Bob Fishman moved on to direct live events outside of the studio. Struck took the job very seriously and felt everyone else should too.

"We've got so many people," Struck told the *Times*, "who can seriously affect a show, off the field as much as on it. Everybody [working on the show] touches the ball, and everybody can fumble it. We don't have any room for prima donnas. Egos are fine during the week, but not here, not on the weekend."

Kentucky governor John Y. Brown with Phyllis George and baby Lincoln. Phyllis sent this photo and thank-you note to the author's mother for her gift of a hand-knit baby sweater. (COURTESY PAMELA BROWN)

In 1982 George Veras became the producer of *The NFL Today*, with Ted Shaker moving up to executive producer. Veras was a little more high-strung than Shaker but he got along well with everyone, especially Brent.

"Brent was not just terrific and brilliant," Veras said when contacted for this book, "he also knew stories. One Thanksgiving Day the copy never got to Brent that he was supposed to track. I was yelling at people, 'Where's the copy?' And Brent just hit the key and said, 'Don't worry about it. Roll the tape, I'll do it.'"

"That's the Brent Musburger I knew," Veras continued. "He took direction. We had disagreements but it didn't matter because we both wanted the same thing—to be the best. He was competitive. We were a steamroller in the ratings. With those four [stars] working together, and the way Brent could make everybody raise their game, no one was close to us."[16]

CHAPTER THIRTEEN

The Greek's Luck Finally Runs Out

"IT WAS THE GREEK'S BAD LUCK," SAID JAY ROSENSTEIN, WHO HAD MOVED up to become the director of programming at CBS Sports in 1988. "Of all the things to happen to The Greek, both the [San Francisco] 49ers and the [Chicago] Bears had to lose as big favorites at home in the first round of the playoffs, to allow the Washington Redskins to sneak in."[1]

What Rosenstein was referring to was how the Redskins got a home game for the second round of the NFL playoffs in early 1988, and that's where *The NFL Today* and Jimmy The Greek would be that weekend. And it was the Martin Luther King Jr. holiday weekend in Washington, D.C., to boot.

"No one expected the Redskins to be there," Rosenstein reasoned, when he was contacted for this book, "because the 49ers and the Bears were the class of the conference as the No. 1 and No. 2 seeds. What were the odds? And that put The Greek and everybody else in Washington, D.C., for the NFC championship game [with the Redskins hosting the Minnesota Vikings]."

Less than a month before, the big news in Washington, D.C., was a visit from Soviet leader Mikhail Gorbachev for a summit with President Ronald Reagan. It was a Peace Summit, and as Gorbachev's limo traversed the D.C. streets, people began to applaud him. Gorbachev stopped the limo, got out, and started shaking hands with everyone. Eleven months later Gorbachev allowed the Berlin Wall to come tumbling down.

"We thought we'd have Jimmy do something similar," said *The NFL Today* executive producer Ted Shaker. "You know, get out of a limo and start shaking everyone's hand. But as we were taping it, the camera broke, and we had to take a lunch break while they got a new one."[2]

Jimmy wanted to go to Duke Zeibert's restaurant, one of his favorites. According to the *New York Times*, "David George 'Duke' Zeibert was, for 44 years, the proprietor of a restaurant in Washington, D.C. that was frequented by Presidents, senators, lawyers, lobbyists, quarterbacks, coaches, and columnists."[3]

On this Friday before Martin Luther King Day, a crew from the local NBC affiliate was at the restaurant asking people, "What does Martin Luther King Day mean to you?" For The Greek it was the perfect storm. He needed both the 49ers and the Bears to lose at home and a camera to break to put him in that restaurant, at that exact moment in time.

WRC-TV's Ed Hotaling, a Black producer-reporter, spotted The Greek having lunch and approached. Snyder may have had a glass of wine or two but he wasn't drunk. Hotaling began by asking Snyder about civil rights in sports. The Greek started explaining how Black athletes became bigger and stronger than white athletes.

"The Black is a better athlete to begin with, because he's been bred to be that way," Jimmy told Hotaling with a microphone in front of him and a camera staring him in the face. "It's because of his high thighs and big thighs that go up into his back. And they can jump higher and run faster because of their bigger thighs, you see." He went on to say that "the Blacks are going to take over everything [in sports]," and that the only thing left for the whites is "a couple of coaching jobs."

Hotaling was stunned, but he kept the camera rolling and allowed The Greek to continue a speech that would ultimately end his broadcasting career. "I'm telling you," Snyder insisted, "that the Black is the better athlete and he practices to be the better athlete, and he's bred to be the better athlete, because this goes all the way to the Civil War when, during the slave trading, the slave owner would breed his big woman so that he would have a big black kid, see. That's where it all started."

Now that might have been okay if it was just table talk between friends or as a famous politician once said, "locker-room talk." But this was for Channel 4 in Washington, D.C., and The Greek just kept talking.

Hotaling went back to WRC and ran the comments on the 5 o'clock news. By 6 o'clock it was everywhere. It was the equivalent of something going viral today.

Shortly after the interview aired, the *Washington Post* reached Snyder at his hotel. "If what I said offended people, I apologize," he said. "I didn't mean for my remarks to come out the way they did. I was trying to emphasize how much harder so many blacks work at becoming better athletes than white athletes. That many black athletes run faster and jump higher than whites is a fact. Using the term 'bred' was wrong on my part, and I apologize for that, as I do for suggesting coaching was the only domain left for whites. Blacks could do well in that area, too, if given the opportunity."[4]

But it was too late. CBS's Shaker arrived at the hotel around 5:00 p.m. that day and was immediately informed by the producer George Veras of what transpired. Back in New York, CBS was covering its tracks. Spokesperson Susan Kerr put out a statement that read: "CBS Sports deeply regrets the remarks made earlier today to a news reporter by Jimmy (The Greek) Snyder. We find them to be reprehensible. In no way do they reflect the views of CBS Sports."[5]

"When I took the job [producing *The NFL Today*]," said Veras, "Shaker told me, 'This job is about handling Brent, Irv, Phyllis, and Jimmy. You'll learn the rest.' [It turned out that] Jimmy was the one who needed the most handling."[6] Perhaps if Veras had "handled" The Greek a little more that day and lunched with him at Duke Zeibert's, he could have prevented Jimmy from making most of those comments.

The Greek was nearly seventy years old when this happened. He had been with *The NFL Today* for twelve full seasons, and his contract was due for renewal after the game that weekend in Washington, which was CBS's last NFL game that season. To most observers of sports, there was no doubt that on average the Black athlete was superior to the white. But where did The Greek get his theories about breeding? Perhaps it was from *Sports Illustrated*.

On January 18, 1971, *S.I.* published a lengthy article by Martin Kane titled "An Assessment of Why Black Is Best." In the article Kane quoted several authorities on the subject. It starts off asking, "Is the black athlete a long stride better than his white counterpart? And if not, what accounts for the immense success of the black in American sport during the last two decades? Scientists are searching for the answers and as they probe for true racial distinctions, fascinating theories have evolved, may of them controversial."

"There is an increasing body of scientific opinion," Kane wrote, "which suggests that physical differences in the races might well have enhanced the athletic potential of the Negro in certain events."

In the same *Sports Illustrated* article, the author quotes Lee Evans, Olympic and world 400-meter record holder. Asked why Black Americans have produced so extraordinarily disproportionate a number of the highest-class athletes in the world, Evans replied: "We were bred for it. Certainly the black people who survived in the slave ships must have contained a high proportion of the strongest. Then, on the plantations, a strong black man was mated with a strong black woman. We were simply bred for physical qualities."

But as far as CBS was concerned, the damage had been done. There was no going back. "At that point everyone was kind of tired of the grind," Shaker said. "Brent for thirteen years, Jimmy for twelve, Irv for thirteen, I'd been on it for ten years. It was still a great show but it was a job."

"When I got to my room [at the hotel], Veras told me what happened," Shaker continued. "I turned on the TV and it was the lead story. They said, 'The things Jimmy The Greek told our reporter about the evolution of slavery.' I had Jimmy come to our suite. [CBS Sports president Neal] Pilson was on his way to an affiliates board meeting in Hawaii. So I got on the phone with [P.R. man] Mark Carlson and we began to figure out what to do."

Then Brent Musburger called Shaker. The fight between Brent and The Greek was nearly eight years earlier, but there was no love lost between them. Brent no longer had respect for what Jimmy did on the show and treated him as such. Some said there might have been some jealousy involved because The Greek was asked for autographs far more often than Brent when they were on the road. So when Brent called, "he was angry and fed up" according to Shaker, and he really unloaded on The Greek.

"I'll tell you, I'm not gonna sit on that field sitting next to that guy," Brent hollered to Shaker. "No chance I'm gonna be on the same show with that guy Sunday."

"It was hunker-down time," Shaker said. "There literally were camera crews walking the halls of the hotel looking for Jimmy. Jimmy was shell-shocked and frightened, and truly didn't understand what was happening."

If there was ever a window where it was still possible for The Greek to save his job, it was at that point. He would have needed lobbying on his behalf from Shaker, producer Veras, president Pilson, and of course Brent, or at least three of those four. But with Musburger coming out so vehemently against him, it was practically a fait accompli.

"Brent panicked," Jimmy told Peter Richmond of *The National Sports Daily* in 1990. "If he'd opened up his mouth that day for me, he could have saved my job. But he didn't. Or if he did, it wasn't to say anything good. Brent and Shaker were the only ones talkin' to 'em [the press]. Nobody stood up for me. When you got the No. 1 producer and Brent against you, nobody's going to go against them. Who's gonna say something?"[7]

When contacted by the *New York Times*, Irv Cross said he was stunned. "[Those comments] don't reflect the Jimmy The Greek I know, and I've known him for 13 years."[8]

Pilson had called Shaker sometime that night, and Gene Jankowski, the head of the CBS Broadcast Group, put out a statement that The Greek was fired. "The statement was written by Jay [Rosenstein]," said Shaker, "and called it [Jimmy's WRC-TV interview] *reprehensible*. That made Jimmy go nuts. He couldn't believe we would use that [word]. He got unglued over that. I remember sitting with him trying to help deal with it, talking to the press. Then Jesse Jackson came to the hotel."

Jackson was there to defend Snyder, whom he had known for years, and told the press that Jimmy The Greek was no racist. Unfortunately, it was too late. Snyder wanted to hold a press conference to explain himself. Shaker told him it would only make things worse. But at that point, he had little to lose. There was no press conference.

"What he said was not necessarily untrue," said *New York Post* columnist Phil Mushnick when contacted for a comment. "He just said it indelicately. They hired him to be a wise guy with an opinion, and they fired him for being a wise guy with an opinion."[9]

The Merriam-Webster dictionary defines reprehensible as "deserving censure or condemnation." The word hurt Snyder badly. "Why'd they have to do it the way they did it?" Snyder asked two years later when interviewed by *The National*. "I begged them not to use 'reprehensible.' It was just a word that wasn't needed. 'Take that word out,' I said. They wouldn't. I said, 'I can't overcome that.'"[10]

Jay Rosenstein takes all the credit for the use of "reprehensible" in the press release.

"I was the one who chose the word reprehensible," Rosenstein said. "It means blame. I disagree with the theories in the *Sports Illustrated* piece. It wasn't accepted science at that time."

The one person who was completely against The Greek getting fired was Ed Hotaling, the reporter who aired the interview. He thought it was "outrageous" that CBS fired him.

"I think maybe one of the few people who might have agreed with me that Jimmy The Greek should not have been fired would have been Martin Luther King," Hotaling told the *Los Angeles Times*. "I think you have to think a little more broadly than firing a sports commentator for expressing stupid comments about civil rights. You should start covering the story and let him learn something."

He suggested putting Snyder on *The NFL Today* with Black and white athletes to discuss civil rights and Snyder's remarks. "His views would be expressed a little more adequately, I think," Hotaling said. "He wouldn't come out to be such a bad guy. They'd have the thing resolved in a positive way instead of a negative way."[11]

Of course, that never happened.

Shortly after the incident, the Alabama A&M football coach Ray Greene told the Associated Press, "You can't change history. He [Snyder] was accurate about the breeding process." After using Coach Greene's quote, *Washington Monthly* columnist Jonathan Rowe wrote: "I've heard numerous other comments along this line. It's not a pleasant subject. In fact, it is one of the most shameful chapters of our national history. But there is just enough historical basis to the breeding notion to see how the street theories of a Jimmy the Greek get started."[12]

The abolitionist and statesman Frederick Douglass is one former slave who wrote about these breeding practices, Rowe recalled. "In his autobiographical narrative, Douglass describes a young landowner who could only afford one slave. So he bought a woman named Caroline, a large able-bodied woman about twenty years old. 'Shocking as is the fact,' Douglass wrote, 'he bought her, as he said, for a breeder.' Then he went out and rented a married male slave. The result was that at the end of the year, the woman gave birth to twins."

That Sunday afternoon, January 17, 1988, at RFK Stadium, during *The NFL Today*'s pregame show, Brent Musburger, with a straight face, made the following statement.

"You know, on Friday afternoon here in Washington," Musburger began, as if he was reading an injury list, "our former colleague Jimmy The Greek made some regrettable and offensive remarks for which he has apologized. Yesterday CBS issued a statement disassociating itself from those remarks. It goes without saying that his remarks do not reflect in any way the thinking or attitudes with the rest of us here at CBS Sports. While we deplore the incident this weekend, we are saddened that our twelve-year association with Jimmy had to end this way. [pause] And *The NFL Today* will continue live from RFK Stadium in Washington, in just a moment."

Shortly after the deed had been done, Brent told the *New York Times*, "I told him [Snyder] he had to be careful what he said on TV. Did he hold those stupid, outrageous beliefs? Well, he said them."[13]

Ted Shaker was slightly more remorseful. "We're going to miss him, no doubt about it," Shaker told Skip Myslenski of the *Chicago Tribune*. "But this is clearly something we had to do. The feeling was we couldn't tolerate what he had said no matter how valuable he had been to us. The feeling was we couldn't be associated with that type of thinking."[14]

Thirty-two years later, when interviewed for this book, Shaker added: "Yeah, he drove everyone nuts sometimes, but he was unique. Then he went out and blew himself up. The unfortunate thing was that it indicated it was beyond his time to be there."

And just like that, Musburger and Shaker and Pilson and Rosenstein dusted their hands of The Greek and moved on. The network just brushed the dirt off its famous CBS eye, and never looked back. Van Sauter, who was president of CBS Sports earlier in the decade, had a different view of the network severing ties with The Greek.

"It was a sad way for him to go," Sauter said, "and it wasn't graceful. At the end of that period of time [twelve years on the air] they should have walked him to the door and patted him on the back and said, 'Thanks.' It didn't happen. It was not an honorable conclusion."[15]

All through the '80s The Greek fought with producer George Veras and Shaker about what he intended to say on the air. One Sunday when Veras asked him during a rehearsal what he had for the show that day, Jimmy said, "I'm going to say something about this guy and drugs." Veras came running out of the control room. "No you're not," the producer told him, "unless you have two sources backing up every word of it."

This was always the problem for the executives with Jimmy. Yes, he was unique, but not so much that CBS could afford a lawsuit.

The Greek understood but it was hard for him to change. "It had gotten to the point where I kept fighting over the show with Shaker almost every Sunday," The Greek told Peter Richmond of The National in 1990. "The last year they almost cut me off completely. Shaker kept wantin' to know what I was going to say beforehand. But I never knew. Which is what made it a great show. Everything was spontaneous."

"But I overcame that. I overcame so much," he continued. "I overcame hittin' Brent. I went to Denver on a speaking engagement and said something about rednecks. I overcame that. I told Phyllis I hated her friggin' husband, right on the air. I overcame that. I overcame everything. Then all of a sudden the thing I was paid to do I was fired for."

Peter Richmond is an award-winning author of six books whose work has appeared in *The New Yorker*, *Vanity Fair*, and *Rolling Stone*. His piece on Jimmy The Greek in April of 1990 for *The National* definitely was sympathetic. He came down hard on those The Greek left behind at CBS.

"Brent Musburger, within days of The Greek's indiscretions, excised Snyder's name from history," Richmond wrote. "In fact, except for a director [Bob Fishman] who has since quit *The NFL Today*, no one from CBS has even given him a phone call since they pulled the trap door. Maybe no one really thought he'd take it this hard. Maybe that's why Brent and Ted Shaker and the rest of the crew haven't bothered to drop so much as a postcard in the mail. Maybe they all said to each other, 'Forget it, guys, it's just The Greek.' As if for The Greek all the rules were different."

"The truth is," Richmond continued, "The Greek had spent the first 50 years of his life in one world and then vaulted, to his surprise, into another, and he wanted, desperately, to finish his life in that second world. The first was a fringe kind of world where a man might be a felon or might not be, where money might flow unnaturally swiftly from sources best left unseen, where distinctions between good and bad were as vague as the distinction between night and day in a town where the neon glowed 24 hours. The second was the network TV world, a place where the morals are similar but the trappings are not. And while it may have never seemed to the people who watched him on Sunday afternoons that it mattered to The Greek that he was on a sound stage instead of at a betting window, it mattered more than you can imagine. A man who'd once been surrounded by federal marshals loosed by Bobby Kennedy had suddenly found himself surrounded by makeup artists and the high-priced talking head spread of Brent and Phyllis and Irv, and it felt not only good, but legitimate. And here he is, living in an overstuffed luxury hotel on Miami Beach, where the other guests glance at him in sidelong fashion as he fills the corner table alone."

Jimmy "The Greek" Snyder didn't hold grudges. He didn't have vendettas, he told Peter Richmond. He said *The NFL Today* was everything to him.

"I thought this was supposedly going to be my life," he said. "*NFL Today* was . . . I mean I had a good PR firm, but little by little I gave everything up because of a show, then all of a sudden I woke up one day and I didn't have it. All of a sudden I was the son-of-a-bitch who said that blacks were better athletes."[16]

Chapter Fourteen

The Firing of Brent Musburger

THE DATE WAS SUNDAY, JANUARY 17, 1988, WHEN BRENT STOOD ON THE field of RFK Stadium and read the statement regarding Jimmy The Greek's departure from CBS. Your first clue that The Greek was fired was when Brent said "our former colleague."

CBS filled The Greek's spot on *The NFL Today* with Will McDonough and Dick Butkus. McDonough was a veteran sports columnist with the *Boston Globe*, known for having a wealth of sources. He actually began making contributions to the program in 1986. Butkus was the fiery Hall of Fame middle linebacker of the Chicago Bears, recognizable from dozens of commercials and cameo film roles.

Brent was happy. The producers were happy, and the show continued to win the ratings war in 1988 and '89. But management also began to think that they had a problem. When Van Gordon Sauter was running the CBS Sports ship in the early '80s, he signaled to Ted Shaker that he wanted one big star as the face of CBS Sports, and that star was to be Brent Musburger.

But as time wore on that became a slight problem, then a bigger one. "Once I became the overall guy [executive producer] in 1986," Shaker said, "I talked to Brent about sharing [some of the plum assignments]. And he didn't want to share. That's where he and I went right down the tubes."[1]

Imagine you were the manager of the New York Yankees and you had terrific starting pitchers. But instead of rotating them every fourth day, you started the same guy every day, and the other three just sat in the bullpen.

As 1990 approached, that was the dilemma Neal Pilson and Ted Shaker had at CBS Sports. Their starting pitchers were Brent Musburger, Jim Nantz, Greg Gumbel, and James Brown, but only Brent was handed the ball.

"When it came to trying [to get Brent] to cut back some," said Shaker, "he didn't want to do it. He became more and more hard to deal with, and it came down to, do we want to move forward [with other lead voices like Nantz] or do we want to stay where we are. Neal [Pilson] and I decided we wanted to move forward."

Musburger was already making $2 million a year. It was a far cry from the $13,500 annual salary he received twenty-two years earlier as a columnist for the *Chicago American*. He was CBS's lead broadcaster for the NBA, *The NFL Today*, NCAA football, U.S. Open tennis, the Belmont Stakes, and the Masters, and he had even been announced as the lead play-by-play voice for CBS's upcoming contract with Major League Baseball. He was also set to be the face of the network at the 1992 and '94 Olympic Games, to which CBS had acquired the rights. Quite a slate.

"We were going to be year-round Brent Musburger," Pilson told the *Sports Business Journal*.[2] Ted Shaker, the network's executive producer, felt they were left with no choice but to fire Brent since he wouldn't give up any of his marquee events.

Plain and simply, they were too dependent on Brent.

Less than a year earlier, Jim Nantz signed a new deal with CBS. The CBS college football executive Kevin O'Malley talked Pilson into giving Nantz what he wanted.

"ABC was hot to trot to get him," said O'Malley. "And they weren't the only ones. I told Neal why he had to pay him: 'Because somewhere along the line Brent Musburger is going to hold you up and you're not going to want to pay. He's hosting the Masters, basketball, NFL football, college football, everything. If someone makes him a big offer, what are you going to do?' He said, 'What should I do?' I told him, 'If you've got Jim Nantz, you've got a backup to Musburger that you can't get anywhere else.' He decided to pay the money to keep Nantz."[3]

It turned out to be money well spent for a moment like this. In the early '80s, when Van Sauter was president of CBS Sports and was looking to add a journalistic touch, he brought Terry O'Neil over from ABC Sports to be his executive producer. O'Neil took one look around at all the things Brent had control over and declared him to be an "anchor-monster." It's no wonder that by 1990 no one knew how to deal with him.

"This is an extremely hard thing to do," Shaker told the *Washington Post*. "But it's our judgment this is something we should do. It's the toughest decision I've been involved in, in my 17 years at CBS."[4]

Looking back twenty-five years later in 2015, Shaker told the *Sports Business Journal*: "It was really, really sad, the end of a major era for us. [Brent] had an insatiable appetite for work and he had the most nimble mind."

When reached by the *Washington Post* in Florida, Jimmy "The Greek" Snyder was neither happy nor surprised by Musburger's dismissal. "We definitely had our disagreements," he said, "but he was a very talented guy. After one of those weeks when he'd do football or tennis or all those things, I'd ask him, 'You going to do volleyball this week?'"

The parting of the ways took place during Final Four weekend in Denver, March 30 and 31, 1990. Brent's new contract was being negotiated with his brother, Todd Musburger, and was due to go into effect in June. There's no telling how much more CBS would have had to pay him.

But Pilson insisted that money wasn't the primary issue, that with great people on the sideline like Nantz, Gumbel, Brown, Andrea Joyce, and Pat O'Brien, CBS had to start grooming someone to eventually take Brent's place. Nantz had been with CBS since '85 and was an obvious talent. In fact, Shaker even told Nantz during his audition five years earlier that he reminded him of Brent.

Greg Gumbel joined CBS Sports for a second time in 1988 and had been a professional broadcaster for fifteen years by then. He certainly could handle a variety of hosting assignments. Much of the same could be said for Joyce and O'Brien. They were pros needing something more constructive to do.

Pilson and Shaker had already made up their minds to allow Musburger's contract to lapse before arriving in Denver for the Final Four, but did not want to tell the Musburgers their decision until after the Final Four. Todd Musburger, however, kept pressing the subject, hounding Pilson, even though there were hundreds of reporters in the vicinity. Pilson begged Todd to wait until after the Final Four to continue the talks.

Todd smelled something fishy. It came down to him and Pilson trying to hash things out late into the night. Kevin O'Malley happened to notice the pair when he was going back to his room that Saturday night.

"The elevator stopped on the fifth floor, at two in the morning," O'Malley said, "and who's sitting there in the two chairs opposite the elevator doors but Neal Pilson and Todd Musburger, wagging fingers at each other. Neal Pilson had never in his life been up at 2 o'clock in the morning. Ever! I said to [my friend] Jim O'Brien, 'What we just saw there—that really means something, but I'm not sure what it is.'"

What it meant was that CBS was not changing its mind. Word got out by Monday, April 1, and most everyone thought it was an April Fool's joke. Despite the decision being made, they all agreed that Brent would still call the NCAA final game Monday night, when UNLV ultimately defeated Duke, and at the conclusion he would say his goodbyes. They even told Billy Packer, Brent's partner on the game, that if Brent didn't end it in a professional manner that Packer was to pull the mic away from him.

"Are you out of your mind?" Packer told CBS. "Brent would never do that."

At the game's conclusion, Brent wrapped it up saying, "Folks, I've had the best seat in the house. Thanks for sharing it. I'll see you down the road. Now, let's send you to Jim Nantz."

Pilson and Shaker tried to take the high road, as reflected in Shaker's comments that weekend. "It was a decision made by CBS Sports. It was not a corporate mandate," he said. "He [Brent] just had a terrific career, and I'm sure his career will continue elsewhere and will be as distinguished. He's traveled the world over for CBS Sports. He's been on more often and longer than most, so it's a very envious record, I think."[5]

At first it looked like Musburger was also going to take the high road. He released a statement that weekend through his assistant that said: "I was surprised, but it was a great run and I have a million fond memories, and I leave behind a lot of good friends at CBS. I'm going to take an extended vacation, and I'll be working again some day, somewhere."

But as the week wore on, Brent burned inside about the contentious ending. As far as he was concerned, he was fired for being too good. In an effort to negate the negative press, he decided to do a prime-time interview with Sam Donaldson from ABC News.

"Let me start out by saying the contract negotiations were a sham," Musburger told Donaldson. "It was a setup all the way. It was unethical. They led us on all the way. Those two men [Pilson and Shaker] had decided I was too big for my britches and uncontrollable. With Shaker, he wants puppets for announcers. And I'm not a puppet."

The clue in that last statement was Brent's use of the word "uncontrollable." Neither Pilson nor Shaker used that word, but in hindsight it seems obvious that Musburger had too much control of too many events and there wasn't anyone brave enough at CBS to say no to him.

Pilson watched the interview from the Masters in Augusta, Georgia, as Musburger told Donaldson that Pilson and Shaker had a "personal vendetta" to get him out of CBS. While Pilson expressed extreme disappointment that Brent did the interview, Shaker also took the high road. "I wish to remember Brent the way he was Monday night [saying good-bye]," he said.

"I'm going someplace," Musburger said to Donaldson. "I'll sit back and take a look at the offers. You don't have to pay me $2 million a year."

Within a month Brent signed on with ABC and ESPN. It was a marriage that lasted twenty-seven years before a hurried exit in 2017.

Two years after Musburger's departure from CBS, in 1992, Shaker left the network to teach at New York University. And in 1994 Pilson retired from CBS and became a sports consultant. That was right after CBS lost the broadcast rights to the NFL.

When interviewed in 2015 by the *Sports Business Journal*, Shaker said he considered going out of the network for a replacement. He considered Vin Scully, Al Michaels, and Bob Costas, but said Scully never was contacted and that Michaels and Costas were under contract to ABC and NBC, respectively.

Funny thing about Al Michaels and Bob Costas—a little over a decade previously, they both had worked for CBS Sports, and Pilson, among others, let them walk out the door.

Chapter Fifteen

Greg Gumbel: Filling Brent's Shoes

With the departure of Brent Musburger after the Final Four in March, CBS decided to go with an entirely new cast on *The NFL Today* for the 1990 season, and an entirely new set. Greg Gumbel was brought in from doing NFL play-by-play to be the main host, with Terry Bradshaw added as a cohost. Dick Butkus was gone, and Will McDonough saw the writing on the wall and switched over to NBC. Joining Gumbel and Bradshaw was Lesley Visser, a veteran *Boston Globe* sports reporter, and Pat O'Brien, a solid TV reporter for years. But as far as Greg Gumbel was concerned, winding up in the sports business seemed like a long shot when he got out of college.

Greg grew up on the South Side of Chicago competing with his brother Bryant (two years younger) for just about anything. And while Bryant found his way to sports broadcasting early on, Greg was going in a far different direction.

"When I got out of school I was going to be an English teacher," Gumbel said when interviewed for this book. "I was an English major in college, and I was going to be an English teacher until I found out how much money English teachers made. Then I thought, maybe there's something else out there."[1]

He went to Loras College, a small Catholic liberal arts college in Dubuque, Iowa. That "something else" turned into quite a few things before he landed behind a microphone.

"While in college, I had been working part-time for a chain of clothing stores in Chicago," Gumbel said, "and they asked me if I'd like to be an assistant advertising director. I wound up spending some time there. [After some time] I told a college friend, who was an assistant buyer with Time Incorporated, that I was displeased with what was happening at the clothing store. He was leaving that job and suggested me to be his replacement. So that happened and I was there about two and a half years. Then I began selling hospital supplies. You know, bedpans."

Meanwhile, Bryant had graduated from Bates College in Maine in 1970 with a degree in Russian history and got a job selling cardboard materials and boxes, according to Greg, before he accepted a freelance job writing for *Black Sports Magazine*.

"Then he became the editor there," Greg explained, "and while doing that he heard about an audition for a weekend sportscasting job at KNBC-TV in Los Angeles in 1972. So he got into the business about three and half years ahead of me."

Then one day Bryant called Greg with an interesting piece of news. This is how the call went:

Bryant: "They're looking for a weekend sports guy at Channel 5 in Chicago. Are you interested?"
Greg: "Let me think about this: Baseball or bedpans? Let's see."

He auditioned at WMAQ-TV, an NBC affiliate, in February of 1973, along with a couple hundred others. "They said, 'Don't call us. We'll call you,'" Greg said. "My college didn't have any journalism or broadcasting courses at all. In the audition I sat down in front of a camera and they basically wanted to see how you look and sounded. I will always admit I was nervous as hell."

But to his amazement, three weeks later they did call and offered him the job as weekend sports anchor. That was March of '73 and he started in April.

"Looking back on those days," he recalled, "I'm kind of surprised I got the job. I certainly wasn't anyone who was polished. By my own reckoning, it took me a good year to start to feel comfortable in front of a camera. I got some heat for having longer than usual hair, down over the collar. It was the look of the day. There are a number of reasons why people survive and some of it is good fortune, and I feel like I've had a fair amount of good fortune. I feel very fortunate that they stuck with me until I figured out what it was all about."

Some might say that while Bryant Gumbel was a natural, Greg Gumbel was a grinder, working hard every day to prepare. Ironically, when he was at the NBC Chicago affiliate, Brent Musburger was the sports director at Chicago's CBS station, WBBM. Greg stayed at WMAQ for seven and a half years doing his three-minute weekend sports roundup. Then ESPN, a brand-new cable network, came calling.

"Sports is not the biggest priority at local news," Greg pointed out. "If there's a currency exchange holdup, that's an extra news story [they have to squeeze in] and you're down to two minutes and thirty seconds [from three minutes]. So when the opportunity arrived to delve into nothing but sports, I was happy to jump at the opportunity.

"ESPN came to me and said, 'Instead of doing three minutes of sports at 10 o'clock at night, would you be interested in doing a half hour at 7 and an hour at 11?' And I said, 'Sure.' I went out [to ESPN headquarters in Bristol, Connecticut] and took a look around, and the parking lot was nothing but mud holes and dirt. The station was in its infancy. I got there the end of January 1981. The people already there—people like George Grande and Lou Palmer and Bob Levy—were doing yeoman-like work."

After seven years in Bristol, Greg left for New York City to work for the Madison Square Garden Network (MSG) doing New York Yankees pregame and postgame shows along with Lou Piniella and Bobby Murcer. He also became WFAN Radio's first morning man, when the station began in 1987.

Many were happy when they could leave Bristol for other assignments or other jobs.

Gumbel described ESPN's parking lot as a "mud hole," but others would have given a similar description for Bristol. When ESPN's boxing reporter, Sal Marchiano, thought he had done his last *SportsCenter* assignment, he signed off that show saying, "Happiness is Bristol in the rearview mirror." The next day Scotty Connal, the head of production at ESPN, called Marchiano and fired him.

Gumbel, however, was just looking for a change. He loved working with Piniella especially. "Ex-athletes are so used to having someone do everything for them," Gumbel said. "One time we were about to fly to Detroit for a game and I get a call the night before from Lou."

Piniella: "Hey Greg, what flight are you on tomorrow?"
Gumbel: "Northwest at 9 a.m."
Piniella: "I guess I'll shoot for that one."
Gumbel: "You mean you don't have your flight yet?"
Piniella: "See you there."

"The next day he asks me when I was flying back. I couldn't believe he didn't book that at the same time. I told him my flight but that it was sold out, and he said, 'Guess I'll just catch the next one.' The great thing about [working with] Lou was that he had a million [George] Steinbrenner stories."

Oddly enough, working at WFAN and doing talk radio was Greg Gumbel's least favorite job, and that might include selling bedpans. "I didn't like talk radio," he said. "I don't like people yelling at me. I disliked it a lot."

He also is no fan of social media, including Twitter. "My conception of what a tweet is comprised of," he explained, "is: type, send, apologize, delete." But, in fact, it was his work on WFAN that enticed Ted Shaker to ask Greg Gumbel to lunch.

"Ted Shaker called me and said, 'We want to talk to you about doing NFL play-by-play,' and I said 'Why? I've never done it.' He said, 'Because we think you *could* do it.' I had lunch with him and producer Chuck Milton; they signed me to do a minimum of five games. I wound up doing eleven or twelve. Talk about another education—my partner was Ken Stabler. Between ex-quarterbacks Bradshaw and Stabler I learned how to drink at an early age. You were just happy if Kenny showed up on game day."

Here's what happened one Saturday night as Greg and Kenny were walking back through the hotel lobby after their production meeting:

Kenny: "Let's have *us* one, Greg."

Greg: "No, I don't do that the night before a game."

Kenny: "Well, I'm gonna have *me* one. What time are they picking us up?"

Greg: "9:15."

Kenny: "Right here?"

Greg: "Right here in the lobby."

Kenny: "OK, see ya buddy."

The next morning at 9:00 a.m. Greg was in line to check out when he sees Kenny coming in the front door of the hotel. "Hey buddy," says Kenny. "I'll get my stuff and be right with you."

His second year at CBS had Greg hosting the college football studio show, and while he liked college football, it didn't compare to the NFL as far as Greg was concerned. "College doesn't hold a candle to the NFL," he said, "but I think it showed them I could host a studio show."

So when the following spring came around, and Brent had departed, Shaker asked Gumbel to host *The NFL Today*. Because it was a new show without Brent, it drew a lot of attention from the media. Here's what Shaker told *Sports Illustrated* on why he hired Gumbel: "I'd been watching him since ESPN. On my drive in to work I would listen to WFAN while he was hosting the morning show. For five minutes he'd talk with Hubie Brown about the NBA, then he'd talk to Sal Messina about the Rangers, then he'd talk to Billy Packer about North Carolina basketball. He would effortlessly take me from one sport to the next, asking the questions I'd have asked. And I thought, Wow!"[2]

At ESPN Gumbel had asked about the possibility of doing play-by-play as well as hosting *SportsCenter*, and was told they like to keep the two areas separate. The only play-by-play work he had ever done was the Chicago high school football and basketball championships between the winners of the public schools and the Catholic schools. But how did Shaker know he could do play-by-play?

"So I thought about it," said Shaker, "and decided we really wanted to get him into CBS Sports. I firmly believed Greg had the talent and intelligence to be a solid, maybe very good play-by-play guy too, if given a good partner, producer, director and time to learn the ropes in the booth. And he turned out to be really good at it, and over time he did both studio anchoring and play-by-play. He also had the personality that was friendly and inviting to the audience."[3]

"They just threw me in and I did it," Gumbel recalled. "I did the best that I could, and when we got past five [games] they kept giving me assignments. I was flattered by that."

He was totally surprised the following year (1989) when CBS brought him back inside to host the college football studio, and even a little more surprised when he was the choice to host *The NFL Today*, along with Bradshaw. Here's what *Sports Illustrated* wrote of the choice:

"Greg Gumbel carries with him none of the baggage of celebrity. Ever so slightly late for a luncheon meeting, he enters a midtown Manhattan restaurant brimming with an apology. Gumbel has arrived at last. For 17 years now, his round, friendly face has been beaming out of television sets. He has covered local sports for WMAQ-TV in his hometown of Chicago, hosted ESPN's SportsCenter, done play-by-play for Madison Square Garden Network and handled a slew of assignments in the past two years for CBS. . . . When Gumbel was named to replace Brent Musburger as the anchor of CBS's *The NFL Today*, it seemed the logical culmination of his peripatetic career."[4]

The changes in the show, with an entirely new cast and set, took some of the heat off of Gumbel. It wasn't just him replacing Brent. It was everyone and almost everything. The ultimate comparisons, however, were inevitable, but Gumbel didn't shy away from talking about them.

"I don't see it as replacing Brent," he said at the time, "though in the technical sense I suppose it is. I'm not going out there trying to be Brent."[5]

When contacted for this book, he added, "I never really appreciated the job that Brent did until I talked with my brother, who was doing that same job at NBC. I think you're doing a good job any time you can make something look much easier than it actually is. Brent and Bryant made it look easy." Gumbel also said, "I thought that if there was any reason [he and Bradshaw] would work, it would be because of the chemistry between Terry and me. We became good friends. We worked well together. We were learning together. And I thought that CBS [Shaker] was very patient with us."

Bradshaw had a phenomenal NFL career, winning four Super Bowls with the Pittsburgh Steelers, before joining CBS as an NFL game analyst, working with Verne Lundquist. He also had a nice little side career going doing commercials and cameo roles in films. Fans and colleagues alike always recognized Bradshaw as a fun guy.

"When we first started," said Gumbel, "we did a lot of Friday night dinners together. Every once in a while we'd go to Elaine's [the celebrity-packed restaurant]. We would take turns picking up the check. We were in Elaine's one night and were ordering expensive cocktails and expensive bottles of wine, when it was Terry's turn [to pay]. The guy brings the bill, which was about $395. Terry looks it over and asks the waiter, '$395 is that right?' And the waiter says, 'Yes.' Then Terry looks at me and says, 'Greg, what's 1 percent of 395?' The waiter visibly shook."

The routine was that Terry would fly in from his ranch in Louisiana on Friday nights. Then he and Greg would have dinner that night and the next night as part of the production meeting, and Terry would fly back Sunday night. In the beginning Bradshaw was concerned about what they'd talk about on the show.

Terry: "What are we gonna do?"

Greg: "We're gonna talk football."

Terry: "What if they tell us to vamp?"

Greg: "Then we vamp."

Terry: "What if I'm wrong?"

Greg: "As long as you start out with, 'Here's what I think . . .' you can't be wrong. And secondly, how are you going to argue about football with Terry Bradshaw?"

The closeness of the relationship came out soon after when a reporter was interviewing the two together. Gumbel recalled: "Terry looks at the writer, and he said, 'I can honestly say that Greg is one of

The new 1990 *NFL Today* cast looked sparkling in this photo. From left are Greg Gumbel, a very thin Terry Bradshaw, Lesley Visser, and Pat O'Brien. (COURTESY CBS SPORTS)

my five best friends.' The guy looked at me, and I said, 'And Terry is one of my ten best.'"

When Lesley Visser was growing up in Massachusetts in the '60s, "women were either schoolteachers, nurses, or homemakers," she often said. "Saying I wanted to be a sportswriter was like saying I wanted to go to the moon."[6]

At Boston College she joined the school newspaper's sports staff, but was stuck covering all of the less popular sports, and was never given a shot at any of the top assignments. But before graduation she found out about, and applied for, a Carnegie Foundation grant. "That grant," she said when contacted for this book, "was given to twenty college women in the country who wanted to go into jobs that were 95 percent male."[7]

Becoming one of those twenty women changed Lesley's life. She was hired by the *Boston Globe* in 1975 and almost immediately was given the job covering the New England Patriots, becoming the first-ever female beat reporter of an NFL team.

"I remember," she said, "that Will McDonough cleared the way for me. He went into the Patriots locker room, stood on a chair, and told them, 'We're going to be having a woman cover the team for the *Globe*. And that's that.'"

Working there was literally a dream come true for Visser. "I'd wanted to be a sportswriter since I was 10 years old," she said, "and the *Globe* was heaven on earth. My assignments included going to Wimbledon with Bud Collins, the World Series with Peter Gammons, the Super Bowl with Will, and the NBA Finals with [Bob] Ryan. And it was a true frontier. The credentials at an NFL game said, 'No women or children in the press box.'"

In 1983 when Ted Shaker and Neal Pilson hired Lesley Visser for CBS Sports, they told her, "We had a woman who knew television [Phyllis George], but didn't know sports; now we'd like to hire a woman who knows sports and teach her television."

Shaker and Pilson and the producer, Mike Burks, and the director, Sandy Grossman, were extremely patient with her until she became somewhat comfortable. "I knew the reporting end," she said, "but the first six months [on the air] I looked like I had rigor mortis."

But she hung in there and kept improving and continued to be the first woman through the door, which was brought up often when Visser was inducted into the Sports Broadcasting Hall of Fame in 2017. She took the hits, the name-calling, and the insults and wound up opening the door for so many other women in sports broadcasting. A typical tribute came from HBO Sports' Andrea Kremer: "If someone like Lesley Visser did not come first, I just don't know that an executive would have had the courage to hire me."

Between 1983 and 1990 Visser covered a variety of events for CBS, and when Shaker decided to change everything up at *The NFL Today*, Lesley became part of the crew, along with Greg Gumbel and Terry Bradshaw and Pat O'Brien. Like Phyllis George and Jayne Kennedy before her, Visser would wind up doing the player profiles for the show.

"When a CBS producer would call an NFL team to line up a feature, we rarely heard the word 'no,'" she emailed. "And the budgets were huge. I went horseback riding with Emmitt Smith, bowling with Jerome Bettis and rode a Ferris wheel with Jim McMahon. Players would let us spend a day in their house, showing us old photos or mementos. And *The NFL Today* had a family feel of its own. We'd all go to dinner in New York the night before, or on NFL seminars we'd go to places like Pebble Beach. Working at CBS always felt like a team."

The first year Visser sat next to Greg and Terry on the set, but she could hardly get a word in with Bradshaw dominating. After that she mainly did profiles in the field and only joined the set to help present her feature. Greg thought she was extremely talented.

"Lesley was as cheerful a person as there could be. Always fun to work with," he said. "She was good for the show. The reason why her interviews were good was because players liked her. She comes off as being a very nice person to talk to. That doesn't mean that she's not good, but that doesn't hurt. And the players were willing to open up more than other people sometimes are. Put Lesley on the field and she lights up the camera."

Midway through the 1992 season, Burt Reynolds wanted to include Terry and Greg in one of his *Evening Shade* comedy shows on CBS. So he wrote a script in which he and his buddy would appear on *The NFL Today*. Both Terry and Greg played themselves.

"I fully expected to be kind of nervous," Gumbel said at the time. "My background didn't make me less nervous or better prepared, but you go in with the knowledge that if you screw up, you go with another take."

Said Bradshaw: "I have nine pictures on my wall at home. Seven are of Burt."

Reynolds said: "We screened the show, and Terry and Greg got the biggest laughs. They're both very real and very funny. Terry could make a living doing this, and so could Greg if he wanted to. Terry is witty, entertaining and knowledgeable."[8]

Gumbel concluded: "It's been referred to as my acting debut, but I don't think it's much of an acting chore to go out there and be who you are."

In 1994 Fox outbid CBS for the rights to the National Football Conference (NFC) package. CBS Network owner Larry Tisch wouldn't go high on the bid because he had just spent a ton of money for the rights to the 1992 and '94 Olympic Games. It was a shock felt throughout the industry. CBS tried to recover and put in a bid for the American Football Conference (AFC) package, but the NFL said they were too late. CBS was faced with the prospect of going without the NFL for the first time since the league put out its first bids in 1962.

Lesley Visser recalled what happened when news got out that CBS lost the NFL package.

"In an effort to cheer everyone up," she said, "Neal Pilson gathered everyone together. 'Hey, look, we've still got a lot,' Pilson told us. 'We've got the Masters. We've got the U.S. Open [tennis].' That's when Bradshaw had that legendary line, 'Does the Masters have a pregame show?'"

CHAPTER SIXTEEN

Who Let the FOX In?

ON DECEMBER 28, 1958, NBC BROADCAST THE NFL CHAMPIONSHIP game. It was the game that pushed the NFL over the top. With Chris Schenkel calling play-by-play, Johnny Unitas led the Baltimore Colts over the New York Giants, 23–17, in sudden-death overtime. Ironically, it was the only NFL game NBC broadcast that year. The next day the newspapers were all calling it "The Greatest Game Ever Played." The marriage of television and the NFL was here to stay.

That game drew tremendous interest. Because it was played at New York's Yankee Stadium, a record sixty-six media credentials were dispensed. On the way to victory, Unitas connected a record twelve times with wide receiver Raymond Berry. It was a championship game mark that stood for fifty-five years. Both players immediately became legends and later were inducted into the NFL Hall of Fame.

CBS started broadcasting NFL games in 1956 after the old Dumont Network folded. In those days CBS would negotiate individual deals with eleven of the twelve NFL teams. (Cleveland, the twelfth team, had its own syndicated network.) And for the next thirty-seven years, CBS was the heart of the NFL's broadcast coverage, until it lost a bidding war to Fox in 1994. The first package sold by the league was in 1962. CBS paid $4.65 million for the right to broadcast the league's games for the next two years. By then, NBC had already begun broadcasting games of the new American Football League (AFL).

CBS lost the NFC package in '94 not only because it bid too low, but also because Fox was desperate. Fox became a national network in

1986 and bid on the NFL packages without success in 1987 and 1990. In December of 1993 when Fox submitted its bids to the NFL, it was a network of only 139 affiliates, of which 120 were on the UHF, or harder-to-find, bandwidth. That compared to at least 200 affiliates that each of the other three networks had. Alan Bell, of the Freedom Newspapers Broadcast Group, saw Fox's overbid coming.

"[Rupert] Murdoch [at Fox] is in a different position," Bell told the entertainment weekly *Variety* at that time. "The growth of Fox is stalled, and he badly needs to broaden his network's demographics and solidify his relationships with his affiliates."[1]

Murdoch, who owned the Fox Network, knew that if he could get his hands on the NFL, he could grow his network and eventually prosper. It didn't matter if he would have to take heavy losses in the beginning, as long as his network was getting larger. Having the NFL meant many more eyeballs watching Fox promos for its primetime shows, which led to higher ratings and the ability to charge advertisers more.

All NFL ratings were down an average of nearly 5 percent in the final year of the previous contract, but that didn't slow Fox down one bit. This wasn't your typical closed-bid auction either. It was a negotiation that the NFL was conducting with the four networks. No one was limited to one bid. When Fox submitted its opening bid, the NFL would tell the other networks what Fox bid. In that previous contract CBS had paid the NFL $265 million a year for its NFC package of games, while NBC paid them $188 million per year for the AFC.

Fox opened the bidding by letting the NFL know it would pay at least $210 million for the AFC or at least $300 million per year for the NFC. Knowing this, NBC raised its offer to $217 million. CBS, thinking Fox would stay at $300 million, only bid $295 million per year—a nice increase considering ratings were down. CBS also thought that if it was within $20 million of Fox's bid that the NFL would stay with CBS out of loyalty for the thirty-seven years CBS had been broadcasting its games.

But instead, Murdoch went for it all. Thinking that CBS would bid more than $300 million per year, Murdoch bid $395 million per year for the NFC, while CBS stood pat at $295 million. CBS had badly misjudged Fox's motives or willingness to lose money. When the NFL announced that Fox had won, it was almost certain that Fox would lose quite a bit of money.

"I've seen those outrageous [estimated] numbers," Murdoch said. "We'll lose a few million in the first year, but even if it was 40 or 50 million, it would be tax deductible. It was a cheap way of buying a network."[2]

It turned out to be an expensive way to buy a network. Fox's parent company, News Corp., wrote off $350 million in unrecoverable costs associated with its $1.58 billion NFC contract in 1995, according to Paul Kagan Media Associates.

When NBC was made aware that Fox would bid at least $210 million per year for its AFC package, it raised its bid to $217 million. CBS was flabbergasted by Fox's bid and turned around and outbid NBC by $30 million per year for the AFC package. The NFL said it was too little and too late.

"At no time [during the entire bidding process] did CBS say they were interested in the AFC package," said Joe Browne, NFL vice president for communications. "After saying 'no' to the AFC for weeks, they became interested after losing the NFC to Fox. By then, frankly, their offer was too late."

"We're mystified," said Neal Pilson, president of CBS Sports. "We don't understand how they can take a larger number from Fox [but] then stay frozen on an agreement with NBC when a higher number had been made by us."[3]

Pilson could not be held at fault. The company was following Larry Tisch's (the owner of the CBS Network) instructions. John Spinola, vice president of operations for Westinghouse Broadcasting's television group, which owned affiliates of ABC, CBS, and NBC, said that losing the NFL wasn't equivalent to losing a hit series like *Cheers*, which is a staple fifty-two weeks a year. "It's a big disappointment for CBS to lose out," he said, "but no one will throw themselves off the bridge over it."[4]

CBS did get over it. And it also got over Murdoch raiding all of its top announcers and production people, starting with Pat Summerall and John Madden. Their agents had wisely coincided their contracts with CBS to expire when the NFL contracts expired. Here's what Murdoch told the *Los Angeles Times* back then: "I think football, and particularly CBS' presentation of it, is about as good an example of sports broadcasting as any in the world today. Our absolute priority would be to be at least that good."[5]

Four years later, in 1998, CBS got back in the game by bidding a whopping $500 million a year for NBC's AFC package, an incredible 130 percent increase from the $217 million NBC paid in '94. After four years of living without the NFL, the affiliates were willing to pay more to help the network get it back. Somehow, CBS thought it wasn't going to lose any money.

"This is a very, very favorably responsible deal we made," Sean McManus, the president of CBS Sports, said. "We are not going to lose money on this deal. [You have to look at] the value it brings to our stations, the savings in promotional time, and the extra value to our affiliates. The AFC from Day One was our number one priority. The AFC is uniquely suited to CBS and CBS is uniquely suited to the AFC."[6]

NBC, on the other hand, might have been more interested in obtaining *Monday Night Football* since it had broadcast the final episode of its top-rated show *Seinfeld* on May 14, 1998. Combining that with its contract for the hit series *E.R.* expiring, and NBC knew it could use a certain top 10 ratings-grabber like *Monday Night Football* to shore up its primetime schedule. But ABC bid more and held on to it.

NBC, however, had previously purchased the rights to the next five Olympics competitions. It was a deal they expected to be profitable. "NBC made an economic decision and dodged a bullet," Chris Dixon, a media analyst with Paine Webber, told *Variety*. "The notion that NBC is in trouble because it lost football and *Seinfeld* is wrong. They'll position themselves for years as the Olympics network. They'll be fine."

NBC Sports president Dick Ebersol confirmed that decision. "We didn't buy five Olympics for billions of dollars for the great promotional opportunities," he said. "We bought them because they'd be wonderfully profitable."[7]

Regardless, CBS was back in the NFL business in 1998, and they were about to unveil their new secret weapon as the host of *The NFL Today*—Jim Nantz.

Chapter Seventeen

Jim Nantz: The Future
of CBS Sports Arrives

Ever since Jim Nantz was in grade school, he imagined himself behind a CBS Sports microphone. Because his father was a port manager for Sealand, the biggest container shipping company in the world, the Nantz family moved frequently during Jim's childhood, from North Carolina to New Orleans to the San Francisco Bay area and finally to Colts Neck, New Jersey, in Monmouth County, just thirty miles from New York City. Along the way, young Jim became enamored with the televised sports personalities that he watched every weekend.

"My dream was to be a sports commentator for CBS," Nantz said when interviewed for this book. "I was so hopelessly in love with the sports realm, and television was a vehicle to take me to all these dream events and dream locations. As young kids do, I felt like there were broadcasters who were my friends, who were coming into my living room and spending some time with me every week. As for CBS Sports, I loved the way CBS broadcast the NFL. I just loved the voices and I loved *The NFL Today*. I also loved how CBS broadcast the Masters tournament. And that was a big hook for me."[1]

His father loved to see the world and wanted his family to experience things and not just read about them. For example, when Neil Armstrong and Buzz Aldrin returned from a moon landing with rocks from the moon, Jim's dad rounded up the family to see the moon rocks at the Smithsonian in Washington, D.C.

"I can still remember my dad saying, 'Guys, get in the car. We're going down to the Smithsonian to see these moon rocks,'" Nantz recalled. "It was a three-and-a-half-hour drive each way. We got down to the Smithsonian and of course there was a long line there. You couldn't touch them. You had to look through a piece of glass. We saw them and then we all got back in the car to go home, and then one of us made a fresh remark, something like, 'That seemed like a long way to go to see rocks that looked like they were in my backyard.' Dad took a little offense to that. 'One day you'll get it, guys,' he said. 'That's a big deal what you just saw right there. I would have walked to go see them.'"

"How passionate he was and how much it meant to him," Nantz continued. "I kind of carry that passion for exploring and discovering and getting exposed to as much knowledge as I can. My dad—he loved to see it all. My dad wanted his kids to be exposed to all sorts of cultural things, to open up our minds, even though we didn't have the means necessarily to experience them."

Jim Nantz grew to be six feet three inches and excelled in sports. He co-captained his Marlboro High School basketball team and was the captain of its golf team. But as he explained, Marlboro High was far from a hotbed for athletes.

"How good a high school basketball player was I?" he asked. "I was a two-year starter, and my high school record as a starter was 2 and 42. We went 0 and 22 my junior year, and we bounced back big my senior year and went 2 and 20."

He was considerably better at golf, having begun swinging a club when he was three or four years old. By the time he was eight, he was playing regularly at a pitch-and-putt course in the Bay area, and played the No. 1 position on his high school golf team his last three years before graduation.

During senior year his parents moved once more, this time to Houston, while Jim stayed with friends in New Jersey to complete his year. He was enrolled at the University of Texas, and he was only weeks away from starting classes when a local golf pro saw him hitting balls at The Woodlands, which has been the site of the Houston Open several times.

"He saw me hitting balls and asked me where I was playing golf in college. When I told him I wasn't, he said, 'Well you should be playing for Houston,' and he set up this fateful meeting with Coach Williams.'"

Coach Williams was Dave Williams, the winningest golf coach in NCAA history, having won sixteen national championships. During his career at Houston, Williams coached two future PGA champions, John Mahaffey in 1978 and Steve Elkington in 1995. He also coached future 1981 British Open champion Bill Rogers, and two future Masters champions, Fuzzy Zoeller in 1979 and Fred Couples in 1992.

"He [Williams] came out to watch me play," Nantz said. "He rode around while I carried my bag and I shot 38 for the nine holes, basically auditioning for him. At the end of the nine holes he said, 'How would you like to be a Cougar?' I got admitted and the next thing you know I had made a life-changing decision to go to U of H. He put me in [a dorm suite] with three of the most decorated freshmen—Freddie Couples and Blaine McCallister, both of whom won events on the tour, and John Horne, who also played on the tour for two years. I look back on it now and I think he had me living with those guys because he saw a very determined goal-minded individual who would be a positive influence on his big decorated recruits. And those are a few of my best of friends today."

Their senior year, Nantz and Couples talked about how one day they would be at Augusta National together—Nantz as a CBS broadcaster, and Couples as the winner of the Masters. "We used to rehearse the green jacket ceremony in our dorm," said Nantz, "with me introducing Freddie as he slipped into the jacket." In 1992 it was a dream that came true when Nantz was in Butler Cabin at Augusta National orchestrating the ceremony after Couples won the event.

At U of H Nantz majored in broadcasting and landed a job as a sports anchor at KHOU-TV in Houston, right out of college. He actually began working there his junior year.

In 1982, KSL-TV in Salt Lake City hired him away to do play-by-play for Brigham Young University football and play-by-play for the Utah Jazz, working alongside Hot Rod Hundley, the West Virginia University All-American guard and No. 1 NBA draft pick who played for the Minneapolis Lakers. Nantz was also their weekend sports anchor.

In 1975, when *The NFL Today* went live, Nantz would watch it each Sunday almost religiously. It was appointment television for him. He had never seen a sports show like that before, or a host like Brent Musburger before. He was riveted to his set.

"And that show packed so much into it," he recalled. "Originally it was just a half an hour show. I didn't miss a second. CBS had some hit shows at that time like *The Mary Tyler Moore Show*, *The Bob Newhart Show*, and *All in the Family*. These were the hit shows that America watched. But the episodic show that I cared about came on Sundays at 12:30 [Eastern time] with *The NFL Today*. I was all in, and I felt like I knew every single person who was in front of the camera."

That familiarity paid off years later for Nantz, when he was brought into that very same studio at CBS Sports for a surprise audition to possibly join the network in 1985. His career had been sailing along beautifully in Salt Lake City when he got a call out of the blue one August day in 1985 from the CBS producer Ed Goren. KSL-TV was not a CBS-owned-and-operated station, so someone was doing some research to recognize that Jim Nantz, age twenty-six, was a talent to be looked at.

"Eddie Goren contacted me on Thursday, August 15, 1985," Nantz recalled. "If you were working for an affiliate, they would often call and ask if you had any B-roll [extra footage used to enhance a story]. I just assumed they wanted footage, and that was why Ed was calling.

"I called Ed and he said, 'Hey, we've been watching your work for the past month and we'd like to bring you to New York to audition.' I thought it was a joke. I honestly thought it was a joke. All my friends knew my dream was to work for CBS. And I thought it was one of my buddies who put somebody up to a call, masquerading as Ed Goren, and that this was some stupid prank and eventually they would identify themselves. So I played along with it, and as the call went on I began to realize that the call was legit and they really wanted me to come to New York."

This was a Thursday afternoon. He would need to fly to New York early the next morning to join Goren and four others who were also auditioning at a dinner Friday night. The actual auditions would be Saturday at the CBS Broadcast Center on West 57th Street. That would all be fine for Nantz except Friday he was scheduled to fill in for the No. 1 sports anchor, who was on vacation. And there was no backup beyond Nantz. Knowing all this, Nantz told Goren he'd see if he could find someone to fill in for him.

"I hung up the phone and found the [KSL] news director on a dinner break and I told him what happened. He said, 'You're going to New York, we'll figure it out. This is your big chance.' So at 8 o'clock the next morning I was on a flight to New York."

Once in New York he checked into Le Parker Meridien Hotel on 57th Street. Dinner was set for the prestigious Russian Tea Room, which was just up the street from the hotel. The four others who were also auditioning were Roy Firestone, the host of *Up Close* on ESPN, who was a weekend anchor at KCBS-TV in Los Angeles; Pat Haden, who was already a college football analyst for CBS; James Brown, who was already working for CBS as a reporter and was the sports anchor for the CBS affiliate in Washington, D.C.; and Fred Wymore, a weekend sports anchor at WCBS-TV in New York. All but Wymore, who was working, met Goren and his wife Patty at the Russian Tea Room.

"So there were guys auditioning from New York, L.A., Washington, D.C., and Salt Lake City," Nantz said. "Most of [Friday] night Roy was telling stories, and they were great stories, and he's an awesome storyteller. I really thought the job was his. I didn't have a whole lot to offer. I was the BYU announcer, I was the weekend anchor at the CBS affiliate, and I did the Jazz games with Hot Rod Hundley since I was twenty-three years old. But Roy Firestone's on national TV, hosting *Up Close*, and he's had the biggest personalities in sports on his show. I was really honored to be sitting there, to be honest. I graduated college and somehow I landed this opportunity to work for KSL in Salt Lake. I had worked for the CBS affiliate since my junior year, anchoring in Houston. But I went to Salt Lake because I wanted to do games and anchor, and I'm working with Hot Rod. I had nothing to lose, but I was never an overconfident person."

Nantz also picked up on the fact that the audition had been in place for several weeks, and that his invitation to join was just forty-eight hours beforehand. "In fact, my name was in a different typeface on the rundown sheet of what was going to happen the next day," he said. "So somebody had typed my name in, and you can tell it was just added to the list."

The next day he was to be the fifth of the five to audition. Goren, who would go on to become the executive producer and later vice chairman of Fox Sports, was producing. The veteran Duke Struck was the director. Also in the control room was CBS executive producer Ted Shaker. The auditions were set up to be as close to actual studio situations as possible, including the roll of commercials in between segments.

Nantz waited for his turn in the Green Room, and while sitting in the makeup chair he got an inkling of what was to come. "As I was sitting in the makeup chair," he said, "Rosemary, the makeup lady, whispered in my ear, 'They're really excited to see what you can do.' I said, 'Really?'"

The audition was taking place in Studio 43, the same studio used for *The NFL Today*.

And it was the same studio where CBS kingpin Brent Musburger had sat behind the desk so many times since 1975. When it was finally Nantz's turn, floor director Jimmy Wall escorted him from behind the set into the studio. Nantz remembered it vividly.

"Suddenly I emerged into the studio, and saw *The NFL Today* set— it was like a dream. They marched me up to the desk and I sat in the chair that had a piece of tape fixed to the back of the chair, with a name on that tape written with a Sharpie. It said 'Brent.' It was one of the thrills of my life. I was twenty-six years old, and I was sitting in Brent Musburger's chair!"

Nantz's reaction was similar to a kid going to his first game at Yankee Stadium, and emerging through the stands to see the field for the very first time. At that moment Nantz was that kid all over again.

The actual audition began with a four-minute segment of the top 20 college football teams' scores with highlights that had been written as if for a live broadcast that Saturday. Nantz and the others were given scant time to prepare. He was then given a stack of blue cards with names of teams and scores on them that he got to thumb through really quickly. There were also some highlight sheets off to the side, with information on highlights that would appear while he was reading the scores.

"They ran the opening, animation, the music, and they cued me," said Nantz. "And I welcomed everyone to the Prudential College Football Report, and I just ripped through some scores and highlights. Ed at some point said [in my ear], 'Last score,' and I went through that score, then he said, 'Take me to commercial,' and I said, 'We'll be back with more of the Prudential College Football Report when we continue on CBS in a moment.'"

They rolled a commercial, and during the commercial someone came over and gave Nantz a new stack of cards that had Ivy League scores on them. Again they rolled the highlights while he was doing the scores, but he suspected that something was up.

"My instincts told me they were going to put something in there upside down to see how I would handle it," Nantz said. "Of course, nothing was scripted. And sure enough, one of those scores was out of order. I knew how to work right out of that. I was ready for that, and I felt like I got the train back on the tracks pretty quickly. I ran through the rest of the scores, and Ed came back [in my ear] and said, 'Take me to commercial,' promising a discussion of the Heisman when we come back. Well, I didn't know [that they'd do this]. So I said, 'When we come back we're going to talk about the favorites for the Heisman, when we continue on the Prudential College Football Report.'"

They rolled another commercial and out from the back came a stocky-looking guy with glasses and a New York accent. He was going to be the expert to discuss the Heisman with Nantz. He stuck out his hand and said, "Hi, I'm Mike Francesa." At that time Francesa was the editor of *College and Pro Football Newsweekly* and he was also a weekend consultant for CBS Sports. He was still several years away from beginning his thirty-three-year career with WFAN Radio.

"Ed [Goren] whispers to me, 'Talk about the Heisman,'" Nantz continued, "and Mike says, 'Ask me anything you want.' So I said, 'Let's talk about the Heisman. I think we need to start with Keith Byars at Ohio State. What do you see?' Fortunately, as a sports fan, I had enough knowledge to go through several names. We did a three- or four-minute segment and at the end, Ed said, 'Throw it back to the game.' I wrapped it up and I felt really good about it."

As soon as they finished, Ted Shaker, whom Nantz had never met or had never seen, came out from the control room with a smirk on his face. He had a wild look in his eye, according to Nantz, and he was all excited, laughing to himself a little bit, almost giggling. Here's how Nantz recalled the conversation went:

Shaker: "Hey, uh, uh. How'd you feel that went?"
Nantz: "I felt it went okay."
Shaker: "Yeah, yeah, yeah [smiling]. Yeah, that was good, that was really good. You remind me a lot of that guy."

Shaker pointed over Jim's shoulder to a monitor that showed CBS's coverage of racing from Saratoga. But by the time Nantz turned to look at the bank of monitors, the image had changed. It was a shot of middle-aged racing analyst Frank Wright. "I remind you a lot of Frank Wright?" Jim asked.

Ted looks over and starts laughing to himself and says, "That's really good you know who he is. No, no, no. Look again." By the time Nantz turns back, the camera had cut back to Brent.

Shaker: "No, you remind me a lot of that guy."
Nantz: "I remind you a lot of Brent Musburger?"
Shaker: "Yeah, you do."
Nantz: "Wow, that's an amazing compliment."
Shaker, somewhat tersely: "It is."

"Holy smokes," Nantz thought. Then the director, Duke Struck, and Ed Goren came out of the control room.

Shaker (to Nantz): "You think you can do this?"
Nantz: "Would I have more time to prepare?"
Shaker: "You'd have all week to prepare. How old are you?"
Nantz: "I'm twenty-six."
Shaker: "You think you can do this?"

Nantz: "If I had more time to prepare, I think I could do a better job than I did today."

Shaker: "Interesting, interesting . . . [shakes his head up and down bobble-head style]. Well, what are you doing tonight?"

Nantz: "I'm going to go back to my room and watch the Dallas–San Diego preseason game."

Shaker: "You have time for a drink?"

Nantz: "Well, sure."

They left the CBS Broadcast Center and went to the lobby bar at Le Parker Meridien, about four blocks away. Meeting Nantz were Shaker and Goren, but Shaker didn't stay for long. After Shaker left, Goren confided to Nantz, "You know you knocked that audition out the park. I haven't seen Ted that excited in a long time. I think something's going to happen with you."

"You've got to realize," Nantz said, summing up the whirlwind audition, "that I had talked to Ed just forty-eight hours before in Salt Lake City, out of nowhere. And he tells me that he talked to Ted in the cab on the way over to the Parker Meridien. 'What we might do,' Goren said, 'is that we might put you into the family [of CBS-owned-and-operated stations], and have you do some part-time work for CBS, but your life's about to change. We're going to do something with you.'"

Two weeks later they flew Nantz back to New York, and he went through a series of interviews with Terry O'Neil, Kevin O'Malley, Shaker, and CBS president Peter Lund. He was meeting all the executive producers. He was told that it came down to CBS either going with Firestone or with Nantz. Firestone was the sure bet, Nantz thought.

"I wound up going to lunch with Ted [Shaker] and Peter [Lund] down 52nd Street at a place called the U.S. Steakhouse," Nantz recalled. "Teddy orders swordfish, then Peter also orders swordfish, and it's my turn to order. And here's the point where I almost lost the job. I look at those two guys and I said, 'What's swordfish?' I never had swordfish in my life. Chalk it up to not being a man of the world at this point, less than four years removed from college. They looked at me and I wonder if they were thinking, 'Can we hire this guy and trust him if he's never even heard of swordfish? Do we have some hick that's so unsophisticated?' I saw eyes that were darting. Teddy later told me that the swordfish story was a big deal. But I wound up getting the job. I wound up being the host of the college football scoreboard show."

Nantz would wind up working with Brent Musburger on many occasions the next four years, especially on CBS's NCAA basketball, where Nantz hosted from the studio or the site of the game and Brent was doing play-by-play.

"I got to know Brent really well," Nantz said, "because in a sense I was his understudy. I did that for four years, and then I replaced Brent on the [college basketball] games. We got along great. His ability to host was just amazing. He strongly influenced me. There never was a show as good [as *The NFL Today* hosted by Brent]."

Jim Nantz wound up doing it all. The following year, 1986, he began his long run reporting on the PGA for CBS. That same year he started a three-year run doing play-by-play of the NBA. In 1987 he began an eight-year run hosting the U.S. Open tennis championships for CBS. In 1989 he was moved up to become CBS's permanent host from the Masters, of which Nantz coined the phrase "A tradition unlike any other." He also had an eighteen-year run calling college basketball games alongside analyst Billy Packer, and in 1990 began calling college football for CBS.

When Brent got fired in 1990, "they felt like Brent was the lead guy on everything CBS had," Nantz recalled. "And he was very skilled at all of it. Ted [Shaker] took me to lunch and said, 'We've got a lot of [good] people here. We're never gonna have another guy here like Musburger who does everything. We're gonna spread it around. We've got you, we've got Greg [Gumbel], we've got J.B. [James Brown].' Then he asked, 'What would you like to do in a perfect world? Would you like to do *The NFL Today*, would you like to do the games with Billy? If you had one, what would it be?' That was too big a question for me to answer. At that point I'm thirty. I had the most experience working with Billy, but in my heart I wanted to host *The NFL Today*. So I walked away and said, 'You guys just tell me what you want me to do and I'll do it.' I wasn't overconfident but I had a pretty good feeling I was going to be there [at CBS] for a long time."

In just a matter of days, Shaker called him and said they were going to put him on college basketball. Greg Gumbel and Terry Bradshaw became the hosts of *The NFL Today*, and things stayed that way for the next four years until CBS lost the broadcast rights to the NFL from 1994 to 1998. Nantz went on the road to do the lead college basketball game with Packer, and they were a team for eighteen years.

In 1998, when CBS regained the rights to the NFL, it brought back *The NFL Today* after a four-year hiatus. But this time it was with Jim Nantz hosting. It was the best way the network could let the NFL know it was putting its best foot forward. Nantz got to live out his dream of sitting in Brent's chair hosting *The NFL Today*.

"I hosted *The NFL Today* the next six years, from 1998 through '03," Nantz said, "they constantly were switching out analysts. We went from being the NFC to the AFC package. We started out the first year with Marcus Allen, Brent Jones, and George Seifert, and that became Craig James, Mike Ditka, and Jerry Glanville, and that became Randy Cross, Deion Sanders, and Boomer Esiason. Then we had Dan Marino come in."

In 2003 CBS wanted to make a change, and Nantz and Gumbel switched assignments. Gumbel returned to hosting *The NFL Today*, while Nantz got to do NFL play-by-play. And after one year James Brown became available—his contract was up at Fox. Gumbel went back to the booth to do the No. 2 NFL game behind Nantz, while Brown became the host of *The NFL Today*, and he's been the host ever since.

Lesley Visser, who was a contributor on *The NFL Today* from 1990 through '93 and then again from 2001 to '06, recalled a few interesting notes about some of the panelists.

"I'd do a feature," said Visser, "then join the others to discuss it on the set: Jim Nantz, Deion Sanders, Jerry Glanville and Mike Ditka—what a group! Glanville had this questionable 'power gum' that he wanted us all to chew. It was like having six cups of coffee in thirty seconds. Deion would send a young, shy runner up to Harlem to get him the chicken wings he wanted for halftime. The show was produced live outside on the GM Building Plaza on Fifth Avenue, and many of the people who came to watch were Asian tourists on their way to Central Park. In 2004, Greg [Gumbel] came back to host, with Shannon Sharpe, Marino, Boomer

[Esiason], and Ditka. Ditka was wonderful, handing out money to every homeless person on the way to a piano bar after the last game ended."[2]

Nantz's relationship with his colleagues grew from his remarkable relationship with his dad, Jim. They had traveled together while Nantz was in high school, going to different events, and developed a warm, loving father-son relationship. In 1995, after Nantz had been with CBS ten years and his dad had retired, he offered his dad an opportunity to travel together again. He asked his dad to be his road business partner, a role he thought perfect for him since his dad's three favorite things in life were traveling, meeting people, and sports. His dad was reluctant to accept.

During that weekend in the sweltering Texas heat, Nantz was broadcasting from Colonial Country Club in Fort Worth. His parents were there, and when his dad climbed up to Nantz's tower location just before they went on the air, something was very wrong.

"His eyes were disoriented. His face looked confused. His speech was halting and barely coherent," Nantz wrote in his book about his relationship with his dad, *Always By My Side*, cowritten with Eli Spielman.[3] Nantz had hoped that his dad was just dehydrated, but when he climbed back down the tower he collapsed at the bottom. It was a mini-stroke and the beginning of a long battle with Alzheimer's.

Slowly, despite all efforts, his dad's condition worsened over the years, and in 2002 when Nantz visited him, he only had faint recognition of his son. Nantz's next stop was the PGA Championship at Hazeltine National Golf Club in Minnesota, and he told his dad that over the weekend he would send out a cryptic message over the air just for him. He told him that he was going to say "Hello, friends" and that would be Jim's way of connecting with his dad. Six years later, in 2008, his dad finally succumbed to the dreaded disease, but ever since that Saturday at Hazeltine, Nantz has opened every broadcast saying, "Hello, friends."

"Jim McKay told me right after I got out of college," Nantz said on Dan Patrick's radio show in 2017, "that when you look into that [camera] lens, to think of one person. I never could quite relate to that. But when 'Hello, friends' came along, suddenly it clicked, and it became a calming effect. I say 'Hello, friends' because my dad had nothing but friends, and I think of my dad and I channel him, and off we'd go."

Jim Nantz continues to be one of the most recognized broadcasters in the history of sports television. Twice (in 2008 and 2009) he's won the Emmy for "Outstanding Sports Personality, Play-by-Play." In 2011 he won the Pete Rozelle Radio and Television Award given by the NFL Hall of Fame, and he's been named National Sportscaster of the Year five times by his peers. There's never been a more popular decision.

In the beginning, Nantz was so low-key and unlike other sportscasters that he needed to be experienced and cultivated for viewers to appreciate him. He never yells, which some play-by-play announcers think is the only way to communicate. Instead, Nantz serenades us with storylines and anecdotes. Analysts take to him like flowers to a rain shower. He always seems to get the most out of them, while never pushing himself to the front. He also has a great sense of history, having been close with former CBS greats like Jack Whitaker and Jim McKay, before McKay moved to ABC.

In college Nantz wrote a fan letter to McKay and eventually became so close with him that McKay's family asked Nantz to do one of the eulogies at his funeral. And through the years he had become so close with Whitaker, who passed away in 2019 at age ninety-five, that Nantz would stop by to see him anytime he was within fifty miles. In fact, Whitaker, at age eighty-eight, attended Nantz's wedding on June 9, 2012, and made a toast on what happened to be the 68th anniversary of the day Whitaker had stormed the beaches of Normandy, tying it all together.

"[These men are] one of the last links to my youth," Nantz told the Sports Broadcasting Hall of Fame upon his induction in 2018. "[They] made such an indelible impression on me, and then to be able to have the gift of friendship from them, that's a pretty amazing thing. I've never taken it lightly."

The Sports Broadcasting Hall of Fame always begins its induction of new members with a five-minute video presentation, followed by the inductee's thank-you speech. The Nantz video was voiced over by none other than Jack Whitaker, who was ninety-four at the time. "I had no idea [he was doing it]," said Nantz. "It was a great gift."

Whitaker opened the video with: "Jim Nantz has always cared about those of us who came before him," and he concluded it saying, "To Jim Nantz the achievements and the accolades have never been as important as the relationships—the connections with other father figures like the 41st president [George Herbert Walker Bush, whom Nantz had also become close with] and the king [video showed Arnold Palmer]. He's modeled himself after them. He's learned from them and along the way he turned into something else—a mentor and a hero for the next generation—a legend in his own right, showing everyone else not just how to do your job, but how to live your life."

Jack Whitaker accurately analyzed the essence of Jim Nantz, whose personality developed friendships and relationships that allowed him to fulfill his teenaged dream of hosting *The NFL Today*. When Nantz finally got to sit in that chair left behind by Brent Musburger, he was right at home. He has left *The NFL Today* in great hands, and it will continue to be the gold standard of pregame shows for years to come.

Epilogue: Where They Are, Where They Went

The NFL Today, started by Bill Fitts in 1970 and re-created by Bob Wussler in 1975, has led the way in sports broadcasting. Its original cast included four broadcasters who became icons in their own right. The program also yielded one of the greatest producer-director teams ever, and executives who have been recognized for their leadership. This epilogue will touch on what happened to them after they left CBS and where they are today.

Brent Musburger: Controversy Followed Him

About a month after CBS fired Brent Musburger in 1990, ABC signed him, and for the next twenty-seven years he voiced just about anything ABC Sports and its owned-and-operated cable network, ESPN, asked. From the Little League World Series to the BCS final, Musburger was able and ready to perform. The one thing he really did miss about the CBS job, however, was hosting *The NFL Today*.

"Was I feeling sorry for myself? Probably not," he later told the Associated Press. "I had a good job with ABC but I missed the live fire of *The NFL Today*. There was no doubt about that. It was extremely difficult for me to leave that show. The opening week of the next season I couldn't bring myself to watch it. I was out in Montana and when I knew it was on I went for a long walk in the hills. It took me, I'd say, at least six or seven weeks before I could watch anything on CBS."

The one thing ABC might have been leery about asking him to do was golf, but in 1992 they assigned him to cohost the U.S. Open with Jim McKay. At CBS Musburger had hosted the Masters broadcast in the late '80s despite his limited knowledge of the game. Former British

Open champion Tom Weiskopf was assigned to "babysit" Brent and help him when possible.

"Brent Musburger was not a golfer," Weiskopf told the *Chicago Tribune*. "Brent did not know or understand the tradition and terminology, or jargon, of the game. I got along with him because I was the baby-sitter for him. I had to get along with him. I was told: 'Your job is to baby-sit Brent and tell him everything you know about Augusta National, the golf course, golf in general, and help him with his terminology.' It was not a pleasant situation."[1]

After Jim Nantz, who played golf for the University of Houston, replaced Musburger, Weiskopf's attitude about his assignment brightened immensely. "Jim's a golfer. Pat Summerall's a golfer," Weiskopf said. "They understand the traditions of the game, the history of the game. And they have the terminology that goes with the game. They know the difference between a chip and a putt. Bunkers are not called sand traps. I just did my job. It's very difficult to be an analyst. When your answers are yes and no, you cease to be an analyst. It's difficult when you're trying to give some facts, and you're trying to really help the telecast . . . and you're sitting next to somebody who doesn't understand what's really going on."

One time Musburger asked Jack Nicklaus if Nicklaus thought he'd be able to recover from his back problems to play the next day. Nicklaus had already withdrawn his name from the tournament. The criticism for that faux pas seemed to roll off Brent's back. He said CBS needed him at the Masters.

"'When I went to Augusta, (CBS) needed some help," he told the *Chicago Tribune*. "I was the person they brought in after they lost Vin Scully, to tell stories about the players. I've lived with the criticism. It'll take time, but I'm more comfortable (with golf) than I was eight or 10 years ago."[2]

CBS Sports golf executive producer Frank Chirkinian was extremely critical of an interview Musburger did with PGA champion John Daly, where he asked about Daly's reputation for living the high life. Chirkinian said that question was "unconscionable," adding, "What you've done is establish in the eyes of other players that you are not to be trusted."[3]

Musburger moved on, and so did ABC. He became their No. 1 college football play-by-play guy. He picked up the nickname of "Big-Game

Brent." It turned out, however, that calling Major League Baseball wasn't his forte either. In October of 1995 Musburger was calling the playoffs for ABC. Richard Sandomir, the former sports media critic for the *New York Times*, took exception.

"Dreadful news," Sandomir wrote. "New York must listen to Brent Musburger of ABC call Games 1, 2 and possibly Game 7 of the Seattle-Cleveland American League Championship Series. Coming off his mistake-strewn work on the Yankees-Mariners divisional series, ABC saw no apparent problem in assigning the former 'anchor monster' of CBS to the ALCS [American League Championship Series]. ABC must be looking to amortize his hefty salary."

"Musburger's weekend in Seattle," Sandomir's article continued, "exposed him as an inattentive baseball naïf, who barely comprehends the game's obvious and nuanced points or its strategy. He is frequently fatuous and noticeably unprepared. 'Buckeye Brent's' digressions to college football reminded me that his overstated style is far better suited to being ABC's No. 2 college football announcer."[4]

At ESPN Brent was the No. 1 college football play-by-play announcer, working alongside former Ohio State quarterback Kirk Herbstreit. His folksy style led him to often call his analysts "pardners" and refer to Herbstreit as "Herbie." In 2011 Musburger was assigned the BCS Championship game between Auburn and Oregon. Here's what the *Times'* Sandomir wrote the next day:

"If Musburger's performances at the Rose Bowl on New Year's Day, and the BCS title game Monday night, are exhibits of the State of the Brent, it is clear that he has veered from the factual precision needed to maintain his status as ESPN's No. 1 college football announcer. Musburger is one of sports broadcasting's great survivors and one of its most recognizable and excitable voices. Fired by CBS in 1990, he was soon picked up by ABC Sports. Being grateful for his second chance, he did virtually anything the network, and then ESPN, asked him.

"But the details add up to inattention to his job or an odd attempt to be the master of a new paradigm of announcing where emotion trumps fact. Musburger's B.C.S. title game performance will be remembered most for his silly recasting of himself as a marketing man. It was probably a

momentary lapse of judgment, a lost trip into humor or an absurd confla-
tion of game and sponsor. But as Auburn lined up for the field goal that
would win the game, Musburger said, 'This is for all the Tostitos.'

"While viewers cringed or laughed nervously, [BCS game sponsor]
Frito-Lay got a bonus for its tortilla chips brand that it could not have
imagined or bargained for. 'Big Game Brent' delivered the snacks."[5]

A few years later in 2013, he was calling Alabama's 42–14 blowout
victory over Notre Dame when ESPN's cameras focused in on Katherine Webb in the stands. Webb, a model and the 2012 Miss Alabama,
was the girlfriend of 'Bama quarterback A. J. McCarron. "You see that
lovely lady there, she does go to Auburn," Musburger began. "But she's
also Miss Alabama and that's A. J. McCarron's girlfriend. You quarterbacks, you get all the good-looking women. What a beautiful woman!
Wow!" When Herbstreit agreed with him, Musburger said, "If you're
a youngster in Alabama, start getting the football out and throw it
around the backyard with Pop."

Within minutes the Twitter universe lit up, complaining about Musburger's comments. Some thought he was acting like a creepy old man
in his seventies.[6]

"It's extraordinarily inappropriate to focus on an individual's looks,"
Sue Carter, a professor of journalism at Michigan State, told the *New
York Times* for its January 8, 2013, edition. "In this instance, the appearance of the quarterback's girlfriend had no bearing on the outcome of
the game. It's a major personal violation, and it's so retrograde that it's
embarrassing. I think there's a generational issue, but it's incumbent on
people practicing in these eras to keep up and this is not a norm."

Referring to a woman as "beautiful" really wasn't the issue. After all,
it was a prearranged camera shot. The bigger issue was telling kids and
their dads that they can have what McCarron had (and married) if they
can be a star quarterback.

Soon after, John Wildhack, ESPN's executive vice president of production, told Musburger through the announcer's earpiece that he had
to "move on." The network apologized for Musburger's comments. "We
always try to capture interesting storylines and the relationship between
an Auburn grad who is Miss Alabama and the current Alabama quarter-

back certainly met that test," the network said. "However, we apologize that the commentary in this instance went too far and Brent understands that." To which Musburger told the Associated Press, "I called a beauty queen beautiful. Are you kidding me?"

When interviewed for this book, Wildhack, who is now the athletic director at Syracuse University, explained his conversation with Musburger after that game.

"I had several chats with him after that," Wildhack said. "They went well. I told Brent, 'You can't say that. It's inappropriate.' He would say 'it's tongue-in-cheek, don't take things literally,' etc. And I believe that's how he felt, but the trouble was, it was still inappropriate. We had a cordial and productive conversation and we may have agreed to disagree on some things, but I said, 'This is the position that the company takes; for better or for worse, I'm the executive in charge of production.' And he respected that."[7]

The following year, 2014, ESPN became the broadcast arm for the new Southeastern Conference (SEC) Network, and Wildhack asked Musburger to take a step back, or down as the case may be, and be the play-by-play voice of the new network. Wildhack made a point of saying that Musburger always was willing to do anything ABC or ESPN asked him to do.

"We always had a great relationship," Wildhack recalled, "including when we assigned him to the SEC Network. Did he like it? No. Did he fight it? No, but he understood what we were doing. It gave the SEC Network instant credibility. When you're launching a new network, you can't have a more credible play-by play person with the conference, with the schools, and with the advertisers."

That credibility recalls what his first boss in television, Van Gordon Sauter, said about Musburger, going back thirty years. "Musburger would talk back to you," Sauter said when interviewed for this book. "'This is dumb, it's a bad idea' or 'I don't know why you want me to do this.' At the end of it all, Musburger knew he was an employee and he would go do what employees did, in spite of all his clout."[8]

But in 2017, with just a few months left to go on his contract, Musburger suddenly announced his retirement effective after a college basketball game he was scheduled to broadcast the following week. He also announced he was starting a new sports betting information business with his family in Las Vegas, but why did he not wait another two months and go out the right way?

"When Brent left ESPN," John Wildhack said, "I had [already] left ESPN [to go to Syracuse] by then. . . . What I heard was that people thought that Brent had lost his fastball, that it's time for him to move on, and we've got to go in a different direction, and all that—and I understand that. But if he didn't go out on his own terms, he was someone who clearly deserved to go out on his own terms. Any assignment we gave him he put 100 percent into everything. If anyone was deserving of going out and being celebrated, Brent's at the top of the list in my opinion."

In 2017, shortly after his retirement from ESPN, Musburger was inducted into the Sports Broadcasting Hall of Fame. He was the only one of the ten inducted that year who did not make it to New York for the ceremony. He gave his acceptance speech on tape from Las Vegas, and in it he once again defended his comments about Katherine Webb, A. J. McCarron's girlfriend. "I became the villain in the eyes of the P.C. [politically correct] press," he said, "because I dared to call a beauty queen beautiful. Oh, my god. How could you do that? And I always thought, what are you talking about?"

ESPN's Jeremy Schaap narrated the accompanying video to Brent's induction. In it he said, "Musburger will always be remembered as one of the giants of sports announcing." In fact, Brent has won many awards, including a Sports Emmy for Lifetime Achievement in 2017, and was named to the National Sports Media Association Hall of Fame. Yet, his peers have never named him National Sportscaster of the Year. It's an award won multiple times by Keith Jackson (five), Vin Scully (four), Chris Berman (six), Bob Costas (seven), and Jim Nantz (five). But if you think you've heard Musburger's voice for the last time, guess again. In 2018, at age seventy-nine, he became the play-by-play announcer for the Oakland Raiders.

His hurried retirement from ESPN came with little notice. Brent simply announced he was retiring after his next college basketball broadcast, January 31, 2017. He was moving to Las Vegas to be the front man for a new family business called VSiN, which bills itself as "The Sports Betting Network."

There's no doubt that Brent Musburger made a tremendous impact on sports broadcasting. But it's ironic that after leaving CBS thirty years ago, he never returned to the one thing that made him famous, the one thing that he did better than anyone else. In the foreword for this book, Jim Nantz wrote that Brent was "the greatest studio host of all time."

PHYLLIS GEORGE: COURAGEOUS AND CREATIVE

Phyllis George left *The NFL Today* a second and final time in 1984 after a four-year run. October of that year she was announced as the new co-anchor of *The CBS Morning News*, along with Bill Kurtis, who had replaced Charles Kuralt. After Kuralt left the program, its ratings began to sag and Diane Sawyer decided to leave early in '84. Several years later, Sawyer became the first female correspondent for *60 Minutes*.

Although Phyllis had interviewing experience, nearly all of her interviews on *The NFL Today* were filmed and edited, as opposed to the live situations she faced on *The CBS Morning News*.

One of those live situations found her doing a joint interview with a woman and the man that the woman had falsely accused of rape. At the end of the interview, Phyllis awkwardly suggested that they could find closure with a hug, which didn't happen. The media backlash of that incident stunned her. In 1985 she told the *Washington Post*, "I'm the least controversial person I know to become controversial."

Tom Shales, the often mean-spirited television reviewer for the *Washington Post*, was the harshest critic. After the "hugging" suggestion, he opened his next column with "Collectors of idiotic remarks made by Phyllis George on *The CBS Morning News* hit a bonanza Wednesday morning. . . . It seemed yet another black mark for the poorly-rated program whose latest in a long series of revampings, installed the personable but klutzy George in the co-anchor seat."[9]

Looking back, Bob Costas had a unique prospective of what it was like at the time for Phyllis. "Luckily there was no social media then," Costas began. "She probably got it from both directions. She was enough of an outward feminist to suit that wing, and there were those who thought a woman had no business being on a football show or any sports show, and she put up with all that from both sides. And the irony was that she had to get tough to put up with all that, but basically she was just a very nice person. She wasn't meant for verbal combat."[10]

Van Gordon Sauter, who was president of CBS Sports when Phyllis returned to *The NFL Today*, had become the head of CBS News in 1982 and was instrumental in her joining *The CBS Morning News.*

"I was an admirer of Phyllis," he said. "I thought when she was on the camera it brightened the set. I used her in News. The News people hated her [because she didn't have a News background] and they did everything in their power to undermine her. I thought it was so unbecoming and it ended up to be damaging . . . but in the right environment—and CBS was not the right environment—she could have done quite well."

Howard Stringer, the new head of CBS News at that time, agreed. "She is under a particularly vicious spotlight," he said. "It is extraordinary and relentless. In the long term what will count will be audience reaction."[11]

She wound up leaving the show after eight months despite having a three-year, no-cut contract at $1 million a year. At age thirty-five she went back to Kentucky to raise her two small children. There she launched a line of pre-marinated chicken breast recipes called "Chicken by George" that she sold to Hormel. She wrote or cowrote five books, including her self-help book, *Never Say Never.* She also created a cosmetics brand, "Phyllis George Beauty," for the Home Shopping Network.

After taking off about ten years to raise Lincoln and Pamela, she returned to do some television and cable, hosting interviews and shopping shows and promoting crafts. And in 2000 she made her movie debut with a small role in *Meet the Parents.*

In 1985, thirty-five years before her death, Phyllis discovered that she had a rare blood disorder called polycythemia rubra vera, a form of leukemia. This is a cancer in which your bone marrow makes too many red blood cells, and also sometimes too many white blood cells and platelets. The real danger is forming clots in your body. Shortly after that, she told the *South Florida Sun-Sentinel,* "We're here on this Earth only once. I have the feeling that I've got to make every day count."[12] And that also may have been on her mind in 1988 when she told the

Louisville Courier-Journal, "I've gone through a lot. I've had a lot of life experiences. . . . From here on out, I want every day to count."[13]

"One of my most distinct memories of her," said her daughter Pamela Brown, "was how she would lie in the bed backwards with her swollen feet propped up after a long day to help with her blood flow. It was very hard for me to reconcile the fact my mom, who was a dynamo in every sense of the word, lived for decades with a blood condition that slowed her down so much."[14]

She kept the blood disorder to herself, and only close friends and family were aware. Even her longstanding friends from *The NFL Today* were unaware she had the illness. After her death there was an outpouring of love for her, and many expressed remorse that they hadn't kept in better touch.

At her memorial service her children, Lincoln and Pamela, told heartwarming stories about their mother. Said Lincoln: "What lived within Phyllis Anne George outshines her career. Her cleaning lady said, 'After all she had done she still made me feel like someone who mattered.'"

"When the doctor called us to tell us how sick she was," Lincoln continued, "she grabbed the phone and started giving him a lecture. 'Don't you know how to deliver bad news?' she said. 'You never start with a negative.' I'm going to send you a copy of my book, *Never Say Never.*"

When contacted for this book, her daughter Pamela related a heartwarming story about Phyllis in high school. "She was raised to always be kind," Ms. Brown said. "As a cheerleader in high school, she befriended a girl with Down syndrome. During the games she'd let her hold Mom's letter jacket, which made her feel so happy. Another time she had mistakenly handed an invitation to a senior party to one of the girls who wasn't invited. 'No, this isn't for me,' the girl said, pointing out the name on the invitation. Phyllis apologized, said she'd be right back, and returned a few minutes later with an invitation that she had hurriedly written the girl's name on.

"That's how my mom was. Her heart was bigger than Texas."[15]

In August of 2020 the Sports Broadcasting Hall of Fame announced that Phyllis George would be among those inducted in its next class. It was an honor long overdue. The induction was scheduled for December

2020 but was postponed to December 2021 because of the pandemic. In a taped tribute Lesley Visser spoke of Phyllis's warmth and kindness, and the doors she opened: "Phyllis' legacy," Visser began, "is that she cleared the path for a role that had been unimaginable until Phyllis got there. Then every young woman could say, 'I can see it. I can be it.' . . . We all remember the gorgeous aura that was Phyllis George."

Mike Pearl: Producing the Best

In 2015 the Sports Broadcasting Hall of Fame inducted Mike Pearl into their club. Al Michaels narrated the accompanying video. He began by saying, "In this crazy and pressure-filled business of sports television, I think of Mike Pearl as always being the calmest guy in the storm. He's been one of the most important figures in the last four decades in sports television, yet even rabid sports fans don't know his name, because not for one second did Mike Pearl ever seek the spotlight. All he ever cared about was producing top-quality sports television."

One reason it was Michaels narrating and not Brent was because Pearl left CBS Sports in 1980 and walked down the street to go to work for Roone Arledge at ABC Sports. Here's how it happened:

Both Pearl and his directing partner, Bob Fishman, were tired of just doing studio shows for CBS. Fishman began directing auto races, and in 1979 when CBS pried the Daytona 500 away from ABC, Pearl joined him for the first historic live broadcast of the race from start to finish. Previously ABC had broadcast it on tape delay.

The race finished with the two leaders, Donnie Allison and Cale Yarborough, neck and neck on the last lap. When Allison tried to pass on the inside, Yarborough cut him off and the two cars collided and careened into the infield. Allison's brother Bobby, who was considerably behind, drove over to see if his brother was okay. When he arrived, Yarborough began yelling at him and before long the two were fighting, and CBS caught almost all of it live. It was thrilling television, and that combined with bad weather in the East produced an audience of 15 million viewers.

"We were on top of every story and there was the fight at the end of the race," said Pearl. "We got a lot of press on Monday. Shortly after that I got a call from Roone Arledge inviting me to lunch. I said, 'Sure.'

I met him at ABC, just two blocks away. Joining Roone were [the director] Chet Forte and producers Dennis Lewin and Chuck Howard. He [Arledge] offered me some great *Wide World* [*of Sports*] shows and the Olympics that winter at Sarajevo."

"I went back and told CBS," Pearl continued, "and [Neal] Pilson said, 'What if we make you executive producer of all of football, all of horse racing, all of auto racing.' I thought about it for a couple of days and I said, 'Nah.' And now when I think about it I wonder if it was the right decision. I always wanted to go where I could learn and do the most. At that point of my career, ABC provided that opportunity for me. I was born at CBS. But I missed the chance to do all those Final Fours that Bob [Fishman] did. In my mind I think I did the right thing."[16]

In 1980 Pearl began an eight-year odyssey producing some spectacular events for ABC Sports, including Super Bowls XIX and XXII, *Monday Night Football*, the 1984 Sarajevo Winter Olympics, the 1984 Los Angeles Summer Olympics, the 1988 Calgary Winter Olympics, and the Indianapolis 500. In 1987 he won Thoroughbred racing's highest honor, the Eclipse Award, for producing all three legs of the Triple Crown.

In 1988 Pearl went back to CBS to serve as coordinating producer for the Winter Olympics in 1992 in Albertville and 1994 in Lillehammer. Feeling restless, he accepted a new challenge after Lillehammer and accepted an offer from Turner Sports. There he oversaw the NFL, Atlanta Braves baseball, NASCAR, Wimbledon, and college football, as well as Turner's cable coverage of the 1998 Nagano Winter Olympics. But the one thing he will always be remembered for during his time at Turner Sports is revamping the *NBA on TNT* and hiring the ultra-opinionated Charles Barkley. It is a show that Bob Costas called "the best studio pregame show in the history of sports television."

"He [Pearl] let me be me," Barkley told the *New York Times* on March 11, 2021. "He didn't try to rein me in, but when I got in trouble, he'd say, 'Let's talk about this.' He was like my grandfather. I didn't want to disappoint him."

"I always believe in looking for the next challenge," Pearl told the Sports Broadcasting Hall of Fame. "I could never handle being stagnant. If it was something that was unknown and seemed like something that wasn't necessarily in my comfort zone, then that's where I wanted to be. That [philosophy] guided a lot of the decisions I ended up making in my career."

The *NBA on TNT* pregame show wound up being so good that it often received higher ratings than the games that followed it. And the Sports Broadcasting Hall of Fame in 2020 announced that Barkley was also being inducted.

"He [Pearl] deserves everything that has come his way—the Hall of Fame and all that," said former colleague Bob Fishman. "Forget CBS, he probably did much more for Turner. His ability, his foresight, was very much like [Bob] Wussler's. I think he learned more from Wussler than anybody in the business because look what Mike did by putting Charles Barkley together with Kenny Smith, very much the same way that Wussler put together the cast for *The NFL Today*."[17]

In 2003 Pearl accepted a new challenge and became senior vice president / executive producer at ABC Sports, overseeing *Monday Night Football*, the NBA, the BCS (Bowl Championship Series), the 2006 FIFA World Cup, the British Open, the Indianapolis 500, and the World Figure Skating Championships. After that Pearl went into semi-retirement in 2014 and started Michael Pearl Productions, consulting with ABC/ESPN and Disney for their bids on the 2014 and 2016 Olympics.

In a strange coincidence, Pearl died a day after Irv Cross, on March 1, 2021. He had been hospitalized for months coping with a series of infections and had returned home to recuperate, only to die there from a heart attack. He was seventy-seven.

Pearl had been in poor health for several years. His good friend Janis Delson recalled how tough it was for him. "He was very sick," she began in an email shortly after he had passed away. "Not just the last few months but for many years with heart problems, diabetes, just to name a few. I was with him many times when he had to go to the hospital or have an angioplasty. When he got sick at the end of last year, I had a feeling that he wasn't going to make it. Too much was wrong—urinary infection, pneumonia, kidney issues and sepsis. I think it was a miracle that they managed to cure all this up. In addition he was in extreme pain from his back and neck problems which they couldn't fix. His brother Bob said to me from day one that 'he is in a better place.' And he is right, as hard as it is for us to accept."[18]

Bob Fishman posted the following: "We did so many iconic broadcasts together: *The NFL Today*, Daytona 500, Belmont Stakes, and so many more. Hundreds, in fact. He was like a brother to me, both in and out of the TV truck."[19]

Some of the posts on social media about Mike Pearl reflected how much he was admired and loved by those who knew him. Among them were these:

> **George Schweitzer:** Sad news. Mike was quite a guy. Larger than life but so approachable and generous. He was a teacher, a leader and a mensch.
>
> **Dan Forer:** Yesterday it was Irv Cross. Today we learn that Michael Pearl, one of the most accomplished, creative and kindest producers ever to enter a TV truck has passed. Throughout my career I consulted with Mike and he always said, "It's simple, just figure out what will make you happy and do it."

Winning sixteen Emmys overall, Mike Pearl has left his mark on sports broadcasting, and he will be remembered with Roone Arledge as one of the greatest producers the business has ever known.

Bob Fishman: A Director for the People

Starting with Michael Jordan's last-minute winning shot for North Carolina over Georgetown at the 1982 Final Four, Bob Fishman has directed a total of thirty-eight Final Fours for CBS Sports. He always looks for that emotional moment. "I have one goal as a director, and that's to capture emotional moments," Fishman said. "Directing for me, whether it's film or sports or anything else, is about capturing those moments that have true emotion."

One of those moments he captured was when North Carolina State coach Jim Valvano was sprinting across the court looking for someone to hug after his Wolfpack pulled a stunning upset of Houston in 1983. Other great emotional moments captured by Fishman include the brawl between Cale Yarborough and Donnie Allison that ended the

CBS Sports' Hall of Fame director Bob Fishman, pictured here after more than forty years with the network. (COURTESY CBS SPORTS)

1979 Daytona 500, and Tonya Harding in tears at the 1994 Lillehammer Winter Olympics.

In 1979 CBS convinced NASCAR to let it broadcast the Daytona 500 by promising to do it live for the first time and broadcast the entire race from start to finish. Fishman was the director, and he immediately began to institute changes that made auto racing seem like it was happening in your living room at home. His innovations included the very first race cam. That live race, with its fantastic fight to the finish, made a huge difference in how the public viewed NASCAR.

"Until that point, NASCAR was just a regional sport," Fishman told the Sports Broadcasting Hall of Fame in 2019, "but the sensational ending vaulted that race to the front page of the *New York Times*. In my mind, that's the moment that took the sport to the next step. And the fact that people were seeing it live for the first time contributed to the success of NASCAR going forward. And, personally, it set my career in motion."

"I think we set a new standard for how to cover auto racing during those years," he continued. "We tried to do a couple things that I found were lacking in racing [coverage]. First, we put out more low cameras to create that sense of speed and show the essence of how dangerous racing can be. Second, my goal was to get farther back into the pack. [CBS analyst] Ken Squier always preached, 'It's not just about the lead two or three cars. It's important to get back in the pack because that's where some of the best battles take place.'"

Fishman directed the Daytona 500 for the next twenty years and also directed tennis's foremost event, the U.S. Open, for twenty-seven years, to go along with his thirty-eight Final Fours. You don't get to direct that many great events by accident.

"Bob has distinguished himself as one of the great directors in the history of sports television," CBS Sports chairman Sean McManus told the Hall of Fame. "His ability to tell the story and set the scene through the camera's lens is simply remarkable. He is both innovative and creative but never loses sight of his main job, which is to cover the action on the field, in the arena, or on the track."

Fishman soared at CBS until he hit a speed bump in 1990—non-Hodgkin's lymphoma, a form of cancer that luckily in Fishman's case was treatable. After experiencing chest pains on a remote, a large mass was discovered in his chest. Chemo worked at first, shrinking the mass to a pimple, but then it began to get larger and his doctor said Bob would need a bone marrow transplant. Fortunately, he was able to transplant his own cells to survive. "First they give you enough chemo to kill an elephant," Fishman revealed, "then they rescue your system with the bone marrow." Six weeks of isolation followed while his white count rose back up. When he was ready to return to work, every assignment he previously had at CBS Sports was waiting for him, thanks to executive producer Ted Shaker.

After recovering, Fishman realized how lucky he was to have his wife Margaret and family there for support during his recovery. He knew there were others getting similar treatments that couldn't afford to have their families there or couldn't even pay for the insurance. So he and friend Christina Merrill, whom he met during his recovery, started the Bone Marrow and Cancer Foundation. In 2019 alone, it distributed over $2 million to families in need.

Fishman has won sixteen Emmys along the way and would gladly share them with the people he worked with through the years. At the Hall of Fame event, Neal Pilson, who negotiated that first Daytona 500 deal, said of Fishman that despite all the recognition he's received, "He remains the same kind, humble, and gracious person we have always known and loved."

At age seventy-one, Fishman was not ready to retire, at least not in 2021. He's one of CBS's top NFL directors as well, and says he'd like to get to fifty years at CBS Sports (he's at forty-five) and forty Final Fours before calling it a day.

Bob Fishman, along with Mike Pearl, were smartly paired together by Bob Wussler back in 1976. Today they are recognized as two of the greatest of all time. And on February 28, 2023, Fishman became only the fifth director in history to receive the Lifetime Achievement Award from the Director's Guild of America.

Irv Cross: Hall of Fame Analyst

In 1994 when CBS lost its NFL rights to Fox, Irv Cross had been working for the network a total of twenty-three years. It was an uncomfortable situation for both Cross and CBS, because they both had to make a decision on whether he should stay.

"We wound up doing Canadian Football for a short time," Irv said. "Neal Pilson was running Sports at that time when we lost the NFL. I probably could have been more aggressive [about staying on]. Instead of pushing and trying to find an opening somewhere, I decided to fade out of there."[20]

After leaving broadcasting, Cross was athletic director at Idaho State from 1996 to 1998. He then moved to Minnesota, as the director of athletics at Macalester College in St. Paul for six years until he accepted the post of chief executive officer of the Big Brothers/Big Sisters of Central Minnesota until May 2010. At that time he did some football commentary for KMSP-TV, the Fox station in the Twin Cities.

In 2009 he was completely surprised to find out that he was named the recipient of the Pete Rozelle Broadcasting Award from the Pro Football Hall of Fame. He said he was shocked when he got the call from the Hall's Joe Horrigan.

"I knew Joe from when I was announcing," Cross said, "and when he said 'dinner,' I thought he meant just getting together for dinner. I was stunned when he told me I won the award. I thought of the great company I was in [of those who had won the award previously]: Jack Buck, Pat Summerall, Lindsey Nelson, Curt Gowdy—those are the greats of broadcasting. I am just fortunate to be in their company. Once they put that plaque of you on that wall, it will be there forever, even when I am long gone."

It was well deserved because there's no question that Irv Cross was one of the true pioneers of sports broadcasting, although he might not think so himself.

"I don't refer to myself as a pioneer," he said, "but in 1975 the sports TV landscape was much different, much whiter. I never focused on that but I was keenly aware that if I failed, it might be a long time before another black person got a similar opportunity. Every time I see James Brown or Greg Gumbel or Tom Jackson on TV, I take pride, knowing in some way I helped create an avenue for them."[21]

In the last few years Irv had been suffering from chronic traumatic encephalopathy (CTE) and early Alzheimer's. He attributed it to all those "dings" he took as a pro, and the countless number of concussions he suffered.

"Owners today, and frankly a lot of today's players, don't have an appreciation of what people went through in the '50s, '60s, and '70s," Cross wrote in his autobiography, *Bearing the Cross*. "Players were like raw hamburger being ground up. We bring the crowds. But nobody thinks about what it looks like in the training room when the game is over. . . . The damage being done is serious. The league is going to have to pay huge sums of money to players, but the NFL will find a way to slow those payments down. Sometimes I think the league's position is to deny, deny until enough of us die. As long as you can play, they're with you. But once the body starts to break, see you later."[22]

After his death, hundreds of posts on social media from former coworkers espoused their love for Irv. One from former CBS producer Sherm Eagan was typical: "The media is making much of the fact that Irv was the 'first black' co-anchor. . . . For those of us in CBS Sports at the time, we didn't think of him as 'black' or 'the first' anything. He was just 'Irv,' a consummate professional that we all looked forward to seeing and working with."

Jimmy The Greek: From Rich to Broke

After CBS parted ways with Jimmy "The Greek" Snyder, he moved into the Alexander Hotel in Miami Beach, just a stone's throw from the Fontaine-bleau Hotel on Collins Avenue. He was there for the winter racing season, leaving his wife Joan back at their home in Durham, North Carolina. With no income from CBS and his public relations business now gone, The Greek's funds quickly dried up, along with his sources of information.

In the early '90s Snyder and his wife separated and The Greek moved to Las Vegas, hoping to re-create the good old days. He took a suite in the Barbary Coast Hotel. Bob Fishman was the only one from CBS who still talked to him.

"We stayed in touch," Fishman said, "and four or five years later I was going to Vegas for a basketball game and I called him up. He asked if we could have dinner. 'Great, I'd love to see you,' I told him. He said to meet him at Michael's, the steakhouse in the Barbary Coast Hotel. I got there first and here he comes. It made you want to cry. His hair was down to his shoulders, there were grease stains all over his jacket, he was still bitter, and he kept wanting to talk about what CBS did to him. I grabbed the check and he then said to me, 'Could you do me a favor? Could you lend me a hundred dollars?' I'm thinking, this guy is broken; his life is over. He and his wife have separated. He's living by himself in Vegas and he's broke. That stayed with me for a long time."

"He passed away shortly after that [April 21, 1996, from a heart attack] and that was another sad moment," Fishman continued. "Hank Goldberg and Mike [Pearl] and myself were at his funeral and hardly anyone came except for about four or five old bookmakers from Steubenville, Ohio. We were sitting in the back pew of the church and before they closed the casket, I slipped a $2 winning ticket from Gulfstream in his casket because I wanted to send him out a winner. It was all bittersweet for me in the end, because I liked Jimmy and I understood his gruffness. Considering his history, background, his upbringing, it was all very sad."

When he was flush in the '70s, a story The Greek occasionally told his friends was about the time he met Bernard Baruch at a dinner party in New York decades earlier. Baruch was a famous financier and advisor to presidents Woodrow Wilson and Franklin D. Roosevelt. Looking for some personal advice, Snyder asked Baruch to meet him the next morning after breakfast. "You'll be broke and rich seven times in your life," Baruch told him that morning. "Just watch the seventh."[23]

Jayne Kennedy: Actress and Mother

After Jayne Kennedy left CBS, she became the first and only female host of the syndicated show *Greatest Sports Legends* for six years. She also played a significant role in the remake of the film *Body and Soul*, which was written and directed by her husband, Leon Isaac Kennedy. In 1981 Jayne was named the recipient of the NAACP Image Award for Best Actress for *Body and Soul*. In 2018 Jayne was honored when the Smithsonian's National Museum of African American History and Culture included her alongside Oprah Winfrey and Della Reese as one of the African American women who pioneered as television hosts and news broadcasters. And in 2021 the National Sportswriters Media Association chose Jayne as the recipient of the prestigious Roone Arledge Award for Innovation.

Jayne married actor Bill Overton in 1985, and they have been together ever since. They have three daughters together, Savannah, Kopper Joi, and Zaire. Jayne is also stepmom to Cheyenne from Bill's first marriage.

In 2020, with her daughters now fully grown, Jayne was planning on relaunching her career.

Bill Fitts: A Pioneering Innovator

Bill Fitts left CBS Sports after more than a dozen years building their NFL product. His first stop was NBC Sports, where he helped develop that network's Sunday pregame show, *NFL '77*. Fitts worked with Bryant Gumbel, who he thought to be every bit as good as Brent Musburger in the host role.

In the early '80s Fitts jumped over to the fledgling cable network ESPN, and stayed long enough to help develop many of that network's top producers and directors. Fitts is among the truly influential figures in the business. At ESPN he built the production department that shaped sports TV for years to come.

In 2018 the Sports Broadcasting Hall of Fame finally got around to inducting Bill Fitts, who without doubt has been one of the true pioneers of sports television for more than five decades.

"He pioneered how to cover the entirety of sports, not just what was happening with the ball," said ESPN's Fred Gaudelli, longtime director of both *Sunday Night* and *Monday Night Football*, in the video for Fitts's induction. "He made you discard your notes after the fact to force you to think anew the next time; he was really teaching us how to keep advancing the production. And, he was deploying women into major production roles far sooner and more sincerely than the rest of corporate America."

Ted Shaker and Neal Pilson: Sharing Their Expertise

Ted Shaker and Neal Pilson both left CBS in the early 1990s, Shaker in '92 and Pilson in '94. Neither sat idle. Shaker, a winner of thirteen Emmys and two Peabody Awards, soon became founder and president of Sports Illustrated Television, where he created branded programs for ABC, CBS, NBC, FOX, and TNT based on *Sports Illustrated*'s legendary storytelling and journalism. He created the first sports video-on-demand test in partnership with the NFL and co-created the first twenty-four-hour sports news channel, CNN/SI.

Shaker then became CNBC's business news executive producer and helped move the financial network forward through various programming, creating seven new series. Among those was *Kudlow & Cramer*, which first introduced Larry Kudlow and Jim Cramer to America. In 2004 he founded Mercury Media Inc., a consulting firm to broadcast, cable, and digital media companies. In 2017 Shaker was executive producer of the ESPN 30-for-30 film *Mike and the Mad Dog*, telling the story of the famous WFAN duo Mike Francesa and Chris Russo. And in 2019 he became founder and CEO of inCourage, a very worthy not-for-profit organization that helps young athletes and adults redefine success in youth sports.

In 1995 Neal Pilson established his sports media-consulting firm, and over the years has represented NASCAR, the Kentucky Derby, the Rose Bowl, and the World Series of Poker in network negotiations. His first client was Bill France of NASCAR. France took a chance in 1979 and allowed Pilson to buy the rights to the Daytona 500 away from ABC. CBS's live coverage of that event helped advance the entire NASCAR industry.

Three months after leaving CBS, Pilson returned to negotiate a new deal for NASCAR. He opened the negotiations, he told *Sports Business Journal*, by pointing his finger at the Sports division's new president, Dave Kenin, and saying, tongue in cheek, "Dave, CBS has been screwing my client for 20 years and it has got to stop now."[24]

Pilson, who turned eighty in 2020, is still looked upon as a fierce negotiator for the clients with whom he consulted.

HALL OF FAME: *THE NFL TODAY* WING

The Sports Broadcasting Hall of Fame inducted its first class in 2007 and now has more than 120 members. More than 10,000 professionals in the industry suggest nominees each year in categories that range from Engineering, Management, Production, Operations, Leagues, and Teams to three different announcing categories: Play-by-Play, Studio Host, and Reporter. A special veterans category recently has also been added.

It's an incredible tribute to *The NFL Today* that nine who worked on the show over the years have been inducted:

Jack Whitaker (2012)

Mike Pearl (2015)

Brent Musburger (2017)

Lesley Visser (2017)

Bill Fitts (2018)

Jim Nantz (2018)

Bob Fishman (2019)

James Brown (2020)

Phyllis George (2020)

In the future I hope the voters will find a way to include Bob Wussler and Irv Cross. Wussler had the great vision to create *The NFL Today* as we know it and show the way to broadcast a live sports studio show, and then had the courage to be the first to do the same at a Super Bowl. Cross was the first Black broadcaster to break barriers in local and national sports television, and in doing his job so well for twenty-three years at CBS, he opened the door for other networks to hire younger outstanding Black broadcasters as well.

Ted Shaker should also be strongly considered by the voters. Shaker was either associate producer, producer, or executive producer of *The NFL Today* from 1978 through 1992. He managed the egos and was the one calming things down when Musburger and The Greek came to blows at Peartrees in 1980, and he was the executive in charge when Snyder made his insensitive remarks on Martin Luther King Jr. Day weekend in 1988. He also had the courage to hire a twenty-six-year-old announcer from Salt Lake City (Jim Nantz) when it wasn't the safe way to go. And finally, Ted Shaker had the gumption, along with Neal Pilson, to fire Brent Musburger in 1990, which opened the door for talents like Nantz, Greg Gumbel, and James Brown to blossom—and become household names on NFL Sundays at 12:30 p.m. Eastern.[25]

NOTES

1. CBS Sports: And That's the Way It Was

1. All Bill Fitts quotes in this chapter are taken from a May 20, 2020, interview by author.

2. Rich Podolsky, "Jack Whitaker—Remembering One of a Kind, Not to be Replaced Soon," *Sports Broadcast Journal*, August 25, 2019.

3. All Ellen Beckwith quotes in this chapter are taken from a May 21, 2020, interview by author.

4. All Yvonne Connors quotes in this chapter are taken from a May 21, 2020, interview by author.

5. Robin Beck, interview by author, December 13, 2020.

6. Unless otherwise noted, all Marjorie Margolies quotes in this chapter are taken from a May 25, 2020, interview by author.

7. All Bob Fishman quotes in this chapter are taken from multiple interviews and email exchanges with author during June, July, and August 2020.

8. All Kevin O'Malley quotes in this chapter are taken from a May 21, 2020, interview by author.

2. Brent Musburger: The Natural

1. "Not Just A Pretty Face," *Sports Illustrated*, January 16, 1984.

2. Tom Schad, "Olympian John Carlos on 1968 Brent Musburger Criticism," *USA Today*, May 30, 2019.

3. Radio.com, May 3, 2018.

4. All Van Gordon Sauter quotes in this chapter are taken from a July 13, 2020, interview by author.

5. Ed Sherman, "With Brent Musburger, a $10,000 Raise Could've Changed Sports Journalism History," *Poynter*, June 23, 2012.

6. Scott Mansch, "Brent Musburger's Montana Roots Run Deep," *Great Falls Tribune*, January 25, 2017.

7. Teddy Greenstein, "Returning to His 1st Love," *Chicago Tribune*, March 28, 2008.

8. "Not Just A Pretty Face."

9. Mike Ferguson, "Centennial Park Diamond Named for Cec Musburger, Founder of Little League Baseball in Billings," *Billings Gazette*, August 23, 2013.

10. Bob Townsley, "Brent Musburger's Love of Sports Journalism Began in Billings," Montana Hall of Fame, February 5, 2020.

11. Norm Clarke, "First Call for Musburger Was as an Umpire," VSiN, February 1, 2017.

12. Townsley, "Brent Musburger's Love."

13. Sherman, "With Brent Musburger."

14. Townsley, "Brent Musburger's Love."

15. Sherman, "With Brent Musburger."

16. Todd Salen, "TV-2's Brent Musburger: He's Young, Enthusiastic and Rising to the Top," *Catching Up with the World* (blog), March 18, 2017, http://toddsalen.blogspot.com/2017/03/tv-2s-brent-musburger-hes-young.html.

17. Tommy O'Neill, interview by author, May 26, 2020.

18. Barry Horn, "Hot Air: Meet Ed Goren," *Dallas Morning News*, January 27, 2017.

19. Bill Fitts, interview by author, May 24, 2020.

3. Phyllis George: More Than a Pretty Face

1. Evan Smith, "Phyllis George: On Life's Rich Pageant," *Texas Monthly*, March 2007.

2. Phyllis George, interview by University of Texas, "Phyllis George: 'Never Say Never' Attitude," Famous Texans series, June 15, 2018.

3. Patricia McConnico, "Phyllis George," *Texas Monthly*, December 1998.

4. Smith, "Phyllis George."

5. Anne Dingus, "Phyllis George," *Texas Monthly*, September 2001.

6. Smith, "Phyllis George."

7. Dingus, "Phyllis George."

8. Neil Dobos, "Walking the Runway with Miss America, Phyllis George," YouTube, March 11, 2011, https://www.youtube.com/watch?v=77NSoSpRPqU.

9. Phyllis George, "The Thrills and Trials of Being Miss America," *Family Weekly*, August 8, 1971.

10. Smith, "Phyllis George."

11. George, "Thrills and Trials."

12. George interview by University of Texas.

13. All Tommy O'Neill quotes in this chapter are taken from a May 26, 2020, interview by author.

14. Bob Stenner, interview by author, July 6, 2020.

15. Amy Argetsinger, "Phyllis George, Miss America Who Became a Trailblazing Sportscaster, Dies at 70," *Washington Post*, May 17, 2020.

16. Rosemary Wussler Boorman, interview by author, September 12, 2020.

17. Phyllis George, *Never Say Never—Yes You Can!* (Louisville, KY: Butler Books, 2009).

18. Neil Amdur, email exchange with author, July 20, 2020.

19. George, *Never Say Never*.

20. Melissa Ludtke, "More Than a Pretty Face," *Sports Illustrated*, August 11, 1975.

21. All Dave Cowens quotes in this chapter are taken from a July 10, 2020, email exchange with author.

22. George, *Never Say Never*.

23. Ted Holmlund, "Phyllis George, Pioneer Sports Broadcaster and Former Miss America, Dead at Age 70," *New York Post*, May 16, 2020.

24. Ludtke, "More Than a Pretty Face."

4. Bob Wussler: The Visionary

1. Robert Feder, "Robert J. Wussler: The Man Who Teamed Bill & Walter," WBEZ Chicago, June 13, 2010, https://www.wbez.org/stories/robert-j-wussler-the-man-who-teamed-bill-and-walter/c0fa19f7-bf48-449d-8217-3910d2cfa2db.

2. All Van Gordon Sauter quotes in this chapter are taken from a May 26, 2020, interview by author.

3. Feder, "Robert J. Wussler."

4. All Bill Raftery quotes in this chapter are taken from a July 23, 2020, interview by author.

5. All Reverend Mike Russo quotes in this chapter are taken from a July 23, 2020, interview by author.

6. Gary Paul Gates, *Air Time: The Inside Story of CBS News* (New York: Berkley Publishing, 1978).

7. Ibid.

8. All Rob Wussler quotes in this chapter are taken from a September 11, 2020, interview by author.

9. Author interview with former CBS Communication executive who did not want to be quoted by name.

10. Joel Banow, interview by author, July 30, 2020.

11. All Bill Fitts quotes in this chapter are taken from a May 20, 2020, interview by author.

12. Kevin O'Malley, interview by author, May 26, 2020.

13. Janet Renz, interview by author, December 13, 2020.

14. All Mike Pearl quotes in this chapter are taken from multiple interviews and email exchanges with author during May, June, and July 2020.

15. "TVTV Goes to the Super Bowl Raw: Bob Wussler," Media Burn, January 1976, https://mediaburn.org/video/tvtv-goes-to-the-superbowl-raw-bob-wussler-2.

16. Rich Podolsky, "Get That Broad Out of the Booth," *TV Guide*, December 21, 1974.

17. "TVTV Goes to Super Bowl."

18. Ibid.

19. All Bob Fishman quotes in this chapter are taken from multiple interviews and email exchanges with author during June, July, and August 2020.

20. Bob Costas, interview by author, July 15, 2020.

21. Neil Amdur, email exchange with author, July 20, 2020.

22. Tony Kornheiser, *PTI*, ESPN, February 22, 2021.

5. Pearl and Fishman: They Made the Magic

1. Unless otherwise noted, all Mike Pearl quotes in this chapter are taken from multiple interviews and email exchanges with author during May, June, and July 2020.

2. Beatles story from Mike Pearl induction video at Sports Broadcasting Hall of Fame, 2015.

3. All Janis Delson quotes in this chapter are taken from a July 7, 2020, interview by author.

4. Hank Goldberg, interview by author, May 28, 2020.

5. Unless otherwise noted, all Bob Fishman quotes in this chapter are taken from multiple interviews and email exchanges with author during June, July, and August 2020.

6. Bill Fitts, interview by author, May 20, 2020.

7. Rich Podolsky, "CBS' Director Bob Fishman Enters the Sports Broadcasting HOF 60 Years after Being Inspired by Vin Scully," *Sports Broadcast Journal*, December 12, 2019.

6. Jimmy The Greek: His Life and Times

1. Unless otherwise noted, Jimmy "The Greek" Snyder quotes are from his autobiography, *Jimmy The Greek, by Himself* (Chicago: Playboy Press, 1975).

2. Gilbert Rogin, "The Greek Who Makes the Odds," *Sports Illustrated*, December 18, 1961.

3. Dave Anderson, "'Greek' Loses an Out Bet," Sports of the Times, *New York Times*, January 17, 1988.

4. All Mike Pearl quotes in this chapter are taken from multiple interviews and email exchanges with author during June, July, and August 2020.

5. Hank Goldberg, interview by author, May 28, 2020.

6. Chuck Milton, email exchange with author, July 10, 2020.

7. All Bob Fishman quotes in this chapter are taken from multiple interviews and email exchanges with author during June, July, and August, 2020.

8. Milton email exchange with author.

9. Frank Deford, "Hey Greek, Who Do You Like?" *Sports Illustrated*, September 8, 1980.

10. Peter Richmond, "Jimmy the Greek: The Living Dead," *National Sports Daily*, April 13, 1990.

11. Deford, "Hey Greek."

7. Irv Cross: Mr. Reliable

1. Irv Cross, *Bearing the Cross*, with Clifton Brown (New York: Sports Publishing, 2017).

2. Unless otherwise noted, all Irv Cross quotes in this chapter are taken from an August 11, 2020, interview by author.

3. Cross, *Bearing the Cross*.

4. Ibid.

5. Ibid.

6. Brent Musburger, interview by Rich Eisen, *The Rich Eisen Show*, NFL Network, March 1, 2021.

7. Frank Fitzpatrick, "Ex-Eagle Irv Cross Tormented by Pain but Not Bitterness," *Philadelphia Inquirer*, September 3, 2018.

8. "Where Are They Now? CB Irv Cross," Philadelphia Eagles website, January 21, 2015, https://www.philadelphiaeagles.com/news/where-are-they-now-cb-irv-cross-14816069.

9. Cross, *Bearing the Cross*.

10. Bob Fishman, interview by author, June 30, 2020.

11. Phyllis George, interview by author, Saratoga Race Course, August 2017.

8. On the Road: Live! from Miami

1. All Janis Delson quotes in this chapter are taken from a July 7, 2020, interview by author.
2. Phyllis George interview with Roger Staubach, *The NFL Today*, December 5, 1975.
3. Rosemary Wussler Boorman, interview by author, September 12, 2020.
4. All Yvonne Connors quotes in this chapter are taken from a June 28, 2020, interview by author.
5. Author interview with former CBS Sports producer who did not want to be quoted by name, July 2020.
6. Mike Pearl, interviews and email exchanges with author, May, June, and July 2020.
7. All George Schweitzer quotes in this chapter are taken from May and June 2020 interviews by author.
8. All Rob Wussler quotes in this chapter are taken from a September 11, 2020, interview by author.
9. All Bob Fishman quotes in this chapter are taken from multiple interviews and email exchanges with author during June, July, and August, 2020.
10. All Al Michaels quotes in this chapter are taken from a May 27, 2020, interview by author.
11. "TVTV Goes to the Super Bowl Raw: Bob Wussler," Media Burn, January 1976, https://mediaburn.org/video/tvtv-goes-to-the-superbowl-raw-bob-wussler-2.
12. Dick Robertson, interview by author, October 6, 2020.
13. Hank Goldberg, interview by author, May 28, 2020.
14. "For the Record," *Sports Illustrated*, June 21, 2010.
15. "TVTV Goes to Super Bowl."
16. Van Gordon Sauter, interview by author, July 7, 2020.

9. Jayne Kennedy: The Greatest Talent Hunt Since Scarlett O'Hara

1. All Jayne Kennedy quotes in this chapter are taken from a June 30, 2020, interview by author and subsequent email exchanges.
2. Carroll "Beano" Cook was a publicist for CBS Sports from 1976 to 1984. A huge proponent of college football, Cook also made it known how much he disliked baseball. "They could hold the World Series in my backyard and I'd pull down the blinds," he often said. During the 1982 NBA All-Star weekend in Cleveland, it was learned that the Iranian hostages were on their way home. Then someone announced to a room full of sportswriters that baseball commissioner Bowie Kuhn would offer the released hostages lifetime passes to baseball. Said Beano after learning the news: "Haven't they suffered enough?"
3. Janis Delson, interview by author, July 7, 2020.
4. Carole Coleman, interview by author, August 5, 2020.
5. Kevin O'Malley, email exchange with author, April 7, 2021.
6. Van Gordon Sauter, email exchange with author, November 1, 2020. (The author was unable to substantiate Jayne Kennedy's quote that Frank Smith told her that CBS's Southern affiliates needed to approve her being hired for *The NFL Today*. No one else the author interviewed was aware of Smith's statement, but no one offered that it wasn't true.)
7. Irv Cross, *Bearing the Cross*, with Clifton Brown (New York: Sports Publishing, 2017).

8. Bob Fishman, interview by author, June 30, 2020.
9. Mike Pearl, email exchange with author, October 13, 2020.
10. All Ted Shaker quotes in this chapter are taken from a May 26, 2020, interview by author.

10. The Fight at Peartrees

1. All Ted Shaker quotes in this chapter are taken from a May 26, 2020, interview by author.
2. All Kevin O'Malley quotes in this chapter are taken from a May 21, 2020, interview by author.
3. All Chuck Milton quotes in this chapter are taken from a July 10, 2020, email exchange with author.
4. All Mike Pearl quotes in this chapter are taken from multiple interviews and email exchanges with author during May, June, and July 2020.
5. Richard Sandomir, "Phyllis George, Trailblazing Sportscaster, Is Dead at 70," *New York Times*, May 16, 2020.
6. Hank Goldberg, interview by author, May 28, 2020.
7. Van Gordon Sauter, interview by author, July 13, 2020.
8. Bob Fishman, interview by author, June 30, 2020.
9. Janis Delson, interview by author, July 7, 2020.

11. Al Michaels's Wild and Crazy Year at CBS

1. Unless otherwise noted, all Al Michaels quotes in this chapter are taken from a May 27, 2020, interview by author.
2. Tommy O'Neill, interview by author, May 26, 2020.
3. Jay Rosenstein, interview by author, July 1, 2020.

12. Phyllis Gets Married . . . Again

1. Kent Demaret, "Kissin' but not Cousins . . .," *People*, October 22, 1979.
2. Myra MacPherson, "Phyllis George and the Kentucky Fried Candidate," *Washington Post*, May 15, 1979.
3. Demaret, "Kissin' but not Cousins."
4. MacPherson, "Phyllis George."
5. Amy Argetsinger, "Phyllis George, Miss America Who Became a Trailblazing Sportscaster, Dies at 70," *Washington Post*, May 17, 2020.
6. Demaret, "Kissin' but not Cousins."
7. MacPherson, "Phyllis George."
8. Ibid.
9. Ibid.
10. Demaret, "Kissin' but not Cousins."
11. Van Gordon Sauter, interview by author, July 13, 2020, and subsequent email exchange.
12. All Bob Fishman quotes in this chapter are taken from multiple interviews and email exchanges with author during June, July, and August, 2020.
13. *The Tonight Show Starring Johnny Carson*, January 10, 1980.

14. The Ginger Man website, accessed July 2020.

15. Yvonne Connors, interview by author, June 28, 2020.

16. George Veras, interview by author, May 31, 2020.

13. The Greek's Luck Finally Runs Out

1. All Jay Rosenstein quotes in this chapter are taken from a July 1, 2020, interview by author.

2. Unless otherwise noted, all Ted Shaker quotes in this chapter are taken from a May 26, 2020, interview by author.

3. B. Drummond Ayres Jr., "Ringmaster of Power Lunches, Duke Zeibert, Is Dead at 86," *New York Times*, August 16, 1997.

4. Leonard Shapiro, "Jimmy The Greek Says Blacks Are 'Bred' for Sports," *Washington Post*, January 16, 1988.

5. CBS statement distancing itself from Jimmy The Greek's comments, January 15, 1988.

6. George Veras, interview by author, May 31, 2020.

7. Peter Richmond, "Jimmy the Greek: The Living Dead," *National Sports Daily*, April 13, 1990.

8. Mark A. Uhlig, "Racial Remarks Draw Furor," *New York Times*, January 16, 1988.

9. Phil Mushnick, interview by author, July 2020.

10. Richmond, "Jimmy the Greek."

11. Jay Sharbutt, "Jimmy 'The Greek' Is Fired by CBS," *Los Angeles Times*, January 17, 1988.

12. Jonathan Rowe, "The Greek Chorus: Jimmy the Greek Got It Wrong but So Did His Critics," *Washington Monthly*, April 1988.

13. Quoted in Skip Myslenski, "CBS Fires 'Greek' for Racial Remarks," *Chicago Tribune*, January 17, 1988.

14. Myslenski, "CBS Fires 'Greek.'"

15. Van Gordon Sauter, interview by author, July 13, 2020.

16. Richmond, "Jimmy the Greek."

14. The Firing of Brent Musburger

1. Unless otherwise noted, all Ted Shaker quotes in this chapter are taken from a May 26, 2020, interview by author.

2. Erik Spanberg, "At Final Four 25 Years Ago, Musburger Provided Drama," *Sports Business Journal*, March 30, 2015.

3. All Kevin O'Malley quotes in this chapter are taken from a May 21, 2020, interview by author.

4. Mark Asher, "CBS Sports Drops Musburger," *Washington Post*, April 2, 1990.

5. Ibid.

15. Greg Gumbel: Filling Brent's Shoes

1. Unless otherwise noted, all Greg Gumbel quotes in this chapter are taken from an August 5, 2020, interview by author.

2. Merrell Noden, "Nice and Easy Does It on *The NFL Today*," *Sports Illustrated*, November 19, 1990.

3. Ted Shaker, interview by author, May 26, 1990.

4. Noden, "Nice and Easy."

5. Ibid.

6. Lesley Visser, *Sometimes You Have to Cross When It Says Don't Walk* (Dallas, TX: BenBella Books, 2017).

7. Unless otherwise noted, all Lesley Visser quotes in this chapter are taken from a July 31, 2020, email exchange with author.

8. John Harris, "NFL Today Has Fan in Burt Reynolds," *Tampa Bay Times*, October 12, 2005.

16. Who Let the FOX In?

1. Jim Benson, "NBC, NFL Shut Out CBS," *Variety*, December 20, 1993.

2. Steve Wulf, "Out Foxed," *Sports Illustrated*, December 27, 1993.

3. Larry Stewart, "CBS's Downfall: Fox's Money, NBC's Agreement," *Los Angeles Times*, December 24, 1993.

4. Benson, "NBC, NFL Shut Out CBS."

5. Stewart, "CBS's Downfall."

6. Leonard Shapiro and Paul Farhi, "ABC Keeps Mondays in Record NFL Deals," *Washington Post*, January 14, 1998.

7. Richard Katz, "Benched NBC Spins Football," *Variety*, January 14, 1998.

17. Jim Nantz: The Future of CBS Sports Arrives

1. Unless otherwise noted, all Jim Nantz quotes in this chapter are taken from July 2020 interviews by author.

2. Lesley Visser, interviews and email exchanges with author, May through September 2020.

3. Jim Nantz, *Always By My Side: A Father's Grace and a Sports Journey Unlike Any Other*, with Eli Spielman (New York: Gotham Books, 2009).

Epilogue: Where They Are, Where They Went

1. Steve Nidetz, "He Was Teed Off as Musburger's Baby-Sitter," *Chicago Tribune*, April 19, 1990.

2. Steve Nidetz, "Criticism Doesn't Tee off Musburger at Open," *Chicago Tribune*, June 19, 1992.

3. Joel Beall, "Remembering Brent Musburger's Infamous Stint with the Masters and Golf Coverage," *Golf Digest*, January 25, 2017.

4. Richard Sandomir, "The Wrong Man in the Baseball Booth," *New York Times*, October 10, 1995.

5. Richard Sandomir, "Brent Musburger Forsakes Facts for Emotion," *New York Times*, January 11, 2011.

6. Greg Hadley, "Remembering All the Creepy Comments Made by Broadcaster Brent Musburger About Women," *Miami Herald*, January 25, 2017.

7. All John Wildhack quotes in the epilogue are taken from a July 24, 2020, interview by author.

8. All Van Gordon Sauter quotes in the epilogue are taken from a July 13, 2020, interview by author.

9. Tom Shales, "Invitation to a Hug: Phyllis George's Gaffe with Dotson & Webb," *Washington Post*, May 16, 1985.

10. All Bob Costas quotes in the epilogue are taken from a July 15, 2020, interview by author.

11. Sally Bedell Smith, "Phyllis George Quits CBS Morning News," *New York Times*, August 31, 1985.

12. Marian Christy, "Phyllis George Working to Make Every Day Count," *South Florida Sun Sentinel*, February 24, 1985.

13. "Phyllis George Makes a New Beginning," *Louisville Courier-Journal*, August 31, 1998.

14. Pamela Brown, CNN opinion piece, updated December 5, 2020, https://lite.cnn.com/en/article/h_620288c9e613d899fc434f5358714a5d.

15. Pamela Brown, interview by author, December 17, 2020.

16. Mike Pearl, interview by author, May 28, 2020.

17. Unless otherwise noted, all Bob Fishman quotes in the epilogue are taken from multiple interviews and email exchanges with author during June, July, and August 2020.

18. Janis Delson, email exchange with author, March 24, 2021.

19. Richard Sandomir, "Mike Pearl, Innovative TV Sports Producer, Is Dead at 77," *New York Times*, March 11, 2021.

20. Unless otherwise noted, all Irv Cross quotes in the epilogue are taken from an August 1, 2020, interview by author.

21. Irv Cross, *Bearing the Cross*, with Clifton Brown (New York: Sports Publishing, 2017).

22. Ibid.

23. *Jimmy The Greek by Himself* (Chicago: Playboy Press, 1975).

24. John Ourand, "Neal Pilson," *Sports Business Journal*, March 22, 2010.

25. Beginning in 1998 *The NFL Today* began at noon Eastern time.

INDEX

Note: Page numbers in *italics* refer to photographs.

Acknowledgments

WHEN I SET OUT TO WRITE THIS BOOK, I KNEW I WOULD NEED A GOOD
editor to work with me as I put it together over the summer and fall of
2020. I reached out to Mike Sisak, whom I met in 1970 when he was
editing my copy for the *Wilmington News-Journal*. Prior to that he had
been a first-rate reporter for the *Philadelphia Bulletin* and went on to be a
top senior editor for both the *Philadelphia Daily News* and the *New York
Times*. Mike Sisak's advice and direction were invaluable. I can't thank
him enough. I also thank my editors at Rowman & Littlefield / Globe
Pequot, Rick Rinehart, Lynn Zelem, and Elissa Curcio, and John Cerullo
for steering me to Rick.

Michael Pearl and Bob Fishman were the key producer-and-director
team of *The NFL Today* in the beginning, and I certainly couldn't have
reconstructed the events from 1974 through the early '80s without their
help. As the writer on *The NFL Today* some of those years, I can attest to
how great they were to work with and the influence they had that made
that show so loved. And on a personal note, I appreciate how welcoming
they were when I first arrived in 1977. Losing Mike Pearl at the end of
this journey is now even more difficult for so many of us.

I also couldn't have made this book complete without the kind words
of Jim Nantz in the foreword and his retelling so much about his early
days at CBS Sports. Jim is one of the most loved and admired men in
the sports broadcasting business. He not only offered his time, but also
advocated in several ways to help get this book off the ground. I'm sure
his name on the foreword was the stamp of approval for any publisher.

I also thank other former CBS Sports colleagues from years past for
their participation and patience while I recorded their interviews. They
include Bill Fitts, Tommy O'Neill, Bob Stenner, Kevin O'Malley, Ellen

Beckwith, George Veras, Carole Ackerman Coleman, Yvonne Connors, Jay Rosenstein, Charles Milton III, Duke Struck, and Ted Shaker. They all went way back in time and were essential to making this book happen. Especially Ted Shaker, whom I went back to with questions several times. And thanks go out to Mark Ganguzza for providing an October 1976 production schedule demonstrating the complexity of a live Sunday broadcast, and to Sarah Podolsky for making that chart publication ready.

I also especially thank Janis Delson, George Schweitzer, and Van Gordon Sauter for their time and their memorable anecdotes of *The NFL Today* and CBS Sports going back four decades. And thanks to the former ESPN executive John Wildhack for recalling his working relationship with Brent Musburger.

Marjorie Margolies was a key figure on *The NFL Today* back in 1970 and I thank her for not only recalling her days with both WCAU and CBS, but also sending me that wonderful *TV Guide* story about her and the Winston cigarette girl Carole Howey.

I also thank Bill Raftery, Joel Banow, Ann Morfogen, and Father Mike Russo for recalling Bob Wussler's years at Seton Hall and CBS News. Thanks also to Wussler's twins, Rob Wussler and Rosemary Wussler Boorman, for their stories about him and for help with photos, and to Gary Paul Gates for supplying background on Wussler at CBS News. And thanks go especially to Pamela Brown for recalling stories about her mom, Phyllis George, and providing some wonderful photos.

Jayne Kennedy Overton, Lesley Visser, Greg Gumbel, and Irv Cross especially are appreciated for their participation. Jayne not only gave her time but also sent along photos for the book and allowed me to go back to her several times with questions. Losing Irv only three months after our interview was devastating.

Others who helped in many ways include Hank Goldberg, who was Jimmy The Greek's ghostwriter and a close friend of Mike Pearl; Clifton Brown, who cowrote the Irv Cross book *Bearing the Cross*; Dave Cowens, who recalled the interview he did with Phyllis George that won her the job; and also Bob Ryan, Neil Amdur, Joe Valerio, Dick Robertson, David Halberstam, Phil Mushnick, and Elizabeth Torsiello.

And my gratitude also goes to Bethany and Gwyn from the Cadence Group and to Sandy Montag.

I also thank those at CBS who helped in so many ways. They include Sean McManus, Jerry Caracciolo, Mary Kouw, and Patrick Turner. And thanks go out to Howard Katz, Bob Costas, Tony Kornheiser, Chris Fowler, and Tim Brando for their terrific blurbs on the back cover of the book. I also want to especially thank Al Michaels for taking the time to go through his entire 1975 season with CBS and remembering details week by week as if they were yesterday.

And last but not least, I offer more than just thanks to my wife Diana, whose patience and support were a key to my following a hunch to write this book during the COVID-19 pandemic.